SCOTLAND IN EARLY MEDIEVAL EUROPE

Sidestone Press

SCOTLAND IN EARLY MEDIEVAL EUROPE

edited by

Alice E. Blackwell

Published by Sidestone Press, Leiden
www.sidestone.com

Lay-out & cover design: Sidestone Press
Photograph cover: The eighth-century cross-slab from Hilton of Cadboll, Easter Ross. Copyright National Museums of Scotland.

ISBN 978-90-8890-752-4 (softcover)
ISBN 978-90-8890-751-7 (hardcover)
ISBN 978-90-8890-753-1 (PDF e-book)

This publication was made possible by a grant from:

HISTORIC ENVIRONMENT SCOTLAND | ÀRAINNEACHD EACHDRAIDHEIL ALBA

Contents

This volume is dedicated to the memory of Alasdair Ross.

List of illustrations and tables

List of illustrations

List of tables

Introduction

Alice Blackwell

This volume explores how (what is today) Scotland can be compared with, contrasted to, or was connected with other parts of Early Medieval Europe. The image chosen for the cover (see also Illus 1), part of an 8th-century Christian carved-stone monument from Easter Ross, embodies this aim. Some elements of this sculpture are local: both the monument type – a substantial relief-carved slab – and the Pictish symbols at the top of the slab are specific to parts of northern and eastern Scotland. Other elements, like the nourishing vine that frames the slab, allude to international Christian connections. The old and the new are likewise juxtaposed: traditional spiral motifs were reimagined into a complex interconnecting design and placed next to a panel featuring a newly emerging figural tradition. Like many pieces of Early Medieval Insular art, the Hilton slab combines connections stretching back in time and links to other parts of the Christian world with new ideas and distinctly local practices (Goldberg 2015, 199-200); it also stands as a visual summary of many of the connections and processes which archaeologists and historians of the period seek. Yet I suspect this piece of sculpture is not well known beyond our modern national border.

The papers in this volume draw on archaeological, artefactual, historical, and place-name evidence, a testament to the healthy cross-disciplinary community that is such a feature of the field today. The contributions consider local expressions of wider developments and practices at a range of scales: through landscapes, places, monuments, burials, objects, and ideas. A number of themes connect these diverse contributions, of which three particularly stand out: the transition from Iron Age to Early Medieval societies and the development of secular power centres; Early Medieval interventions in prehistoric landscapes; and the management of resources necessary to build kingdoms.

The majority of the papers have their origins in contributions delivered to the Society of Antiquaries of Scotland's 2013 conference 'Scotland in Early Medieval Europe', one in a series of international conferences and resulting volumes (Saville 2004; Shepherd and Barclay 2004; Hunter and Ralston 2015). Here, we open with a pair of papers that present agendas. The 2013 plenary lecture was delivered by Ewan Campbell and addressed the liminalisation of Scotland in recent publications on Early Medieval Europe. Ewan illustrates the ways in which Scotland has variously been ig-

Illustration 1 The eighth-century carved stone cross-slab from Hilton of Cadboll, Easter Ross. Copyright of National Museums of Scotland.

nored or seen as deviant from the normative trajectory of Early Medieval Europe, and the effects this has had on archaeological study. This liminalisation, he argues, results from a perspective that sets the Carolingian kingdom as the ideal, against which other areas are measured and found lacking. Rather than make a value judgment about, for example, the apparent absence of stone architecture in Early Medieval Scotland, he argues that we should instead recognise difference as an alternative and no less valid strategy, for example in the harnessing of portable material culture and stone sculpture for the purposes that architecture fulfils on the continent.

The second contribution, by Sally Foster, reviews the state of Church archaeology in Scotland, and echoes Ewan's (and others) critique of models that marginalise the north and west and allow only for a unidirectional effect of the notional 'core' on the 'periphery'. She seeks ways forward that allow Scotland a European stage whilst recognising local difference in conversion and Christian belief and practice, posing the important question: how do we employ regional studies to better understand diversity and local response to the Church? By way of one answer, she presents an exciting prospect (with an excellent acronym): a research project – The Early Christian Churches and Landscapes (or ECCLES) – that is part of European-wide umbrella initiative, and which seeks to foster meaningful comparison between Scottish and European evidence for the early Church.

Sally also raises a theme echoed by several contributions to the volume: the prehistoric roots of early Christian practice and the development of power centres with cult significance, an area where Scotland has rich evidence to contribute to an established Europe-wide research topic. Meggen Gondek and Gordon Noble outline an integrated exploration of the architecture, sculpture and material culture of power in the 5-6th centuries through their excavations at Rhynie, Aberdeenshire. They identify a cultic element to the site and interpret it through models applied to the 'central places' of southern Scandinavia, as well as pointing to Rhynie's landscape context, dominated by an imposing hillfort. Rhynie is a key part of an AHRC-funded research network hosted at the University of Reading 'Monumentalising kingship: places of royal residence and the making of Early Medieval British kingdoms AD 500-800', while the University of Aberdeen's ongoing Leverhulme-funded 'Comparative kingship' project offers an exciting prospect: a cross-disciplinary approach to the development of social, political and ideological frameworks across northern Britain and Ireland.

The material culture of power in this early transition period is explored in my own contribution with Martin Goldberg. We examine the reinvention of Late Roman bullion into the material that underpinned the developing Early Medieval power relations in Scotland. The practice of Early Medieval hacksilver hoarding is compared with strategies for managing the precious metal elsewhere along the fringes of the crumbling western Roman empire, particularly in Denmark. There is difference here too, in the particular role of silver in Scotland in place of gold, and in the deposition of early hacksilver hoards, not at settlement sites as in Denmark, but in a Bronze Age burial cairn and by a stone circle. A growing awareness of the re-imagination of earlier monuments and landscapes in Scotland, at sites such as these and at Rhynie and Forteviot, provides links to scholarship on the development of Early Medieval power centres in Ireland, Anglo-Saxon England and Scandinavia, and there is still much to do to exploit these parallels fully. Martin and I also created an international AHRC-funded research network, with the aim of building links between scholars working on the role of silver in social and political transformation across first millennium AD Europe.

Following this, we return to powerful places. First, Campbell et al explore the development of a 9th-century lowland power centre and its landscape context in Strathearn, Perthshire. Drawing on excavation by the University of Glasgow under the auspices of the long-running SERF project, Ewan and his co-authors reveal unprecedented evidence from Scotland for Early Medieval intervention in a major prehistoric landscape at Forteviot, identified through extensive sampling and dating programmes. Martin Carver then profiles the development of Portmahomack, Easter Ross – an estate centre that changed direction to become a monastery, and then turned its attention to secular production – and notes similar trajectories in Ireland. Martin likens early activity at Portmahomack to a type of site that has emerged in recent years in Irish scholarship, the 'cemetery-settlement', a development with wider implications for Early Medieval Scotland which have not yet been explored fully. As at Rhynie, Martin also draws a comparison with the changing status and use of 'central places' in Scandinavia, as well as with monastic developments elsewhere in Europe, providing a useful summary of Portmahomack's European context.

Adrián Maldonado's contribution shows the potential of mortuary archaeology to bring fresh insights into local practice and wider connections. Despite a substantial body of inhumation burial evidence that is readily comparable with data elsewhere, Early Medieval mortuary archaeology in Scotland has not had the attention it deserves. Adrián explores here one practice, that of interment within a log coffin: previously regarded as abnormal or rare, over a hundred Scottish examples are now recognised. Adrián argues that this is a mainstream (and probably under-recognised) part of the spectrum of burial practices attested in Early Medieval Britain, and one which can only be understood in its European context.

From here, the volume turns to managed landscapes and the harnessing of resources to build kingdoms. The late Alasdair Ross explores the division of land across Early Medieval Europe and the fundamental importance of such units to the formation of the state apparatus. This is valuable context to his work on one such unit found in parts of Scotland, the *dabhach*, a subject that has often been mired in murky waters. Although study of *dabhaichean* has been poorly integrated into wider understanding of similar processes elsewhere in the Early Medieval world, he concludes that they would have been recognisable in many parts of Europe as a 'common unit of land assessment imposed by a superior authority as an effective way to assess and raise taxation, and to aid in a state building process'. He also raises the interesting question of why Scotland's rulers never introduced a truly common unit of land assessment across the whole country. Mapping *dabhaichaen* and understanding their relationship with parishes provide exciting opportunities for the future: to develop integrated case studies that investigate the placement and meaning of Early Medieval archaeological sites and monuments within their organised landscape context, and to compare these case studies with similar approaches undertaken elsewhere in Europe.

The final contribution considers identity and ethnicity – issues pertinent across Early Medieval Europe. Nicholas Evans explores what origin legends tell us about the aspirations and agendas of the societies that created, changed and maintained them. In the context of strategies of dynastic elites in England, Ireland and continental Europe,

Nick explores issues of ancestry and language within the origin legends of the Picts, Gaels, Britons and Anglo-Saxons. In Early Medieval Scotland, as in contemporary Ireland and England, there seems to have been little correlation between kingdoms and ethnic groups, a contrast with most of the rest of Christendom. Within Scotland there are also hints of difference in the relative importance of ancestry for royal dynasties, playing a significant role among the Gaels, Anglo-Saxons and maybe Britons, but less so for Pictish overkingship.

While the majority of contributions grew out of the 2013 conference, there are some omissions from the programme, together with some additions commissioned by the editor (by Ross, Foster & Maldonado). The conference built on an initiative by the St Andrews Institute for Dark Age Studies, begun twenty years earlier. *Dark Age Scotland in Europe*, edited by Barbara Crawford (1994), arose from a conference held in 1993, a year that Barbara noted marked the beginning of the single European market. There is some thematic crossover with the present volume, published as very different changes to Scotland's place in Europe remain unsettled. Stuart Airlie's 1994 paper on role of cults in Frankish kingdoms, and Peter Heather's contribution exploring the development of kingdoms in other parts of Europe beyond the western imperial borders echo themes of cult and political transition explored here, while Alan Lane's paper, drawing on the thesis of his former student and our plenary speaker Ewan Campbell, explored the long-distance trade networks bringing pottery and glass (amongst other things) to sites in Scotland, including, we know now, to the north-east at Rhynie (see Gondek and Noble, this volume). On the other hand, the reuse and manipulation of prehistoric landscapes, picked up repeatedly within this volume, is a theme that has emerged since the 1994 collection. Indeed, Airlie's 1994 discussion focussed on royal palaces and used Forteviot as an example; the present contribution by SERF team is less about Airlie's 'state formation' and more about ritual landscape.

As well as the models critiqued in Ewan and Sally's contributions, the perceived peculiarity particular to one part of Early Medieval Scotland – the Picts – must also be responsible for some missed connections beyond our borders. Leslie Alcock made tentative comparisons with Europe in his contribution to the 1987 volume *The Picts: a new look at old problems*, in which he made the case to demythologise the Picts, rejecting supposed characteristics that had set them apart. Part of his intention was to set the Picts in their European context, and though the examples he explored were relatively few in number, he concluded that 'they are a typical northwest European Barbarian society, with wide connections and parallels not merely throughout Britain and Ireland, but across northern Europe into hither Asia, and into the Mediterranean as well' (Alcock 1987, 90-1). Within this volume, the emphasis has not been on 'typical', but on the value of combining an awareness of regional difference with a European perspective. But there is still much to do. Ewan reiterated an important point made elsewhere by James Fraser (2009) about the need to engage particularly with scholarship and material from Anglo-Saxon England, to transcend the modern political boundary and contemporary national identities. But this is only part of the issue; we need more research applications and networks that look beyond national borders, creating links with rest of Britain, Ireland and continental Europe. Fundamentally, we need to build better connections with those working on Early Medieval archaeology outside Scotland, and to help foster a stronger awareness of the Early Medieval material culture of Scotland amongst a European audience. I hope this volume is a useful step along this road.

Acknowledgements
I would like to thank the contributors and all the peer reviewers for their patience over what has been a protracted editing process, and particularly Sally Foster for overseeing the peer review and editing of my own contribution. Thanks are also due to my fellow members of the conference organising committee, Sally as well as Mark Hall, and to the Society of Antiquaries of Scotland staff for making the 2013 event such a success. Historic Environment Scotland kindly supported the volume through a financial contribution which is gratefully acknowledged.

Finally, I and all of the volume's contributors were extremely sad to hear of the sudden death of Alasdair Ross in 2017, during the preparation of this volume. He is greatly missed, and *Scotland in Early Medieval Europe* is dedicated to his memory.

Bibliography
Airlie, S 1994 'The view from Maastricht', in Crawford, 33-46.

Alcock, L 1987 'Pictish studies: present and future', in Small, A (ed) *The Picts: a new look at old problems*, 80-92. Dundee: The Graham Hunter Foundation.

Crawford, B (ed) 1994 *Dark Age Scotland in Europe: proceedings of a day conference held on 20 February 1993.* St Andrews: The Committee for Dark Age Studies, University of St Andrews.

Fraser, J 2009 *From Caledonia to Pictland. Scotland to 795.* Edinburgh: Edinburgh University Press.

Goldberg, M 2015 'At the western edge of the Christian world, c AD 600-900', in Farley and Hunter (eds) *Celts: art and identity*, 173-205. London: British Museum.

Heather, P 1994 'State formation in Europe in the first millennium AD', in Crawford, 47-70.

Hunter, F and Ralston, I (eds) 2015 *Scotland in later prehistoric Europe.* Edinburgh: Society of Antiquaries of Scotland.

Lane, A 1994 'Trade, gifts and cultural exchange in Dark-Age western Scotland', in Crawford, 103-15.

Saville, A (ed) 2004 *Mesolithic Scotland and its neighbours: the early Holocene prehistory of Scotland, its British and Irish context and some northern European perspectives.* Edinburgh: Society of Antiquaries of Scotland.

Shepherd, I and Barclay, G (eds) 2004 *Scotland in ancient Europe: the Neolithic and Bronze Age of Scotland in their European context.* Edinburgh: Society of Antiquaries of Scotland.

1

Peripheral vision: Scotland in Early Medieval Europe

Ewan Campbell

1.1 Introduction

The catalyst for this paper was a review by Richard Hodges of the excavation monograph for the royal Scottish site of Dunadd, Argyll and Bute (Lane and Campbell 2000). Hodges, one of the leading Early Medieval archaeologists, described Early Medieval Scotland as 'marginal in European terms', having 'an aboriginal level of material culture', and as an area which 'failed to engage in the Post-Roman rebirth of Europe' (Hodges 2004, 725). He is not alone in this view – Chris Wickham's 2005 monumental survey of Early Medieval Europe and the Mediterranean, *Framing the Early Middle Ages*, deliberately excludes Scotland as being of little interest, one of only three regions (the others being Bavaria and Cyrenaica) to have this distinction (Wickham 2005, 6, n 6; see Barrett 2008, 675 for a critique). The Society for Medieval Archaeology's recent fiftieth anniversary volume (Gilchrist and Reynolds 2009) barely mentions Scottish archaeology at all in its survey of European Medieval archaeology. I hope to show this view of Scotland is an old trope, based on the notion that Scotland is peripheral in importance as well as in geography, and to offer an alternative view – if you like, a view *from* the periphery, rather than a view *of* the periphery. My title, 'Peripheral vision', was chosen because I also want to examine vision in the metaphorical sense of innovation, and make comments on how being geographically peripheral to mainland Europe might have actually encouraged the development of new ways of looking at the world. In a word, because Early Medieval Scotland is different from the rest of Europe, it does not mean that it is less important. To ignore or side-line Scotland runs the danger not just of bad scholarship, but also of missing important questions which are raised by comparing the achievements of a liminal society with those of an economic core.

On the matter of terminology, though this volume is themed on Scotland, at the period I am discussing 'Scotland' of course did not exist. I will be focussing on the Gaelic-speaking kingdom of Dál Riata, but much of what I say also applies to the wider Gaeldom of Ireland, to Pictland in the eastern part of modern-day Scotland, and the British and Anglian areas of southern Scotland. Of course, there were strong re-

in: Blackwell, A.E. (ed.) 2019: *Scotland in Early Medieval Europe*,
Leiden: Sidestone Press, pp. 17-34.

gional differences in material culture within Scotland, though these do not necessarily coincide with the four 'peoples' mentioned by Bede as living in Scotland – the Scots, Picts, Britons and Angles. Within the scope of this paper these differences can only be briefly alluded to, but further detail can be found in recent accounts (Lowe 1999; Henderson and Henderson 2004; Clarke et al 2012; Foster 2014).

1.2 Visions of the periphery

In the classical imagination, Britain and its outlying islands occupied a symbolic place at the ends of the known world, a remoteness similar to our recent use of Timbuktu or the use of 'Far Cathay' in the nineteenth century. These lands were as far as you could go before falling into the abyssal Ocean which was imagined to surround the three known continents (O'Loughlin 1997). Roman conquerors of Britain saw the *Orcades* (Orkney) as the furthest habitable part of the world (*Ultima Thule* was not habitable) and therefore its conquest symbolically represented Imperial rule of the whole world (Scully 2005). Both Claudius and Agricola were said to have conquered the *Orcades* – because they were the furthest extent possible of the Empire.

This view persisted into Christian times but was adapted and enhanced, particularly because the ocean was seen in the Old Testament as the realm of monsters and demons – an untamed region outside the civilised world and therefore a suitable site for spiritual warfare between good and evil. As examples one only has to think of Columba's miracles of calming the waters (*Vita Columbae*, VC II.12), and the search for 'a desert in the ocean' by early monks. So, for example, in the fifth century Patrick says Ireland was 'at the ends of the earth' and thus that the Christian message has reached all parts of the world (O'Loughlin 1997, 14; Hood 1978, 49). In the late seventh century Adomnán described Iona as being 'on the edge of the ocean' (VC III.23). It is here worth remembering that it was Adomnán who established the location of Jerusalem as at the geographic centre of the world (O'Loughlin 1997, 19). As late as the twelfth century, Giraldus Cambrensis was comparing Henry II to Roman Emperors because he ruled Britain as far as the Orkneys.

When we turn to more recent times we see the rise of the stereotype of the wild and uncivilised Highlander, a view strengthened by reaction to the eighteenth-century Jacobite rebellions. Dr Johnson in his *Tour of the Hebrides* says that for most people

> [The Highlands and islands] ... are equally unknown with that of Borneo or Sumatra: of both they have only heard a little, and guess the rest (Bray 1986, 13).

Note that in this passage he paraphrases the work of Martin Martin (1716, viii), a Gaelic-speaking writer whose work he scathingly dismisses. The prejudiced view of the Scottish Highlander was more forcefully put by Thomas Pinkerton, an Edinburgh historian

> [The Celts] have not yet advanced even to the state of barbarism … they are incapable of industry or civilisation … fond of lies and enemies of the truth … For the Celts were so inferior a people, being to the [Scots] as a negro to a European, that, as all history shows, to see them was to conquer them (Pinkerton 1787, 73, quoted in Ferguson 1998, 253).

The Gaelic Highlanders are therefore seen as the Other – and to be feared and destroyed if possible. This 'Great Ill-will of the Lowlander' (Broun and MacGregor 2007) has deep historical roots, and the viewpoint of the Celts as being backward continued to influence scholarship. For example, in his discussion of the Celtic Iron Age torques, Simon Birch describes them as being of excellent workmanship, but despite this they are

> productions of a rude, simple, and unartistic people, and are evidence of their intellectual inferiority to the other great nations of antiquity (Birch 1846, 38).

Similar, though more subconscious, views coloured scholarship up to the modern period. Netzer (2001; 2009) has detailed how the interpretation of Insular manuscript art continued to have a history of nationalist bias until very recently, showing how preconceptions and politics have skewed art historians' reading of the evidence. It is only recently that critical reading of the sparse historical sources has become widespread (Fraser 2009, 6-8), with the understanding that these sources tell us about the period they were written in rather the period they purport to describe. These new readings have revealed biases that have distorted archaeologists' (Campbell 2000, 291) and linguists' (Forsyth 1997, 13) interpretation of their evidence. More generally, there has been a prolonged but recently intensified debate on the whole notion of Celticity (for summaries see Chapman 1992; Sims-Williams 1998; 2012). These debates arouse passions because of individual's self-identification with supposed ancestral peoples. While the more strident views are easy to spot, the more unconscious biases are less obvious, but just as capable of distorting views of the past, as evidenced by Hodges' view of Scotland as having an 'aboriginal level of culture'.

1.3 A vision from the periphery

In contrast to these negative views of Early Medieval Scotland, I would like to present what is I hope a more balanced, or perhaps balancing, view. The core/periphery model of Early Medieval Europe sees the Carolingian Empire as the ideal of a core, and the monetised and urbanised society there as unproblematic and normative. By comparing what was happening there with contemporary Scotland, both in material culture and intellectual development, it is possible to challenge this viewpoint, as has been done for Scandinavia, an area which has also been seen as peripheral (Geary 2013).

1.3.1 Material culture

There is no doubt that Carolingian society was sophisticated and economically advanced, and that its material culture shows high levels of technical and decorative skill by artisans, access to exotic materials, and considerable concentrations of wealth, resulting in some outstanding architecture. In contrast, Scotland is almost entirely lacking in stone buildings in the Early Medieval period. Despite this lack of stone architecture, when we look at Insular art we see an explosion of artistic and technical creativity in the seventh and eighth centuries, where the traditions of Germanic animal art, Late La Tène abstract geometric motifs, Pictish art, and late classical human figurative art become combined to produce vibrant new artworks. Items such as the Book of Kells and the Book of Durrow, the Hunterston brooch (North Ayrshire) and the St Ninian's Isle treasure (Shetland Islands), or St John's Cross on Iona (Argyll and Bute) and the Nigg cross-slab (Easter Ross, Highland) all exhibit levels of design and innovation at least equal to that of corresponding artefacts of the contemporary Merovingian/Carolingian world. This is a generalisation of course; many works, such as manuscripts, produced in continental Europe were themselves influenced by the Insular tradition (Henderson 1994, 271) and others show equally skilful technique. I should make it clear that I am not talking here about subjective judgements on the merit of Insular versus classical art. What I am saying is that the *innovation* is expressed very differently from that in Carolingian examples. The intriguing questions to me are why there is this difference, and why is it expressed only in certain areas of endeavour, particularly metalwork, manuscripts and sculpture, but not widely in stone architecture? Although the influence of monastic centres such as Iona can partly explain investment in manuscript art and stone crosses, this is not the full story: secular metalwork also shows these innovative qualities, and monastic centres on the continent did not always show the same creativity in combining disparate traditions and creating entirely new art forms. I will return to this question in my conclusions after looking at other areas of innovation.

If we look in detail at individual examples of the types of material culture surviving from Scotland (and Ireland), they show a great deal of experiment, assimilation of a variety of artistic traditions, and innovation. Some of these types of artefact, particularly in the fields of sculpture and metalwork, have no close parallels within Francia. For example, the eighth-century Ardagh chalice has a complex construction, using a series of techniques including filigree panels, *Pressblech* panels, multi-colour enamelling, and wire-inlaid glass studs. The contemporary Tassilo chalice in contrast uses only chip-carved decoration. Although the Insular examples fall into the general tradition of Late Antique metal-ware chalices, they differ in details of construction and decoration, showing local craftworkers were experimenting and innovating (Ryan 1989; 1990). In a similar fashion, although techniques of gold filigree work were known and used in Frankish brooches, these tend to be early and simpler in design (Whitfield 1990, vol 2, 25-7) and do not show the types of technical innovation in design and construction found in the Insular examples (Whitfield 1987; 2014). Thus there are no Carolingian brooches with the innovation of the Hunterston brooch, and even items of the highest status (such as the crown of Charlemagne), which displayed wealth through the lavish use of gold and precious stones, were relatively poorly constructed. In Francia there are no lavishly decorated stone crosses comparable to the Iona or Pictish monuments, and most sculpture is in the form of decorated capitals and other structural components of buildings. Despite evidence for Insular innovation in figural sculpture (Henderson and Henderson 2004; Stalley 2014), the Insular material has often been ignored or side-lined in discussions of European art (Stalley 1990). On the other hand, Carolingian ivories are of the highest quality of workmanship, and are unmatched in

Insular contexts, though their designs are entirely based on Late Antique exemplars. Carolingian art was directly derived from Late Antique traditions, consciously copying styles and objects from the Mediterranean area. Of course, there is an exception where some manuscript art was directly influenced by Insular developments, due to the presence of monks trained in Britain and Ireland. In general however, materials and craftsmen were brought from Italy and Byzantium to create what has been termed the 'Carolingian Renaissance'. There was also wholescale importation of building materials such as stone columns, mosaics and marble panelling to build Charlemagne's palace at Aachen and other churches (eg Peacock 1997). Although the results are monumental and imposing, and the dome at Aachen has been shown to use new construction techniques not seen in Roman and Byzantine domes (Rollason 2015, 446), there is little sign of innovation in the decoration, something that has been noted by some art historians (Webster 2012; Januszczak 2012; Henderson 1994). This is not surprising, as the intention was to re-create a vision of the Roman Empire in north-west Europe.

Architecture is the area where the disparity of investment between the continent and Scotland is most apparent. We have almost no Early Medieval stone buildings (other than domestic dry-stone constructions) surviving in Scotland, and most buildings were probably of organic materials. This does not necessarily mean these buildings, such as the timber churches at Whithorn (Dumfries and Galloway; Hill 1997, 134ff), were not highly decorated or sophisticated structures (indeed contemporary literary references suggest they were richly elaborated) – we just don't have the evidence. Tomás Ó Carragáin (2010, 78) has suggested that Columba's chapel on Iona may be the first example of a founder's tomb in the Gaelic world and might date to the mid-eighth century, making it the earliest post-Roman mortared stone building in Scotland. The Forteviot arch (Perth and Kinross) and other Pictish sculptural fragments show that there could have been complex decorated stone church or palace buildings in the ninth century, but these are nonetheless very scattered pieces of evidence. I suspect it is this lack of 'proper' buildings that particularly influenced Hodges in his view of Scotland's 'aboriginal level of culture', especially given his experience of excavating the late Roman town of Butrint in Albania, and the San Vincenzo al Volturno monastic complex in Italy. This surprising lack of engagement with contemporary continental trends in stone architecture mirrors the situation in Ireland, where Ó Carragáin (2010, 143-66) has argued that the notion of churches as repositories of social memory resulted in a conservative approach to church architecture as a conscious choice, rather than as the result of any 'backwardness'. All these examples are intended to show that Early Medieval Scotland was different from the core of Carolingian Europe, but that does not make it inferior.

1.3.2 Economy

Let us turn to another area where the Atlantic west is seen as being backward: economy and trade. There is no doubt that Early Medieval Scotland did not have any of the normal markers of a developed economy – markets, merchants, towns and coinage. These did not appear until at least the eleventh century, and some later still, lagging well behind England for example. The inhabitants of Scotland were however aware of these economic aspects – they travelled and read widely, but never adopted these particular practices. But in some ways they were economic pioneers, at least in British terms.

From the late fifth century to the later seventh century the Atlantic west was part of a series of trading networks which linked it to the Mediterranean and later to the western continent. The residue of these contacts can be seen in the pottery containers and glass drinking vessels found on (mainly) high-status sites in Ireland, Wales, south-west England and Scotland (Campbell 2007). I have shown that this was the result of direct contact with the eastern Mediterranean in the early sixth century (and Carthage by the mid-sixth century). A remarkable example of the extent of this trade has recently been found at Rhynie in Aberdeenshire, where the most northerly examples of sixth-century Mediterranean amphorae in the world have been excavated (Noble et al 2013). An extraordinary effort was involved in transporting these heavy items (weighing up to 50kg when full) some 5000km by sea, then overland up the Great Glen or across the Central Valley and up the east coast, then a further 40km inland. These direct contacts had the potential to serve as conduits for people, objects, stories and ideas from the core of the Byzantine Empire.

Later in the sixth century a new trading system developed from western France (Aquitania), but this time the focus of the trade was in the north of the Atlantic zone, with Dunadd and Whithorn as the two most significant import centres. The characteristics of both these systems of trade are peculiar in many respects and do not fit neatly into the economic systems put forward by Hodges and others. In Scandinavia, similar systems have been described as 'between gift and the market' (Gustin 2004). I have suggested that both systems were driven by imperial or royal agents, and suspect that metals were the economic driving force for the earlier system, and slaves for the later one. These connections gave Dál Riata direct access to the highest levels of European society, and a rapid means of communication with them, creating what network theorists have described as 'a small-world network', where hubs enable long-distance communication of materials and ideas (Sindbaek 2007). But what is interesting about the system is that it pre-dates the beginnings of organised trade in Anglo-Saxon England, which does not really get going until the later seventh century with the founding of the trading towns of *Hamwic*, *Ipswic*, *Lundenwic* and *Eorfwic* (Campbell 2007, fig 3). There, towns appear simultaneously with silver coinage, a variety of imported pottery types, and mentions of both merchants and taxes in contemporary documents.

But why do we not see towns, merchants and coinage in the Atlantic west? One difference is that the major trading places in the west are situated at royal sites, whereas in England they are at a distance from royal sites and administered by a royal official or reeve. In the west the kings seem to want to keep personal control of the trade – I suspect the exchange still functioned on the level of personal contacts and the feasting and redistribution of the foreign luxuries to client lords took place on these central sites. It thus falls into what Offer (1997) calls 'the economy of regard', and Bourdieu 'the accumulation of symbolic capital' (1990, 112-21), at least on the Gaeldom side of the transaction. But clearly such exposure to Gallic merchants, their methods and coinage did not inspire emulation. There are only two imported coins of this period (AD 450-700) in the whole of Gaeldom, both from Ireland, so that it seems even hoarding for bullion value was not taking place, as it did later in the Norse period. Writers like Adomnán were perfectly aware of towns, merchants and coinage, and we know that many clerics and others would have visited places like Rome. I would suggest that the decision not to have these 'civilised' attributes was at least partly a conscious one, because personal interaction and social standing were more important than personal gain, rather than because they were too unsophisticated to produce them. The view that towns are necessary for civilisation is an old one, and was used to justify the colonisation and eradication of indigenous peoples in North America and other areas. There is surely no place for such views today when we are aware of the complexities of pre-industrial societies.

1.3.3 Administration

One of the most important documents from Early Medieval Scotland is the *Miniugud Senchusa fer nAlban* (Bannerman 1974; Dumville 2002). This is a highly complex text, repeatedly revised and rewritten and fiendishly complex to interpret, but at its core is a civil survey of the landholders and their wealth (in terms of client households) in Dál Riata. Two major strands can be separated, one part dating to the 640s and another to the 740s, and in it we see the names not just of kings and whole peoples, but of individuals and their obligations to the king. There is no equivalent attempt to carry out this detailed type of survey anywhere else in northern Europe at this early period – the *Tribal Hidage*, for example, merely gives total numbers of people in a polity rather than individual named persons. The original purpose is now obscure, though my colleague Professor Dauvit Broun (pers comm) suggests that its restructuring reflects periods of change in overkingship in Dál Riata. The important point here, however, is that this survey is not just innovative, but shows both literacy, and some sort of administrative development at a very early period in European terms. The writing, re-writing and consultation of these secular documents pre-supposes someone to produce, store and interpret them in the secular contexts of military service and food renders of clients. I have suggested elsewhere that literacy was more widespread in the Atlantic Insular world than commonly acknowledged (Campbell 2010). This is shown by mention of penalties in the Irish Laws for stopping 'learning' by young people and tenant farmers living on monastic estates; many recorded instances of secular pilgrims and penitents living on monastic sites; failed monks who return to the secular world; the widespread use of ogham script including casual use on small objects; as well as direct archaeological evidence of graffiti from secular sites such as Dunadd and Tintagel, Cornwall. I have also suggested that the reconstructed satchel from the secular site of Loch Glashan (Argyll and Bute) was a book satchel (Crone and Campbell 2005; Campbell 2010, 141), though this interpretation has been disputed (Clarke 2012, 112).

Another aspect which is well-known but perhaps not receiving just attention in European terms is the creation of the 'Iona Chronicle', possibly as early as the 560s (Charles-Edwards 2006, 8, 58). The Insular annals developed from Late Roman annalistic accounts such as those of Prosper of Aquitaine and Isidore of Seville, which continued into the fifth to early seventh centuries on the continent, but the concept of keeping a year by year contemporary record of political, social and natural events was a re-innovation by the monastic houses of Early Medieval Europe. The Iona Chronicle formed the basis of many other annals, particularly the 'Chronicle of Ireland' assembled in the early tenth century, and many insular monasteries kept their own records of this type. Despite debate about exactly when the Iona annals become regular contemporary entries, rather than back-dated accounts from other sources, most scholars agree that it was happening by the 640s if not in the late sixth century (Woolf 2007, 3;

Herbert 1996; Evans 2010, 172ff; Charles-Edwards 2006). The Frankish annals in contrast mainly originated in the late seventh and early eighth century (Burgess and Kulikowski 2009, 172; Scholz 1970), as was the case with the North British annals (Dumville 1974; 1977). The earliest entries of the Anglo-Saxon annals may belong to the 660s (Swanton 1996). Whether or not Iona produced the earliest examples, it was at the forefront of these new developments. This new phase of record keeping suggests a new way of looking at and ordering the world was developing in Atlantic Britain. Yet, well-known as this is to local historians, general accounts of chronicle writing emphasise the contributions of Isidore and Bede, while tending to ignore the Irish tradition altogether (eg Scholz 1970, 3), or sometimes dismissing these as 'mere annals' (Burgess and Kulikowski 2009, 154).

1.3.4 Learning

Although we are familiar with the idea of monasteries such as Iona being centres of learning, it is not always appreciated just how much they contributed to the intellectual development of the wider European community. This is being established by much new scholarship in recent years, for example by Thomas Clancy, Gilbert Márkus, Thomas O'Loughlin, James Fraser and many others (Wooding et al 2010). Convincing arguments have been made for the wide variety of books available in the library on Iona by the late seventh century (Clancy and Márkus 1995, 211-22; O'Loughlin 1994), and this library is similar in size and composition to those described for the earliest known Carolingian monastic libraries of the mid- to late eighth century (McKitterick 1989, 166-75). Iona is accepted by many scholars to be the production site of illuminated manuscripts, notably the Cathach of Columba, the *Book of Kells* and possibly the *Book of Durrow*. These works exhibit great artistic invention, but more important in terms of the intellectual content are the original writings produced in Iona. These include: Cumméne's 'book of the miracles of Columba' in the 640s; Adomnán's *Vita Columbae, De Locis Sancis*, and *Cáin Adomnáin* (the *Law of Innocents*) in the late 600s; and at least in part, the *Collectio Canonum Hibernensis*, of the early eighth century; as well as numerous poems (Clancy and Márkus 1995). Adomnán was described by Medieval commentators on the continent as 'the Illustrious', the only Gael in the Middle Ages to achieve this distinction (O'Loughlin 1995), a testament to his learning which expressed itself in the *De Locis Sanctis*, which was repeatedly copied and was the standard work for many centuries (despite Adomnán never leaving these islands). O'Loughlin (2007) has shown that this was not a simple work of description but a sophisticated liturgical and exegitical text in which Adomnán felt confident enough to identify the problems with Augustine's solution to the inconsistencies in the accounts of the four gospels, and to provide his own solution. The *Vita Columbae* is similarly a complex document showing a sophisticated understanding of biblical sources, commentaries and presenting a subtly directed message to its audience. The *Law of Innocents*, which sought to guarantee the rights of women, children and non-combatants in times of warfare, can be seen as a precursor to the United Nation's Universal Declaration of Human Rights, and Adomnán managed to assemble over 30 kings from Scotland and Ireland to witness it (Ni Dhonnchadha 1982; Márkus 1997; O'Loughlin 2001). Adomnán has also been suggested to be the route by which Virgil reached Anglo-Saxon England, as Lapidge has claimed in his analysis of Aldhelm's career (Lapidge

2007). The *Collectio Canonum Hibernensis,* co-authored by an Iona monk in the early eighth century, is also a pioneering work, for the first time codifying the canon law of the Church. This work was the standard for four centuries, and was widely copied in continental Europe. All these works show that Iona was at the heart of intellectual life of Europe and innovation, and in no sense a backwater or periphery. It seems that from at least the 640s onwards Iona was a major centre of innovation in learning just as it was in sculpture and art, and that this innovation ultimately contributed to the Carolingian renaissance.

1.4 Distorted visions

Does all this matter? I think it does, and by way of example I would like to look at a few instances of how a distorted view of Early Medieval Scotland as a backward place incapable of indigenous development has distorted archaeological interpretations.

1.4.1 Glass vessels

When I started working on my PhD in the 1980s, the sherds of glass found on western British sites were interpreted as 'cullet' brought in from Anglo-Saxon areas to make trinkets and beads (Harden 1956). Although many complete vessels were known from Anglo-Saxon pagan graves, no-one thought that people in the west could have access to such objects, and documentary references, such as Adomnán's account of the Pictish king Bridei drinking from a glass vessel, were dismissed as anachronisms (Foster 1965, 234), or in the irrefutable case of a surviving complete glass phial from Mullaroe, Sligo, as 'an exception' (Mytum 1986, 376). My own work on the taphonomy of imported glass and pottery from Dinas Powys (South Glamorgan) allowed me to prove that these sherds were in fact derived from complete glass vessels in use on the site, and this interpretation can now be extended to the over 60 sites which have produced this material (Campbell 1995; 2000; 2007). These luxury items, all used for drinking in the feasting hall or monastic refectory, were in as widespread use as in contemporary European contexts, and some may even have been made in Scottish monastic centres, as there is some manufacturing evidence from Whithorn (Campbell 1997, 314) and Iona (Barber 1982, fig 42, 108, 23). Iona has produced a reticella rod used in the production of highly decorated eighth-/ninth-century vessels, and sherds from these vessels have been found at the ecclesiastical establishments at Inchmarnock, Argyll and Bute (Lowe 2008, fig 6.40), Portmahomack, Highland (Campbell 2016), and Whithorn (Hill 1997, 314, fig 10.12).

1.4.2 Iona vallum

Scotland has not just been written out of European narratives but also Insular ones. Before the widespread use of Insular as a label, older terms such as 'Hiberno-Saxon' specifically excluded Scotland as a locus. The Hunterston brooch, for example, was often referred to as being 'Irish' (eg Youngs 1989, 91), and it was only archaeological evidence of production of similar brooches at Dunadd which revealed Scotland as a possible place of manufacture (Campbell and Lane 1993). The interpretation of the monastic vallum at Iona has suffered a similar fate. I have mentioned Iona several times, but here want to look at the layout of the site. It has always been realised that Iona's vallum was unusual. Unlike all the Irish parallels for Early Medieval monasteries, the vallum was not circular, but quadrangular or D-shaped. It has been regarded as an oddity, perhaps because it occupied the site of an earlier Iron Age enclosure. New geophysical work by the National Trust for Scotland has clarified the picture and shown that there are complex multiple versions of this shape of enclosure on Iona (Derek Alexander pers comm). However, I would suggest that the search for Irish parallels is misplaced. When we look at other major Scottish monastic sites it turns out that not one has a circular vallum, and all are similar to Iona, despite repeated attempts to force the evidence into an Irish pattern. All these C- and D- shaped enclosures have the long side open to the landscape, along a scarp, shoreline or river terrace. Examples are now known from aerial photography, excavation and other surveys at Portmahomack, Fortingall (Perth and Kinross), Forteviot, and St Blane's, Kingarth (Argyll and Bute). Previous attempts to impose a circularity on the evidence derived from very short excavated stretches of enclosure ditches at sites such as Whithorn (Hill 1997, 30-5, fig 2.6), Inchmarnock (Lowe 2008, 252, figs 5.9, 9.2) and Dunning (Perth and Kinross; Cook 2008, illus 4) can be shown to be misplaced, and were explicitly based on the notion that Ireland must be the progenitor of monasticism and therefore all cultural traits. In fact, the Iona form of enclosure seems to be the norm for the larger sites in Scotland, though some smaller sites may have circular boundaries. Interestingly, this layout is shared by some monasteries in Anglo-Saxon areas, such as Hoddom (Dumfries and Galloway; Lowe 2006, fig 8.11), and probably Lindisfarne (Northumberland; David Petts pers comm). At a recent workshop on Iona, organised to prepare for the new museum display of sculptured stones, I suggested that the reason for this relates to the landscape position of these sites. At Iona the open side of the D-shaped enclosure allows an extensive view over the sea and small islands towards the imposing mountains of Mull. Similarly, the other sites mentioned each has a view over an outstanding landscape towards hills, perhaps reflecting Psalm 12 – 'I will lift up mine eyes unto the hills: from whence cometh my help'. So even at this micro-scale, the attitude was outward-looking (physically and metaphorically), rather than just the inward contemplation of one's sins.

1.4.3 Anglo-Saxon Scotland

National blindspots can work both ways of course. In the Early Medieval period much of southern Scotland was under the political and cultural influence of Northumbrian Bernicia. The Anglo-Saxon material culture of this region has been largely ignored by Scottish archaeologists until recent years, perhaps because it was thought to relate to another national narrative, that of the English. Perhaps surprisingly, Anglo-Saxon scholars have also tended to ignore this material and most distribution maps stop at the border (eg Lucy 2000, fig 5.9). Different legal and organisational structures in the two countries compounded this problem; for example, the Portable Antiquities Scheme only covers England (Marzinzik 2011). A particularly perverse example of this is the decision to exclude Scotland from the British Academy's series on Anglo-Saxon sculpture, which thereby excludes one of the finest examples of all Anglo-Saxon sculpture, the cross from Ruthwell, Dumfries and Galloway (and fine examples from Jedburgh, Scottish Borders, Aberlady, East Lothian and Hoddom, amongst others). Perhaps it is because the concept of an Anglo-Saxon identity is so tied up with the notion of England – there is, for example, no *Anglo-Saxon Britain* to compare with *Anglo-Saxon*

England (Stenton 1971) – that Anglo-Saxon material outside of England is not seen as important by Anglo-Saxon scholars. Recent research by Alice Blackwell has begun to address this issue (Blackwell 2007; 2010; 2018). The surprising fact is that there is more high-status gold and garnet jewellery from East Lothian than in parts of Bernicia further south (Blackwell 2010, 370). It seems that people in Scottish Bernicia were no less eager to adopt Germanic material culture than those in England. Of course, whether this means there was an invasion of genetically Germanic peoples is a hotly debateable topic, with several scholars suggesting a more nuanced approach seeing Bernicia as a largely British kingdom which adopted Germanic material culture (Lucy 2000, 174-81; Campbell 2009; O'Brien 2012; Loveluck and Laing 2011).

1.5 Vision and liminality

In the Carolingian Empire mortared stone buildings seem to have been one of the key modes of expressing material power. In Scotland, sculptured monuments, set not just in monasteries, but also in the landscape at key points, performed a similar function (Carver 2005; Forsyth and Driscoll 2009), though wooden buildings and drystone forts (Ralston 2006; Noble et al 2013) may have been large and elaborate. Alongside these monuments, personal jewellery was a key means of expressing wealth and position in society (Nieke 1993; Whitfield 2004) – these objects are both at a more intimate scale than the massive buildings of sites such as Aachen. Perhaps this was just because this was a smaller scale society. Certainly, in Scotland the move from a kin-based society to the incipient Medieval kingdom took a different trajectory from other areas such as England and the continent, but this did not prevent the emergence of a unified kingdom in the ninth century, an early date in European terms.

What I think is most important is that from at least the early seventh century we see a process of innovation at work Scotland. This innovation takes place in the practical fields of art (the development of the Insular art style at sites such as Dunadd and the Mote of Mark, Dumfries and Galloway, as well as in the monastic centres throughout Scotland), sculpture (the invention of the ringed cross on Iona, Pictish animal art), metalwork (the complex, highly-decorated brooches and ecclesiastical vessels), but also being at the forefront of new ways of learning (Canon Laws, biblical exegesis and liturgy), and ordering the world (annal writing, the civil survey of the Dál Riata, the *Law of Innocents*). This could well be described as the First Scottish Enlightenment. Throughout this period Scotland was in constant contact with other areas – Ireland, Anglo-Saxon England, the continent and the Mediterranean world. Local traditions were transformed into new art styles and new ways of thinking about the world. I hope the evidence presented here has shown just how influential and important places like Iona were in the Early Medieval period in European terms. Yes, Scotland did not have the normal attributes of a capitalist market economy, but given recent events in the financial world, it is possible to view this as a sane choice rather than an indication of backwardness! I would also like to suggest that it was the lack of a monetised economy which resulted in the diversion of available surplus into the support of artists and craftsmen, with the resulting explosion in output from the later seventh century. Gaeldom also had a social system which privileged people of learning and people of high artistic skill – a poet could have the same honour-price as a king, a master carpenter the same honour-price as a lord (Kelly 1988). A major difference from other areas of Europe was that high status could be gained through acquired skills, and that secular intellectuals were highly valued (Charles-Edwards 1998). The reason for this was that the Iron Age learned orders were not terminated by Rome, but survived into the Early Medieval period having been transformed by Christianisation. In this process, these new understandings were written down by the newly literate intellectuals. Thus, paradoxically, Irish vernacular literature and law far exceeds in quantity that of any other area of contemporary Europe, areas which had enjoyed the benefits of Roman civilisation. What I would also like to propose is that Scotland was innovative precisely *because* it was in a liminal, non-mainstream situation; the people were exposed to constantly changing conditions, political, economic and social as well as environmental, making survival imperative on being adaptable, but also allowing native traditions to flourish. Coupled with its geographical position at a crossroads of Irish, Pictish, British and Anglo-Saxon (and later Norse) cultural influences, integration and innovation were perhaps inevitable. Stability does not produce change, by definition.

I hope I have begun to redress the balance in response to the entrenched stereotypes I described in my opening remarks, and that we can appreciate the place of Scotland in Early Medieval Europe. To ignore the differences apparent in Early Medieval Scotland is to lose important insights into how relatively small polities managed to transform themselves into Medieval kingdoms without the full panoply of political structures often deemed essential to the formation of early states (cf Broun 2013).

I leave you with a quote from another Iona product, the monk Colman Elo writing around 600, which I think illustrates the openness of viewpoint 'from the edge of the world', rather than a parochial society unengaged in the Post-Roman rebirth of Europe.

> What is best for the mind? Breadth and humility, for every good thing finds room in a broad, humble mind (Clancy and Márkus 1995, 206)

Acknowledgements

This paper has benefitted greatly from many helpful discussions with present and past colleagues at the University of Glasgow, particularly Alice Blackwell, Dauvit Broun, Thomas Clancy, Stephen Driscoll, Katherine Forsyth, Sally Foster, Meggen Gondek, Gilbert Márkus, Gordon Noble and Simon Taylor; the responsibility for the paper is, of course, entirely my own. I would also like to thank Derek Alexander, Alice Blackwell, Martin Goldberg, Fraser Hunter, and Peter Yeoman for help with various aspects of the paper and its presentation to the *Scotland in Early Medieval Europe* conference.

References

Bannerman, J 1974 *Studies in the history of Dalriada.* Edinburgh: Scottish Academic Press.

Barber, J 1982 'Excavations on Iona, 1979', *Proceedings of the Society of Antiquaries of Scotland* 111, 282-380.

Barrett, J 2008 'What caused the Viking Age?', *Antiquity* 82, 671-85.

Birch, S 1846 'On the torc of the Celts', *Archaeological Journal* 3, 27-38.

Blackwell, A 2007 'An Anglo-Saxon figure-decorated plaque from Ayton (Scottish Borders), its parallels and implications', *Medieval Archaeology* 51, 165-72.

Blackwell, A 2010 'Anglo-Saxon Dunbar, East Lothian: a brief re-assessment of the archaeological evidence and some chronological implications', *Medieval Archaeology* 54, 361-71.

Blackwell, A 2018 'A reassessment of the Anglo-Saxon artefacts from Scotland: material interactions and identities in Early Medieval northern Britain', unpublished PhD thesis, University of Glasgow.

Bourdieu, P 1990 *The logic of practice.* Stanford: Stanford University Press.

Bray, E 1986 *The discovery of the Hebrides.* Glasgow: Collins.

Broun, D 2013 'State-formation in Scotland before the twelfth century', unpublished O Donnell Lecture, Oxford 2013.

Broun, D and MacGregor, M (eds) 2007 *Mìorun Mòr nan Gall, 'The great ill-will of the lowlander'? Lowland perceptions of the highlands, Medieval and Modern.* Centre for Scottish and Celtic Studies, University of Glasgow: Glasgow.

Burgess, R W and Kulikowski, M 2009 'The history and origins of the Latin Chronicle tradition', *The Medieval Chronicle* 6, 153-77.

Campbell, E 1995 'New evidence for glass vessels in western Britain and Ireland in the sixth/seventh centuries AD', *in* Foy, D (ed) *Le Verre de l'Antiquité tardive et du Haut Moyen Age*, 35-40. Association Française pour l'Archéologie du Verre: Musée Archéologique du Val D'Oise.

Campbell, E 1997 'The Early Medieval imports', *in* Hill, P, 297-322.

Campbell, E 2000 'A review of glass vessels in western Britain and Ireland AD 400-800', *in* Price, J (ed) *Glass in Britain and Ireland,* AD *350-1100*, 33-46. British Museum Occasional Paper 127. London: British Museum Press.

Campbell, E 2007 *Continental and Mediterranean imports to Atlantic Britain and Ireland,* AD *400-800.* Council for British Archaeology Research Report No 157. York: Council for British Archaeology.

Campbell, E 2009 'Anglo-Saxon/Gaelic interaction in Scotland', *in* Graham-Campbell, J and Ryan, M (eds) *Anglo-Saxon/Irish relations before the Vikings.* Proceedings of the British Academy 157, 253-63.

Campbell, E 2010 'The archaeology of writing in the time of Adomnán', *in* Wooding et al, 139-44.

Campbell, E 2016 'Glass and glass-working', *in* Carver, M O H, Garner-Lahire, J & Spall, C *Portmahomack on Tarbat Ness. Changing ideologies in north-east Scotland, sixth to the sixteenth century.* Edinburgh: Society of Antiquaries of Scotland.

Campbell, E and Lane, A 1993 'Celtic and Germanic interaction in Scottish Dalriada: the seventh-century metalworking site at Dunadd', *in* Spearman and Higgitt, 52-63.

Carver, M O H 2005 'Sculpture in action: the Early Medieval cross-slabs on the Tarbat peninsula, Easter Ross', *in* Foster, S (ed) *Able minds and practised hands,* 13-36. Society for Medieval Archaeology Monograph 23. Leeds: Society for Medieval Archaeology.

Chapman, M 1992 *The Celts: the construction of a myth.* Basingstoke: Macmillan Press.

Charles-Edwards, T 1998 'The context and uses of literacy in early Christian Ireland', *in* Pryce, H (ed) *Literacy in Medieval Celtic societies*, 62-82. Cambridge: Cambridge University Press.

Charles-Edwards, T 2006 *The Chronicle of Ireland*. Liverpool: Liverpool University Press.

Clancy, T and Márkus, G 1995 *Iona: the earliest poetry of a Celtic monastery*. Edinburgh: Edinburgh University Press.

Clarke, D, Blackwell, A and Goldberg, M 2012 *Early Medieval Scotland: individuals, communities and ideas*. Edinburgh: National Museums Scotland.

Clarke, D 2012 'Communities', *in* Clarke et al, 68-139.

Cook, M 2008 'An Early Christian vallum in Dunning?', *Tayside and Fife Archaeological Journal* 14, 9-15.

Crone, A and Campbell, E 2005 *A crannog of the first millennium* AD*: excavations by Jack Scott at Loch Glashan, Argyll, 1960*. Edinburgh: Society of the Antiquaries of Scotland.

Dumville, D 1974 'Some aspects of the chronology of the *Historia Brittonum*', *Studia Celtica* 10/11, 439-45.

Dumville, D 1977 'Sub-Roman Britain: history and legend', *History* 62(205), 173-92.

Dumville, D 2002 'Ireland and north Britain in the Early Middle Ages: contexts for Míniugud Senchasa Fher nAlban', *in* Ó Baoill, C and McGuire, N R (eds) *Rannsachadh na Gàidhlig 2000: papers read at the conference, Scottish Gaelic Studies 2000, held at the University of Aberdeen 2-4 August 2000*, 185-211. Aberdeen: University of Aberdeen.

Evans, N 2010 *The present in the past in Medieval Irish chronicles*. Woodbridge: Boydell Press.

Ferguson, W 1998 *The identity of the Scottish nation: an historic quest*. Edinburgh: Edinburgh University Press.

Forsyth, K 1997 *Language in Pictland: the case against 'non-Indo-European Pictish*. Series: Studia Hameliana, 2. Utrecht: De Keltiche Draak.

Forsyth, K and Driscoll, S T 2009 'Symbols of power in Ireland and Scotland, eighth-tenth century', *in* Conde, F and Valdés, C (eds) *Territorio, sociedad y poder, revista de estudios Medievales*, 31-66. Gijon: Ediciones Trea.

Foster, I 1965 'The emergence of Wales', *in* Foster, I and Daniel, G (eds) *Prehistoric and Early Wales*, 213-35. London: Routledge and Paul.

Foster, S M 2014 *Picts, Gaels and Scots: Early Historic Scotland*. Edinburgh: Birlinn.

Fraser, J 2009 *From Caledonia to Pictland: Scotland to 795*. Edinburgh: Edinburgh University Press.

Geary, P 2013 'Concluding remarks', *in* Salonen, K, Jensen, K V and Jørgansen, T (eds) *Medieval Christianity in the north: new studies*, 261-68. Turnhout: Brepols.

Gilchrist, R and Reynolds, A (eds) 2009 *Reflections: fifty years of* Medieval Archaeology*, 1957-2007*. Leeds: Maney.

Gustin, I 2004 *Mellan Gava och Marknad: Handel, Tillit och Materiell Kultur under Vikinatid* . Lund Studies in Medieval Archaeology 34. Lund: Lund University.

Hamerrow, H, Hinton, D and Crawford, S (eds) 2011 *The Oxford handbook of Anglo-Saxon archaeology*. Oxford: Oxford University Press.

Harden, D B 1956 'Glass vessels in Britain and Ireland, AD 400-1000', *in* Harden, D B (ed) *Dark Age Britain: studies presented to E T Leeds*, 132-67. London: Methuen.

Henderson, G 1994 'Emulation and invention in Carolingian art', *in* McKitterick, R (ed) *Carolingian culture: emulation and invention*, 248-73. Cambridge: Cambridge University Press.

Henderson, G and Henderson, I 2004 *The art of the Picts.* London: Thames and Hudson.

Herbert, M 1996 *Iona, Kells and Derry: the history and hagiography of the Monastic familia*. Dublin: Four Courts Press.

Hill, P 1997 *Whithorn and St Ninian. The excavation of a monastic town, 1984-91*. Stroud: Sutton/Whithorn Trust.

Hodges, R 2004 'The shaping of Medieval north-western Europe', *Antiquity* 78, 723-7.

Hood, A B E 1978 *St Patrick: his writings and Muirchu's Life.* Phillimore: London.

Januszczak, W 2012 *The Dark Ages: an age of light*. Episode 4 – 'The men of the north'. http://www.bbc.co.uk/programmes/p00zbtmp/episodes/guide. Accessed 4/6/14.

Kelly, F 1988 *A guide to early Irish Law.* Early Irish Law Series 3. Dublin: Dublin Institute for Advanced Studies.

Lane, A and Campbell, C 2001 *Dunadd: an early Dalriadic capital.* Oxford: Oxbow.

Lapidge, M 2007 'The career of Aldhelm', *Anglo-Saxon England* 36, 15-69.

Loveluck, C and Laing, L 2011 'Anglo-Saxons and Britons', *in* Hamerrow et al, 550-71.

Lowe, C 1999 *Angels, fools and tyrants: Britons and Anglo-Saxons in southern Scotland* AD *450-750.* Edinburgh: Canongate Books.

Lowe, C 2006 *Excavations at Hoddom, Dumfriesshire: an early ecclesiastical site in south-west Scotland.* Edinburgh: Society of Antiquaries of Scotland.

Lowe, C 2008 *Inchmarnock: an Early Historic island monastery and its archaeological landscape.* Edinburgh: Society of Antiquaries of Scotland.

Lucy, S 2000 *The Anglo-Saxon way of death.* Stroud: Sutton.

Márkus, G 1997 *Adomnán's 'law of innocents': Cáin Adomnán.* Glasgow: Blackfriars.

Martin, M 1716 *Description of the western islands of Scotland.* London.

Marzinzik, S 2011 'Anglo-Saxon archaeology and the public', *in* Hamerrow et al, 1025-42.

McKitterick, R 1989 *The Carolingians and the written word.* Cambridge: Cambridge University Press.

Mytum, H 1986 'High-status vessels in Early Historic Ireland: a reference in the *Bethu Brigte*', *Oxford Journal of Archaeology* 5, 375-8.

Netzer, N 2001 'Style: a history of uses and abuses in the study of Insular art', *in* Redknap, M, Edwards, N, Youngs, S, Lane, A and Knight, J (eds) 2001 *Pattern and purpose in Insular art*, 169-78. Oxford: Oxbow.

Netzer, N 2009 'Framing the Book of Durrow inside/outside the Anglo-Saxon World', *Anglo-Saxon Studies in Archaeology and History* 16, 65-78.

Ni Dhonnchadha, M 1982 'The guarantor list of Cáin Adomnáin, 697', *Peritia* 1, 178-215.

Nieke, M 1993 'Penannular and related brooches: secular ornament or symbol in action?' *in* Spearman and Higgitt, 135-42.

Noble, G, Gondek, M, Campbell, E and Cook, M 2013 'Between prehistory and history: the archaeological detection of social change among the Picts', *Antiquity* 87, 1136-50.

O'Brien, C 2012 'Yeavering and Bernician kingship: a review of debate on the Hybrid Culture Thesis', *in* Petts, D and Turner, S (eds) *Early Medieval Northumbria: kingdoms and communities,* AD *450-1100*, 207-20. Turnhout: Brepols.

Ó Carragáin, T 2010 *Churches in Early Medieval Ireland: architecture, ritual and memory*. New Haven: Yale.

O'Loughlin, T 1994 'The library of Iona in the late seventh century: the evidence from Adomnán's *De Locis Sanctis*', *Ériu* 45, 33-52.

O'Loughlin, T 1995 'Adomnán the illustrious', *Innes Review* 46, 1-14.

O'Loughlin, T 1997 'Living in the ocean', *in* Bourke, C (ed) *Studies in the cult of Saint Columba,* 11-23. Dublin: Four Courts Press.

O'Loughlin, T 2001 *Adomnán at Birr: essays in commemoration of the Law of Innocents*. Dublin: Four Courts Press.

O'Loughlin, T 2007 *Adomnán and the holy places: the perceptions of an Insular monk on the location of the biblical drama*. London: T and T Clark.

Offer, A 1997 'Between the gift and the market: the economy of regard', *Economic History Review* 50, 450-76.

Peacock, D P S 1997 'Charlemagne's black stones: the re-use of Roman columns in Early Medieval Europe', *Antiquity* 71, 709-14.

Pinkerton, J 1787 *Discussion on the origin and progress of the Scythians or Goths*. London.

Ralston, I 2006 *Celtic fortifications*. Stroud: Tempus.

Rollason, D 2015 'Review article: Charlemagne's palace', *Archaeological Journal* 172, 443-48.

Ryan, M 1989 'Church metalwork in the eighth and ninth centuries', *in* Youngs, 125-69.

Ryan, M 1990 'The formal relationships of Insular Early Medieval eucharistic chalices', *Proceedings of the Royal Irish Academy* 90C, 281-356.

Scholz, B W 1970 *Carolingian chronicles: royal Frankish annals and Nithard's Histories*. Ann Arbor: University of Michigan Press.

Scully, D 2005 'Bede, Orosius and Gildas on the early history of Britain', *in* Lebecq, S Perrin, M and Szerwiniak, O (eds) *Bède le Vénérable*, 31-42. Lille: Ceges – Université Charles-de-Gaulle.

Sharpe, R (ed and trnsl) 1991 *Adomnán of Iona: Life of St Columba*. London: Penguin.

Sims-Williams, P 1998 'Celtomania and Celtoscepticism', *Cambrian Medieval Celtic Studies* 36, 1-35.

Sims-Williams, P 2012 'Bronze- and Iron-Age Celtic-speakers: what don't we know, what can't we know and what could we know? Language, genetics and archaeology in the twenty-first century', *Antiquaries Journal* 92, 427-49.

Sindbaek, S M 2007 'The small world of the Vikings: networks in Early Medieval communication and exchange', *Norwegian Archaeological Review* 40, 59-74.

Spearman, M and Higgitt, J (eds) *The age of migrating ideas. Early Medieval art in northern Britain and Ireland*. Edinburgh: National Museums Scotland.

Stalley, R 1990 'European art and the Irish High Crosses', *Proceedings of the Royal Irish Academy* 90C, 135-58.

Stalley, R 2014 'Irish sculpture of the early tenth century and the work of the "Muiredach Master": problems of identification and meaning', *Proceedings of the Royal Irish Academy* 114C, 141-79.

Stenton, F 1971 *Anglo-Saxon England*. Oxford: Oxford University Press.

Swanton, M 1996 *The Anglo-Saxon Chronicle*. New York: Routledge.

VC *Vita Columbae*, see Sharpe 1991.

Webster, L 2012 *Anglo-Saxon art: a new history*. London: British Museum Press.

Whitfield, N 1987 'The motifs and techniques of Celtic filigree: are they original?', *in* Ryan, M (ed) *Ireland and Insular Art* AD *500-1200*, 75-84. Royal Irish Academy: Dublin.

Whitfield, N 1990 'Celtic filigree from the seventh to the ninth century AD with particular reference to that on brooches', four volumes, unpublished PhD thesis, University of London.

Whitfield, N 2004 'More thoughts on the wearing of brooches in Early Medieval Ireland', *in* Hourihane, C (ed) *Irish art historical studies in honour of Peter Harbison*, 70-108. Dublin: Four Courts Press.

Whitfield, N 2014 'Hunterston/"Tara" brooches reconsidered', *in* Hawkes, J (ed) *Making histories: proceedings of the sixth international conference on Insular art, York 2011*, 145-61. Stamford: Paul Watkins Publishing.

Wickam, C 2005 *Framing the Early Middle Ages*. Oxford: Oxford University Press.

Wooding, J with Aist, R, Clancy, T and O'Loughlin, T (eds) *Adomnán of Iona: theologian, lawmaker, peacemaker*. Dublin: Four Courts Press.

Woolf, A 2007 *From Pictland to Alba 789-1070*. Edinburgh: Edinburgh University Press.

Youngs, S (ed) 1989 *The work of angels: masterpieces of Celtic metalwork, sixth-ninth centuries*. London: British Museum.

2

'A bright crowd of chancels': whither early church archaeology in Scotland?

Sally M Foster

> He brings northward to meet the Lord a bright crowd of chancels – Colum Cille, kirks for hundreds, widespread candle

2.1 Introduction

From this opening verse of Thomas Clancy's translation of *Tiurgraind Beccáin* (The Last Verses of Beccán), a poet, hermit and saint associated with Rum, Iona and the Hebrides (d AD 677), we learn of the perceived extent of St Columba's influence in promoting Christian beliefs and converting people beyond his monastic base on Iona (Clancy and Márkus 1995, 147, 156). Today we acknowledge that a change of belief need not immediately correlate with Christianisation – a change in ritual practices – and that the lived experience of religion might often involve just small-scale and repetitive actions quite difficult for archaeologists to detect in most contexts, which extend technically anywhere (see Petts 2011). We struggle to recognise whether some structures associated with early burial places *are* actually early churches. Indeed, we appreciate that for the majority of people, the earliest Christian worship could have taken place in the home, and that prior to the eighth century burials rarely took place in a church graveyard (see for example, O'Brien 2003; Maldonado 2011; 2013). Yet, written while Iona was energetically developing the cult of Columba, this seventh-century poem with its reference to 'chancels' reminds us how the presence of churches was, and still is, an important index of the spread, nature and broad impact of Christianity in Early Medieval Scotland. This paper offers a brief commentary on the present state of play with early church archaeology in Scotland, some of the issues, and the rationale for a future approach that on the one hand puts Scottish church archaeology on the European stage while at the same time responding to and celebrating its diversity and local idiosyncrasies.

in: Blackwell, A.E. (ed.) 2019: *Scotland in Early Medieval Europe*,
Leiden: Sidestone Press, pp. 35-50.

2.2 Current state of early church archaeology in Scotland

Although they both focus on materialised ideology (cf de Marrais et al 1996) and are part of a continuum, the archaeology of religion is greater than the archaeology of the Church (there can be a tendency to conflate these: Maldonado 2012); each needs understanding in the context of wider society and landscape, and from an interdisciplinary perspective. That the rituals of religion are everywhere and in the every day, and it is impossible to separate the domestic and ritual (cf Bradley 2005, 210), does not negate or diminish the need for a greater modern focus on the archaeological evidence for its most recognisable physical expressions, and their materiality (cf Insoll 2011, 1): our Christian sculpture and early churches, their associated ecclesiastical complexes, and landscape contexts. These were still places where people performed formalised as well as personal rituals, and where individual and group memory was exteriorised through the production of artefacts, monuments and landscapes (cf Gilchrist 2012, 13-14). And they help us to answer the most basic what, when and where questions that we still sorely need answers to.

Stephen Driscoll's comments on the Pictish Church apply to the country as a whole:

> ... almost nothing is known about the origins of the Church and its development before the eleventh century ... This must be considered a priority for the future (Driscoll 2011, 270).

The Medieval section of the 2013 *Scottish Archaeological Research Framework* (ScARF 2012) mirrors this need, although the reader needs to piece together what is relevant to the Church and early Christianity (a reflection of the document's thematic structure as well as the interests of its many authors). Charles Thomas, in 1971, is the first and last person so far to have attempted any significant overview of the different sources for the early church across Scotland, with his inspirational *The Early Christian archaeology of north Britain* (Thomas 1971). In relation to burial, the influential paradigms inherited from Thomas, in particular, are only now being revisited (Maldonado 2011; 2013). Scotland still lacks a modern version of the *Early Christian monuments of Scotland* (Allen and Anderson 1903), although there is the excellent *Early Medieval sculpture in the West Highlands and Islands* and *Art of the Picts* (Fisher 2001; Henderson and Henderson 2005). Since Thomas, Ian Smith and Ian Fisher published short overviews of the current state of knowledge and issues in Scottish church archaeology, and more recent books provide basic introductions (Smith 1996; Fisher 1996; eg Carver 2008, 37-42; and Foster 2014, ch 5; Jones 2013 is useful for broader British developments).

The absence of any overarching archaeological research strategy for the early church in Scotland may, with hindsight, help to explain Historic Scotland's regrettable decision in 2005 not to excavate to its earliest levels the Anglian church at Auldhame (East Lothian). This exceptionally rare beast – a previously unrecognised abandoned church with pre-twelfth-century origins – was discovered when ploughing brought up human remains. We should also allow for how, in the last couple of decades, we have glided to a new norm of expectation and perception of the early church. In good measure, this arises from recent publication of large or largish-scale excavations that mostly took place in the 1990s. With the exception of Iona (an earlier project), Hoddom and Auldhame, these were research-driven initiatives rather than prompted by rescue needs. In order of full publication, the key projects are:

- Iona (Argyll and Bute) 1979 (Barber 1982; see also St Ronan's chapel: O'Sullivan 1994)
- Whithorn (Dumfries and Galloway) 1984-91 (Hill 2006; McOmish and Petts 2008)
- Hoddom (Dumfries and Galloway) 1991 (Lowe 2006)
- Inchmarnock (Argyll and Bute) 1999-2004 (Lowe 2008)
- Isle of May (Fife) 1992-7 (James and Yeoman 2008)
- Hirsel (Scottish Borders) 1979-82, 1984 (Cramp 2014)
- Portmahomack (Easter Ross, Highland) 1994-2007 (Carver 2004; 2008; Carver et al 2016; Carver, this volume)
- Auldhame (East Lothian) 2005 (Crone and Hindmarch 2016; Hindmarch and Melikian 2006)
- Govan (Glasgow) 1994-6 (Driscoll 2003).[1]

Jerry O'Sullivan's analysis and commentary on the terribly piecemeal excavation history on Iona forcibly makes the point for large-scale, strategic fieldwork rather than 'death by many cuts' (O'Sullivan 1998). Archaeology now begins to provide the necessary counter-balance to church histories written from the surviving documentary sources, with their bias towards the Columban church. The archaeological evidence for greater late- and sub-Roman Christianity among those living on or close to the periphery of the Roman Empire – Britons in western and northern Britain, and quite probably the southern-most Picts – forces us to question the traditional, literary-derived modes and routes of conversion, from north to south (Petts 2003; Fraser 2009, 68-115; Seaman 2012). This Columban dominance is something that place-names studies are also redressing (eg Clancy 2008). Place-names add nuance to our appreciation of the workings of the Columban Church in Pictland (eg Clancy 1996; Taylor 1997), although the historian James Fraser now plays down the extent of impact that the Columban church had in Pictland prior to the late seventh century, and this has implications for how we understand the subsequent Verturian support for the Columban church (Fraser 2009).

In terms of excavated remains, we still have very little to go on for the church and sacred core of a site, and certainly nothing to compare with the excavations, however partial still, of the Anglo-Saxon monastery at Wearmouth and Jarrow (Co Durham). Like Wearmouth and Jarrow, however, we need to recognise that churches, their internal fittings and associated buildings for any ecclesiastical community will combine external architectural influences as well as native traditions in layout and construction (Cramp 2005, ch 24 in particular). Although no churches are standing in Scotland, and we only glimpse bits of possible ground plans (notably St Ninian's Isle, Shetland: Barrowman 2011), we can now more readily allow that the Picts built a small number of technically accomplished and ornate stone churches. At Portmahomack, the excavators are not certain if the lower levels of the east wall of the present crypt is the vestige of an eighth-century building, but sculpture surely implies a church enclosing some decorated stone sculptures,

1 The text lists key sources for excavations at their first mention only.

both architectural (a small corbel), fittings (such as thin slabs and an upright post grooved to hold a slab in place) and furnishings (a possible stone chair and an elaborate sarcophagus). The overall volume of fine stone sculpture leaves us in no doubt of the inhabitants' capacity to quarry, transport and finely work stone. Until Tómas Ó Carragáin's recent research on the early Irish church architecture, there had also been generally low expectations of this material (Ó Carragáin 2010). Ireland has a decent number of pre-Romanesque upstanding stone churches to work with, although few pre-date the eleventh century. Notably, Ó Carragáin has been able to consider liturgical aspects of the architecture (Ó Carragáin 2009a). His work also explores the Irish shrine church, the earliest example of which, he argues, was St Columba's Shrine on Iona, most likely built over Columba's burial place at the time of the enshrinement of his relics in the mid-eighth century (reconstructed in the late twentieth century without its characteristic *antae*). The choice of building materials for church buildings and sculptures reflected availability of resources, and the ability to procure and transport them, a little studied subject (but see Miller and Ruckley's 2005 study of the geological source of Pictish sculptures). We now have evidence in Scotland for how elaborate and large a timber church might be – the Minster church at eighth-century Whithorn with its complex internal sub-divisions (on the continent large and important churches were also built of timber, summarised by Ó Carragáin, above) – to which we might add the nice evidence from Iona for skilfully made timber fittings. At Whithorn and St Ronan's, Iona, ecclesiastical buildings were clay-bonded. Coloured window glass comes from Whithorn and now Iona (pers comm Ewan Campbell). In the largely tree-less Northern Isles, timber could still be a building component, but combined with stone and turf, as at the Norse chapel on the Brough of Deerness, Orkney, with its possible pre-Norse predecessor (Morris 1986). Corbelled upstanding structures in the Western Isles, such as on the Garvellachs and North Rona, are fiendishly difficult to date, and cannot be proved to be contemporary with what may be seventh- to ninth-century carved stones; Ireland's examples seem unlikely to pre-date the tenth century (O'Sullivan et al 2014, 169-70). A few of the upstanding or grassed-over foundations of small, single-cell structures in western Scotland and their associated remains, such as Sgòr nam Bán-Naoimha (cliff of the holy women) on the island of Canna (Highland), are generally assumed to be early Christian, but lack scientific dating.

For these larger sites, from excavation we now have some understanding of what takes place in their outer extremities but exceedingly little of the church and sacred core. From the University of York excavations at Portmahomack, we know that a massive sub-rectangular ditch and bank enclosed a graveyard and a series of workshops for fine metalworking and vellum working, built on either side of and connected by a well-laid road. This is interpreted as a large monastery established in the eighth century on the site of an earlier Iron Age settlement and burial place, possibly after a break in settlement. Regardless of the presence/absence of building material of any church building, these discoveries have finally given the lie to the notion that Picts were not capable of major intellectual, ecclesiastical, architectural, technological and artisanal enterprises.

Ecclesiastical sites clearly ranged in size, status and function. It is from Portmahomack and the other large-scale excavations mentioned earlier that we have begun to gain an important insight into their economic and technological basis. Work focussing, in particular, on the extremities of enclosed sites (the zones most readily available for investigation, and most vulnerable to development) reveals evidence for a hierarchical and zoned use of space for functions that include not just worship, burial, living, education, industry and crafts, but also large-scale food-processing enterprises (at Hoddom). Disappointingly, given the surviving outputs, we have yet to discover a sculpture workshop.

From the eighth century onwards, excavated church sites comprise our main visible evidence for power centres of any form. As in Anglo-Saxon England, the church had apparently become part of the aristocratic Establishment (cf Wormald 2006, ch 2), although what this means in practice on the ground is generally far from certain. Indeed, we must learn from the example of Flixborough in Lincolnshire. Here a seventh- to ninth-century Anglo-Saxon, high-status rural settlement is difficult to distinguish on archaeological grounds from a contemporary monastic site, with its evidence for literacy, burials, long-distance exchange and specialist craft-working (Loveluck 2007). From excavations it is now more widely recognised that Early Medieval settlements can incorporate burials, but not necessarily associated (or leastways distinctive) church buildings. Meantime, mortuary chapels, oratories or churches, not necessarily associated with burial evidence, are a component of Anglo-Saxon and continental settlements that are excavated on a large scale (Loveluck 2007, xvi; Ó Carragáin 2009b). So, we might also think of the Picts and their neighbours supporting diverse settlements that might incorporate a church, or a religious presence indicated in some way by sculpture. 'Church-settlement' embraces the notion of a major complex church site with multiple functions and possibly sited at a royal centre; this is what we might envisage for St Vigeans (Angus) or Meigle (Perth and Kinross) (Woolf 2013, 56), to name but a few examples.

Beyond excavations, re-examination of Early Medieval sculpture is also offering new insights into the architecture of church buildings. Long recognised as including some architectural sculpture, the interpretation of new and existing material is expanding the range of this assemblage (an arch, lintels, decorative architectural panels, some possibly for dividing space, internal fittings, chair finials, etc), and there may be other possibilities. Some of the sculpture was surely also intended for use *in* buildings, such as cross-slabs and recumbent stones in mortuary chapels (Henderson and Henderson 2005, ch 7; Clarke et al 2012, 92-7). By way of example, Jane Geddes' research on the assemblage of Pictish sculpture from St Vigeans enables her to evoke a stone church with ornate furnishings and possible internal divisions, enclosing highly valued relics and high-status burial monuments. The iconography tells of intellectual and theological rigour, and of concerns with pre-Christian practices such as bull sacrifice and pagan priesthood. Some of the monuments stood outside, and we get a sense of how the church's cycle of rituals extended from the church's distinctive knoll and into its wider estate (Geddes 2017).

We do not have descriptions for Wearmouth and Jarrow, but, in our mind's eye, our churches are also better equipped. For,

> who could imagine, for example, that the Pictish churches, patrons of vigorous schools of sculpture were without the necessary books and place for the celebration of the Eucharist or a range of scholarly texts for teaching purposes? Indeed, what we know of Pictish metalwork and sculpture encourages us to think that patronage of the arts in the service of the Church was of a high order (Ryan 2013, 8; as illustrated by, for example, Henderson and Henderson 2005, ch 4).

The extraordinary series of slates inscribed with texts and sketches recovered from the monastery on Inchmarnock vividly illustrates how the Church provided learning in the west. We should expect monastic schools in eastern Scotland too. George and Isobel Henderson challenge historians and archaeologists to 'allow for a political maturity and economic infrastructure' that is the match for the production of the Christian art that they interpret as evidencing a deeply erudite mindset (Henderson and Henderson 2005, 13, 180). Historians' revelations about Picts' use of literary sources to shape their identity provide indirect support for the prevalence, degree and influence of ecclesiastical scholarship, despite the lack of surviving Pictish documents (Evans 2011; Fraser 2011; Maldonado 2012).

2.3 Scottish early church archaeology in Europe

So, with some sense that our perception and expectations of the archaeology of the early church in Scotland is transforming, although the archaeological evidence-base and landscape perspective is still very slight, we should now consider some of the implications of thinking about the church in Scotland *in Europe.* The spread and universalising nature of the Church, and its inter-weaving with the social and political landscape, arguably facilitated the earliest Europeanisation. When we work with church archaeology, we are dealing with a connected people who are part of an extensive network, as the material culture, in particular, suggests. The influences of this process can be felt even before places convert, as in Scandinavia (Andrén 2005, 130). It is probably fair to say that most European scholars do not generally appreciate or necessarily value what happens in northern Britain in relation to their own work, or see how what happened in what is now Scotland more generally makes a contribution to European evolution as a whole; they are not helped by the tendency to focus on the contribution of the Irish and Anglo-Saxons, omitting the other peoples of northern Britain from European surveys (see Driscoll 2011; Campbell, this volume). Patrick Geary's analysis of the roots of this issue for Scandinavia is just as pertinent for Scotland (Geary 2013). He identifies two different scholarly traditions at the heart of the problem.

The first sees the northern and western peripheries of Europe as marginal in some way – continental Europe is normative and elsewhere is deviant. The scholarly 'home' predilection for finding 'resistance' to Christianity in interpretations of the Scottish archaeological evidence is conceivably the flip side of this. To add to this, the anthropologist Jon Holtzman's study of the global in the local explores how the marginal nature of the local/periphery (as opposed to the global/centre) is bound up with the idea that it is spatially distant and historically prior, offering a window to a *past* something (Holtzman 2004). In passing, Holtzman's work also invites us to reflect on the perceptions that our Early Medieval peoples themselves had of what local was in relation to the thing that was Christianity, and how this could have affected the ways in which they expressed their beliefs through material culture.

Geary's second scholarly tradition sees expansion from a centre (in this case Rome) to peripheries (what Holtzman refers to as the explicit social hierarchy, in which the centre moves to the rest). This approach leads to a common, homogenised culture rather than considering how what was 'colonised' might have contributed to European culture in general, or had an impact on particular forms of culture in different parts of Europe. This is a perspective that has traditionally dogged discussions about the contribution of the Picts to Insular art, for example (see Barclay 2001 on this and related issues in regard to Scottish prehistory, much of which has resonance for other periods too).

Overall, Geary's point is that there are universal aspects of Christian belief and practice that are shared wherever they are found, but that the realities on the ground, which include geographical position and prehistoric precursors, make for differences whether at the 'self-proclaimed centre or self-proclaimed periphery' (Geary 2013, 267); peoples converted Christianity, rather than the other way around (Maldonado 2011, 42). The implication of this is for how we as a community of researchers work on the church across Europe, given the reality of current practice is that our work is regionally and chronologically fragmented. Working in different places, with different resources, and emerging from a multitude of historiographical traditions, we have very different emphases and approaches (cf Turner 2011). To the south there is a tendency to be 'boxed in by antiquated visions of [the legacy of] Roman governance and Christianity' (Carver 2014, 201). In Scotland, we are comfortable looking to Gaelic and Scandinavian areas for comparison, but risk doing so at the expense of exploring linkages with, for example, Northumbria, and other areas that were part of the Roman Empire. Fraser tellingly observes how the Northumbrian dimensions of our Early Medieval history have been downplayed at the expense of Gaelic ones (Fraser 2009). Early Medieval Scotland, from around AD 300-1100, is where prehistory and history meet. Its study demands interdisciplinary and international approaches, but most of us need shaking out of our usual territories and comfort zones to re-invigorate this process.

2.4 Whither early church archaeology in Scotland?

The key questions are therefore:

- what we do by way of regional studies to understand the basis of our diversity and local idiosyncratic responses to the relentless expansion and domination of the universal church
- what do we do that better links what happens here to what happened and is happening elsewhere in Europe?

In terms of the latter, we have begun the necessary journey of joining our Gaelic, Scandinavian and Germanic neighbours from non-Roman parts of Europe in seeking to understand the prehistoric roots of Christianity (Carver 2009; Driscoll 2011,

270). This is an approach given a massive boost by the discovery of what appears to be a Pictish royal cult centre at Rhynie (Aberdeenshire; Gondek and Noble, this volume), but we must also remember to look south too. Geary refers to this as the sacralisation of the religious landscape while introducing Christianity and desacralisation of the pagan religious and social landscape (Geary 2013, 263), a process of change in which we should remember there is a difference between pagan beliefs and secular values, and what happens to them (Wormald 2006, 67). The work of scholars such as Stefan Brink and very recent archaeological discoveries in Scandinavia have revolutionised the appreciation of how polities there developed from a network of votive cult sites that changed significantly with the arrival of Christianity (Brink 2004; 2013; Andrén 2013). Continuity, or not, is a key issue, and one that requires greater critical treatment (eg Andrén 2011; Shaw 2013, 6-7). New excavations and landscape studies in Scotland illuminate the rich and scarcely tested potential of Scottish archaeology to contribute to this broad, European-wide research theme: Forteviot, Perth and Kinross (Driscoll 2011); symbol-incised stones in the landscape (Fraser and Halliday 2011; Noble et al 2013); and Portmahomack. To this we can add the new evidence of Iron Age ritual practices from sites such as Mine Howe, Orkney, High Pasture Cave on Skye, 'shrines' on brochs, or Roman hoards deposited on later prehistoric settlements, such as Birnie, Moray (Card and Downes 2003; Birch et al nd; Ritchie 2003; Hunter 2007). In places such as Orkney, this might also be pursued within the context of an excellent later prehistoric settlement record and understanding of later parish formation (Gibbon 2006).

The trajectory of the early church in what was the Roman Empire, and of its scholarship, working from an enviable range of upstanding buildings, sculptures and documentary sources, is quite different, and not an area this writer is well qualified to comment on. Relevant in this context though is the Corpus Architecturae Religiosae Europae (CARE) initiative, with its ambition to catalogue Europe's fourth- to early eleventh-century religious buildings in a unified way that will allow comparison across countries for the first time (Brogiolo and Jurković 2012; see also the entire content of vol 18 of *Hortus Artium Medievalium*, the Journal of the International Research Center for Late Antiquity and Middle Ages, based in Croatia). CARE is best described as an 'academic confederacy' of projects (there is no centralised funding). While in some countries the rationale and focus may appear fairly focussed on the architectural history of church buildings (this was certainly the starting point, and remains a core consideration), others, such as Spain and France, are developing a tool for landscape-based analysis, driven by the questions prompted by their local resources (pers comm Gisela Ripoll and Pascale Chevalier).

In the Isles of Britain and Ireland, Dr Tom Pickles (University of Chester), Professor Nancy Edwards (University of Bangor), Dr Tomas Ó Carragáin (University of Cork) and the author (University of Stirling) are, at the time of writing, actively developing a project within the umbrella of CARE that will enable us to make meaningful comparisons across Europe while reflecting our own research interests in Early Christian Churches and Landscapes (ECCLES). Our surviving evidence better lends itself to this (see above). For Scotland, the main objective is to lead to a wider understanding and appreciation of the nature, value and significance of pre-Romanesque architecture to AD 1100. The aim is that this will include:

- increased knowledge and understanding of surviving evidence for Early Medieval ecclesiastical architecture (where 'architecture' embraces church buildings, including architectural fittings/sculpture, settlements, associated monuments and landscapes);
- increased availability and accessibility of information about such places, their value, significance and potential for future research;
- facilitated interpretation, presentation, management and protection of the surviving archaeological resource and early church sites; and
- increasing the cultural, social and economic potential of such places for wider public benefit.

We do need more work on church structures, not least to date them (reworking existing sources; exploring new ones). We need a greater understanding of the activities taking place around these foci, inside and outside the enclosures. The areas around churches can be vulnerable to destruction without recording since the presence of enclosures and what happened in these is not always recognised or confirmed. Cadw's approach in Wales to assessing the nature and extent of church sites would, with some remodelling, be valuable in Scotland too (Ludlow 2009 and the report that underpinned this are the best starting point). Perhaps most exciting, is the potential for greater interdisciplinary working on a landscape-scale, by joining forces with historians and toponymists and reflecting on the outcomes of their work. In addition to our sculpture, church-related place-names are the main tangible legacy of the Church's transformation of the social, political and economic landscape, and with it the eclipse of the pagan one (cf Geary 2013, 263). Since the end of 2014, we can now access the University of Glasgow's *Saints in Scottish place-names* website (University of Glasgow 2014). Names containing saints names, or allusions to incidents in their lives, are one of approximately six categories of place-names that reflect different aspects of the early church, the others being: places for worship, usually a church or chapel; places where religious communities lived and worked; places set aside for sanctuary; places whose income supported the Church; and places to which people have attached some sort of religious quality (Taylor 1998). The *Saints in Scottish place-names* database will therefore highlight many but not quite all relevant place-names of interest to understanding the early church. Other projects and the longer-term visions for a Scottish place-names database offer the opportunity to capture these (pers comm Thomas Clancy and Simon Taylor). Such place-names help us to identify and categorise early sites, and to explore saints' cults and their relationship to secular polities, which we will shortly also to be able to do in comparison to early units of land assessment – davachs and their equivalents (see Ross 2006; 2011, ch 1; 2015; Ross, this volume). *The survey of dedications to saints in Medieval Scotland* website also contains some relevant and complementary material (University of Edinburgh nd).

A series of detailed interdisciplinary case studies could therefore provide explanatory narratives for landscape parcels in different parts of Scotland linked to questions such as 'How do we explain the regional character of archaeological evidence in relation to processes of Christianisation and the preceding landscape', and 'What can we learn from ecclesiastical architecture about when and in what ways Scotland first became "Europeanised"?' Potential early church sites can also be pinpointed and assessed in-depth with an eye to a future era of research. Small-scale and community-led initiatives can also play important roles here (see eg Dunning, Perth and Kinross: Campbell 2013; and Coldingham, Scottish Borders: Rhodes and Bowles 2014).

2.5 Conclusion

In a feisty short article in *Antiquity*, Martin Carver reviewed a tranche of recent publications on the Picts, a people he describes as either 'lost, found, repossessed or argued away' (Carver 2011). Recognising the tensions that arise from current scholarship in 'normalising' them, he pleas for some serious archaeological investment, to give the Picts an *archaeological* voice, to enliven them through situating them in their local landscapes. So, we must make sense of the Picts and their neighbours in their prehistoric context, but we must also look at their contribution to the study of *European* social evolution, indeed to Europeanisation. We will look to Scandinavia and Ireland because they have a better understanding of how polities developed from a landscape served by a network of votive cult sites, and in time they will look more to us. This is not, however, an excuse for not being historically informed or ignoring the ideas and questions that arise from the work of historians and toponymists. Archaeology has the unique potential to tease out the nuances of how and why people did things differently at different times in different places, to establish the impact *on the ground* of that tension between local practices and the centralising force of the church, and for uncovering pre-Christian practices.

Ultimately, we need more nuanced and tailored approaches for studying the evolution of early Christianity. We need to look back into prehistory, and seek to understand our regional diversity, but at the other extreme we also need to give fuller attention to what happened in the early Viking Age in Pictland, which is when major establishments such as Meigle (Perth and Kinross) and St Vigeans (Angus) were clearly still blazing with energy and action, at least until around 900 (Woolf 2007, 312). The general assumption (up for critical scrutiny) has been that the early 'creative' spirit of Christianity evaporated from the ninth century as Christianity and the Establishment bedded together, albeit with, until the twelfth century, only a 'semi-autonomous "chain of command" stretching back to Rome' (ScARF 2012). Our ninth- to eleventh-century churches demand as much attention as the legacy of prehistory. We also need to link better with the church archaeology of our Isles (often the domain of those with a north Atlantic focus), where Christianity gets a second bite at the cherry as the Norse convert. The historians have done a fantastic job at reworking their finite sources, we will all shortly be able to benefit from more useful and usable information about place-names and units of early land assessment, but excavations such as Portmahomack illustrate the potential difference that archaeology can and should make, as well as the unique public interest this generates.

Acknowledgements

This paper develops ideas first presented at the First Millennia Studies Group 'Reconsidering the Archaeology of the Early Church' event on 24 June 2014. I thank the organisers and participants, Rod McCullagh, Jeff Oliver, the reviewers and editor for their direct and indirect input. I gratefully acknowledge a grant from the Royal Society of Edinburgh to develop ECCLES.

References

Allen, J R and Anderson, J 1903 (repr 1993) *The early Christian monuments of Scotland.* Balgavies: The Pinkfoot Press.

Andrén, A 2005 'Behind *heathendom*: archaeological studies of Old Norse religion', *Scottish Archaeological Journal* 27(2), 105-38.

Andrén, A 2011 'Old Norse and Germanic religion', *in* Insoll, T (ed) *The Oxford handbook of the archaeology of ritual and religion*, 846-62. Oxford: Oxford University Press.

Andrén, A 2013 'The significance of places: the Christianization of Scandinavia from a spatial point of view', *World Archaeology* 45(1), 27-45.

Barber, J 1982 'Excavations on Iona, 1979', *Proceedings of the Society of Antiquaries of Scotland* 111, 282-330.

Barclay, G 2001 '"Metropolitan" and "parochial"/"core" and "periphery": a historiography of the Neolithic of Scotland', *Proceedings of the Prehistoric Society* 67, 1-18.

Barrowman, R 2011 *The chapel and burial ground on St Ninian's Isle, Shetland: excavations past and present.* The Society for Medieval Archaeology Monograph 32. Wakefield: Society for Medieval Archaeology.

Birch, S, Wildgoose, M and Kozikowski, G nd *High Pasture Cave.* Available: http://www.high-pasture-cave.org/ [accessed 31 July 2014].

Bradley, R 2005 *Ritual and domestic life in prehistoric Europe*. London: Routledge.

Brink, S 2004 'New perspectives on the Christianisation of Scandinavia and the organisation of the early church', *in* Adams, J and Holman, K (eds) *Scandinavia and Europe 800-1350: contact, continuity and coexistence*, 163-75. Turnhout: Brepols.

Brink, S 2013 'Myth and ritual in pre-Christian Scandinavian landscape', *in* Walaker Nordeide, S and Brink, S (eds) *Sacred sites and holy places. Exploring the sacralization of landscape through time and space*, 33-51. Turnhout: Brepols.

Brogiolo, G-P and Jurković, M 2012 '*Corpus architecturae religiosae Europae (IV-X Sec.)* Introduction', *Hortus Artium Medievalium* 18(1), 7-26.

Campbell, E 2013 'St Serf's Church tower, Dunning, Perthshire. Data Structure Report SS13.07'. Unpublished report for SERF project. Available: http://www.gla.ac.uk/media/media_296377_en.pdf [accessed 10 April 2015]

Card, N and Downes, J 2003 'Mine Howe – the significance of space and place in the Iron Age', *in* Downes and Ritchie, 11-19.

Carver, M O H 2004 'An Iona of the east: the Early Medieval monastery at Portmahomack, Easter Ross', *Medieval Archaeology* 48, 1-30.

Carver, M O H 2008 *Portmahomack. Monastery of the Picts*. Edinburgh: Edinburgh University Press.

Carver, M O H 2009 'Early Scottish monasteries and prehistory: a preliminary dialogue', *Scottish Historical Review* 88:2 (226), 332-51.
Carver, M O H 2011 'Lost, found, repossessed or argued away – the case of the Picts', *Antiquity* 85, 1479-83.
Carver, M O H 2014 'Medieval archaeology: families and freedoms', *in* Gelichi, S (ed) *Quarant' anni di Archeologia Medievale in Italia. La rivista, i temi, la teoria e i metodi*, 197-204. Florence: All'Insenga del Giglio.
Carver, M O H, Garner-Lahire, J and Spall, C 2016 *Portmahomack on Tarbat Ness. Changing ideologies in north-east Scotland, sixth to sixteenth century* AD. Edinburgh: Society of Antiquaries of Scotland.
Clancy, T O 1996 'Iona, Scotland, and the Céli Dé', *in* Crawford, B E (ed) *Scotland in Dark Age Britain*, 111-30. St Andrews: St John's House.
Clancy, T O 2008 'Deer and the early church in north-eastern Scotland', *in* Forsyth, K (ed) *Studies on the Book of Deer*, 363-97. Dublin: Four Courts Press.
Clancy, T O and Márkus, G 1995 *Iona. the earliest poetry of the Celtic monastery.* Edinburgh: Edinburgh University Press.
Clarke, D V, Blackwell, A and Goldberg, M 2012 *Early Medieval Scotland. Individuals, communities and ideas*. Edinburgh: National Museums Scotland.
Cramp, R 2005 *Wearmouth and Jarrow monastic sites.* Two vols. London: English Heritage.
Cramp, R 2014 *The Hirsel excavations.* Society for Medieval Archaeology Monograph 36. Leeds: Society for Medieval Archaeology.
Crone, A and Hindmarch, E with Woolf, A 2016 *Living and dying at Auldhame: the excavation of an Anglian monastic settlement and Medieval parish church*. Edinburgh: Society of Antiquaries of Scotland.
de Marrais, E, Castillo, L J and Earle, T 1996 'Ideology, materialization, and power strategies', *Current Anthropology* 37(1), 15-31.
Downes, A and Ritchie, A (eds) 2003 *Sea change. Orkney and northern Europe in the later Iron Age* AD *300-800*. Balgavies: Pinkfoot Press.
Driscoll, S T 2003 'Govan: an Early Medieval royal centre on the Clyde', *in* Welander, R D E, Breeze, D J and Clancy, T O (eds) *The Stone of Destiny: artefact and icon*, 77-83. Edinburgh: Society of Antiquaries of Scotland.
Driscoll, S T, Geddes, J and Hall, M A (eds) 2011 *Pictish progress. New studies on northern Britain in the Early Middle Ages*. Leiden: Brill.
Driscoll, S T 2011 'Pictish archaeology: persistent problems and structural solutions', *in* Driscoll et al, 245-79.
Evans, N 2011 'Ideology, literacy and matriliny: approaches to Medieval texts on the Pictish past', *in* Driscoll et al, 45-65.
Fisher, I 1996 'The west of Scotland', *in* Blair, J and Pyrah, C (eds) *Church archaeology: research directions for the future*, 37-42. York: Council for British Archaeology Research Report 104.
Fisher, I 2001 *Early Medieval sculpture in the West Highlands and islands*. Edinburgh: Society of Antiquaries of Scotland.
Foster, S M 2014 *Picts, Gaels and Scots: Early Historic Scotland.* Third edition. Edinburgh: Birlinn.

Fraser, I and Halliday, S 2011 'The Early Medieval landscape of Donside, Aberdeenshire', *in* Driscoll et al, 307-33.

Fraser, J E 2009 *From Caledonia to Pictland. Scotland to 795*. Edinburgh: Edinburgh University Press.

Fraser, J E 2011 'From ancient Scythia to *The Problem of the Picts*: thoughts on the quest for Pictish origins', *in* Driscoll et al, 15-43.

Geary, P J 2013 'Concluding remarks', *in* Salonen, K, Villads Jensen and Jorgensen, T (eds) *Medieval Christianity in the north*, 261-8. Turnhout: Brepols.

Geddes, J 2017 *Hunting Picts: Medieval sculpture at St Vigeans, Angus*. Edinburgh: Historic Environment Scotland.

Gibbon, S J 2006 'The origins and early development of the parochial system in the Orkney Earldom', unpublished PhD Thesis, University of the Highlands and Islands Millennium Institute, Orkney College.

Gilchrist, R 2012 *Medieval life. Archaeology and the life course*. Woodbridge: Boydell Press.

Henderson, I and Henderson, G 2005 *The art of the Picts*. London: Thames and Hudson.

Hill, P 2006 *Whithorn and St Ninian. The excavation of a monastic town 1984-91*. Stroud: Sutton Publishing.

Hindmarch, E and Melikian, M 2006 'Baldred's Auldhame. An Early Medieval chapel and cemetery', *Church Archaeology* 10, 97-100.

Holtzman, J 2004 'The local in the local: models of time and space in Samburu district, north Kenya', *Current Anthropology* 45(1), 61-84.

Hunter, F 2007 *Beyond the edge of empire – Caledonians, Picts and Romans*. Rosemarkie: Groam House Museum.

Insoll, T 2011 *The Oxford handbook of the archaeology of ritual and religion*. Oxford: Oxford University Press.

James, H and Yeoman, P 2008 *Excavations at St Ethernan's monastery, Isle of May, Fife 1992-7*. Tayside and Fife Archaeological Committee Monograph 6. Perth: Tayside and Fife Archaeological Committee.

Jones, M J 2013 'Recent research on the archaeology of the early Christian church in Britain, c 300-800', *in* Cresci, S, Quiroga, J L, Brandt, O and Pappalardo, C (eds) *Atti Del XV Congresso Internazionale Di Archeologia Cristiana (Toledo 8-12.9 2008) – Episcopus, Civitas Territorium – Studi Di Antichità Cristiane LXV*, 1163-78. Vatican: Studia di Antichita Cristiana.

Loveluck, C 2007 *Excavations at Flixborough vol. 4. Rural settlement, lifestyles and social change in the later first millennium* AD*: Anglo-Saxon Flixborough in its wider context*. Oxford: Oxbow.

Lowe, C 2006 *Excavations at Hoddom, Dumfriesshire*. Edinburgh: Society of Antiquaries of Scotland.

Lowe, C 2008 *Inchmarnock. An Early Historic island monastery and its archaeological landscape*. Edinburgh: Society of Antiquaries of Scotland.

Ludlow, N 2009 'Identifying Early Medieval ecclesiastical sites in south-west Wales', *in* Edwards, N (ed) *The archaeology of the Early Medieval Celtic churches*, 61-84. Leeds: Maney Publishing.

Maldonado, A 2011 'What does early Christianity look like? Mortuary archaeology and conversion in Late Iron Age Scotland', *Scottish Archaeological Journal* 33(1-2), 39-54.

Maldonado, A 2012 'Review of *Pictish Progress*', *Innes Review* 63(1), 91-101.

Maldonado, A 2013 'Burial in Early Medieval Scotland: new questions', *Medieval Archaeology* 57, 1-34.

McOmish, J M and Petts, D 2008 *Fey Field, Whithorn: excavations by David Pollock and Amanda Clarke.* York: York Archaeological Trust. Available: http://www.iadb.co.uk/yat/publish.htm?PUB=58 [Accessed 12 March 2015]

Miller, S and Ruckley, N A 2005 'The role of geological analysis of monuments: a case study from St Vigeans and related sites', *in* Foster, S M and Cross, M (eds), *Able minds and practised hands. Scotland's Early Medieval sculpture in the twenty-first century*, 277-91. Leeds: Society for Medieval Archaeology.

Morris, C D 1986 'The chapel and enclosure on the Brough of Deerness, Orkney: survey and excavations, 1975-77', *Proceedings of the Society of Antiquaries of Scotland* 116, 301-74.

Noble, G, Gondek, M, Campbell, E and Cook, M 2013 'Between prehistory and history: the archaeological detection of social change among the Picts', *Antiquity* 87, 1136-50.

O'Brien, E 2003 'Burial practices in Ireland: first to seventh centuries AD', *in* Downes and Ritchie, 62-72.

Ó Carragáin, T 2009a 'The architectural setting of the mass in Early-Medieval Ireland', *Medieval Archaeology* 53, 119-54.

Ó Carragáin, T 2009b 'Cemetery settlements and local churches in pre-Viking Ireland in light of comparisons with England and Wales', *in* Graham-Campbell, J and Ryan, M (eds) *Anglo-Saxon/Irish relations before the Vikings. Proceedings of the British Academy 157*, 329-66. London: Oxford University Press for the British Academy.

Ó Carragáin, T 2010 *Churches in Early Medieval Ireland.* New Haven and London: Yale University Press.

O'Sullivan, A, McCormick, F, Kerr, T T and Harney, L (eds) 2014 *Early Medieval Ireland,* AD *400-1100. The evidence from archaeological excavations*. Dublin: Royal Irish Academy.

O'Sullivan, J 1994 'Excavations of an early church and a women's cemetery at St Ronan's Medieval parish church, Iona', *Proceedings of the Society of Antiquaries of Scotland* 124, 327-65.

O'Sullivan, J 1998 'More than the sum of the parts. Iona: archaeological investigations 1875-1996', *Church Archaeology* 2, 5-18.

Petts, D 2003 *Christianity in Roman Britain.* Stroud: Tempus.

Petts, D 2011 *Pagan and Christian. Religious change in Early Medieval Europe. Debates in Archaeology*. London: Bristol Classical Press.

Rhodes, D and Bowles, C 2014 'From monks to mausolea', *Archaeology Scotland* 21, 5-10.

Ritchie, A 2003 'Paganism among the Picts and the conversion of Orkney', *in* Downes and Ritchie, 3-10.

Ross, A 2006 'The dabhach in Moray: a new look at an old tub', *in* Woolf, A (ed) *Landscape and Environment*, 57-74. St Andrews: St John's House.

Ross, A 2011 *The kings of Alba c1000-c1130*. Edinburgh: John Donald.
Ross, A 2015 *Land assessment and lordship in Medieval northern Scotland.* Turnhout: Brepols.
Ryan, M 2013 'Ireland and Insular art', *in* Hawkes, J (ed) *Making histories. Proceedings of the sixth international conference on Insular art, York 2011*, 1-12. Donington: Shaun Tyas.
ScARF 2012 Hall, M and Price, N *Medieval panel report.* Available: http://www.scottishheritagehub.com/content/Medieval [accessed 3 March 2013]
Seaman, A 2012 'Tempora Christiana? Conversion and Christianisation in western Britain AD 300-700', *Church Archaeology* 16, 1-22.
Shaw, J 2013 'Archaeology of religious change: introduction', *World Archaeology* 45(1), 1-11.
Smith, I 1996 'The origins and development of Christianity in north Britain and southern Pictland', *in* Blair, J and Pyrah, C (eds) *Church archaeology: research directions for the future*, 19-37. York: Council for British Archaeology.
Taylor, S 1997 'Seventh-century Iona abbots in Scottish place-names', *Innes Review* 48(1), 45-72.
Taylor, S 1998 'Place-names and the early church in Scotland', *Records of the Scottish Church History Society* 28, 1-22.
Thomas, C 1971 *The early Christian archaeology of north Britain*. Oxford: Oxford University Press.
Turner, S 2011 'Christianity', *in* Insoll, T (ed) *The Oxford handbook of the archaeology of ritual and religion*, 948-66. Oxford: Oxford University Press.
University of Edinburgh nd *Survey of dedications to saints in Medieval Scotland.* Available: http://www.shc.ed.ac.uk/Research/saints/Project.htm [Accessed 12 March 2015]
University of Glasgow 2014 *Saints in Scottish place-names.* Available: http://www.saintsplaces.gla.ac.uk/ [Accessed 12 March 2015]
Woolf, A 2007 *From Pictland to Alba 789-1070.* Edinburgh: Edinburgh University Press.
Woolf, A 2013 *The churches of Pictavia*. Cambridge: Hughes Hall and Department of Anglo-Saxon, Norse and Celtic.
Wormald, P 2006 *The times of Bede. Studies in early English Christian society and its historian. Edited by Stephen Baxter*. Malden (MA), Oxford and Victoria: Blackwell.

3

The fifth-sixth-century Early Medieval Pictish power centre at Rhynie, north-east Scotland, and its European context

Meggen Gondek and Gordon Noble

3.1 Introduction: northern Pictland in the fifth-sixth centuries

The fifth-sixth centuries AD are crucial for examining how Iron Age social groups were transformed into the kingdoms of Early Medieval Europe. In this article this transition is examined in north-east Scotland, a region often seen as peripheral to the emergence and maintenance of new forms of authority in the post-Roman period. That various groups now north of the Roman frontier were significant on a political and military level in northern European affairs in Late Antiquity seems to be suggested by the role of late Roman period groups such as the Di-Calidones and Verturiones in the barbarian conspiracy of AD 367 (Fraser 2009, 43-4, 55-7). However, there are only limited historical records to inform our understanding of the early social and political life and the European connections of the Picts following early references in the late Roman period. Whilst the historical sources are sparse, the archaeological evidence for Early Medieval Scotland is rich and includes carved stones, hillforts, enclosures and artefacts, although our evidence for the fifth and sixth centuries has been harder to address.

Despite persistent questions regarding their practical and social functions and chronology, the carved stone monuments of Pictland are interpreted as an iconic marker of Pictish material culture and monumentality, though they are also part of a much wider late Antique and Early Medieval tradition of carved stone monuments that flourished from the fifth century AD (Handley 2003, 177; Edwards 2007, 30; Fraser 2008, 2). The north-east of Scotland (especially Aberdeenshire and Morayshire) is the focus of a dense concentration of carved stone monuments bearing incised Pictish symbols and with no apparent Christian iconography (Class I stones), monuments we can connect to the expression and creation of new forms of power

in: Blackwell, A.E. (ed.) 2019: *Scotland in Early Medieval Europe*,
Leiden: Sidestone Press, pp. 51-66.

and authority in the fifth-sixth centuries AD (Driscoll 1988; Gondek 2006; Noble et al 2013). It is clear there were a wide variety of types of enclosure and settlement in existence, including hillforts, promontory forts, coastal forts, ringforts and palisaded enclosures (Ralston 2004; Noble et al 2013). Assessment of the dating available for these enclosed sites in Pictland shows a concentrated construction period in the fifth-sixth centuries AD with forts built and rebuilt until the late first millennium AD (Noble et al 2103, 1143-4). In some regions at least, there may have been a trend after the fifth-sixth century AD for larger sites to predominate. In Aberdeenshire, for example, smaller enclosures tend to show evidence of construction and activity in the fifth-sixth centuries AD, with little evidence of use after this, but the larger forts and complexes seem to continue into the seventh-eighth-centuries AD and later (Noble et al 2013, 1143). This emerging evidence for consolidation of power at the more dramatic and intensively defended sites in the north-east is one way in which we can perhaps begin to relate the historical records for increasing evidence of a hierarchical society from the seventh century onwards to the archaeological evidence for post-Roman society in northern Scotland (Woolf 2006).

This paper presents a summary of excavations conducted by the University of Aberdeen and the University of Chester at Rhynie that demonstrates that this area of Aberdeenshire was home to a substantial power centre in the fifth-sixth centuries, with extensive connections and parallels with other parts of Scotland, Britain and the northern world. Evidence from Rhynie also shows that in northern Pictland, like neighbouring areas to the west and east, from Ireland to Scandinavia, defended settlement, cult and the acquisition of exotic material culture appear to have been key elements of a transition to more hierarchical forms of power. The high-status complex uncovered at Rhynie shows that even modest programmes of excavation can illuminate the sparse historical record of fifth-sixth-century northern Britain, offering insights that allow the social and political life of this period to be reconstructed and placed in its northern European context.

3.2 Rhynie in the fifth-sixth centuries

The site at Rhynie offers an intriguing avenue for more in-depth research into the nature of what in Scandinavia might be termed a central place – a location where concentrated evidence for high-status settlement, trade, burial and perhaps cult activity seem most evident in the archaeological record and may indicate particular nodes in a network of power in the Early Medieval landscape (eg Brink 1996). Rhynie has long been known for its remarkable group of eight Pictish Class I stone monuments, discussed below (Fraser 2008, 38-41; Allen and Anderson 1903, ii, 182). But the site is important not only for its collection of carved stones, one of which – the Craw Stane (Illus 3.1) – is likely to be *in situ*, but also because of a series of aerial photographs that revealed a spectacular cropmark complex at the Craw Stane and in the vicinity of the findspots of two other Class I stones (Aberdeen Archaeology Surveys 1979). The cropmarks at Rhynie consist of at least three concentric enclosures encircling the knoll on which the Craw Stane stands (Fraser and Halliday 2007, 119-22). Geophysical survey conducted in 2005-6 suggested a range of interior features such as pits and postholes (Gondek and Noble 2011; Noble and Gondek 2011; Noble et al 2013). Several years

Illustration 3.1 The Craw Stane Class I Pictish stone and Tap O Noth hillfort in the background. Copyright Cathy MacIver.

of evaluative excavation at the main Craw Stane complex (2011-12; 2015-17) and another site closer to Rhynie village (2013) have revealed a complex high-status landscape that has the potential to change interpretations of the contexts of carved stones and assumptions about the power and reach of this area of north-east Scotland (Gondek and Noble 2011; Noble and Gondek 2011; Noble et al 2013).

3.2.1 The carved stones

The eight carved stones were found along a ridge and natural routeway (now reflected by the route of the modern road), with their southernmost extent marked by the Craw Stane and findspots of Rhynie nos 7 and 8 (numbering follows Fraser 2008) and the northernmost reported as being just outside the modern village area (Table 3.1; Illus 3.2). In many ways the group at Rhynie represent 'classic' Class I monuments: in original form the stones all seem to be glacial erratics or only roughly shaped; they are incised; they usually have paired symbols sometimes accompanied by a mirror or mirror/comb symbol; some of them may have been re-used prehistoric monuments; and the circumstances and locations of their finds follow a general pattern seen elsewhere (Clarke 2007). However, a few aspects of the group stand out amongst the Class I corpus. The Craw Stane shows two paired animals – a fish and a Pictish beast. Both of these symbols are common in the corpus, but the pairing of them together is unusual, with only two other examples known, as is the pairing of two animals in general: animals either tend to appear alone or are paired with one of the geometric/abstract symbols (Alcock 1989, 13; Fraser 2008). Another unusual feature is the presence of two stones carved with single human figures: only six examples of lone figures are known in total. The two figure-bearing stones were found at either end of the symbol stone distribution at Rhynie and appear to be

Stone	Pictish symbol	Findspot
No 1, Craw Stane	Fish, Pictish beast	In situ
No 2	Double disc and Z rod, Crescent and V rod	Found near village
No 3	Man with spear and shield	Found near village
No 4	Now lost: Pictish beast, Crescent and V rod?, Mirror	Fragments in local buildings
No 5	Beast head, Double disc and Z rod, Mirror, Comb (13 cupmarks)	Foundations of church
No 6	Double disc and Z rod, Crescent and V rod, Mirror	Foundations of church
No 7, Rhynie Man	Man with axe	Ploughed up near Craw Stane
No 8	Pictish beast, Mirror, curving symbol	Ploughed up near Craw Stane

Table 3.1 Carved stone monuments from Rhynie (collated from Fraser and Halliday 2007, 119-22; Fraser 2008, 38-41).

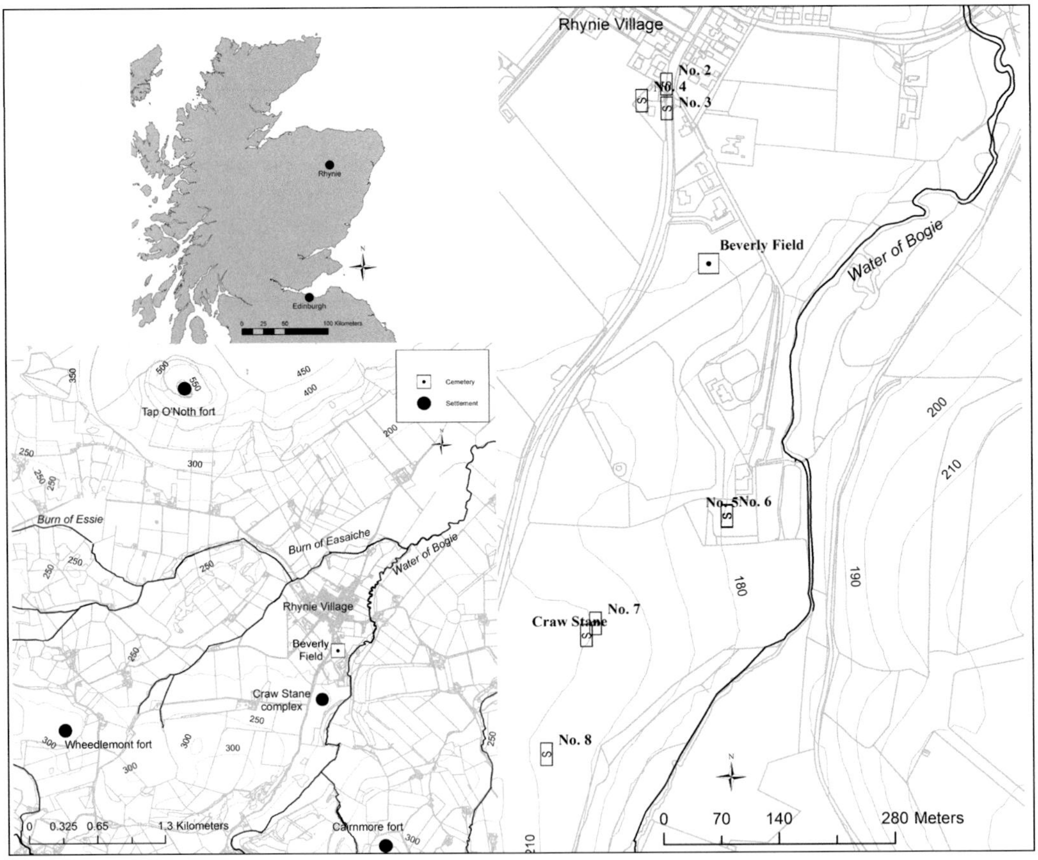

Illustration 3.2 Location of Rhynie, key features in the landscape and distribution of symbol stones. Base map: Crown Copyright/database right 2013. An Ordnance Survey/EDINA supplied service.

opposites of each other in that they face/walk in different directions, carry different 'weapons' and are dramatically different in size (Gondek and Noble 2011, 288-90). None of these monuments can be unequivocally dated to the fifth-sixth centuries by direct archaeological dating. However, that is true of most Early Medieval carved stones and the other archaeological evidence from Rhynie provides a strong case for a fifth-sixth-century context for the monuments.

3.2.2 The high-status settlement/ritual centre

The aerial photographs and geophysical surveys of the Craw Stane field highlighted the juxtaposition between the Pictish Class I stones known from this field (nos 1, 7 and 8) and the cropmark enclosures. Five seasons of large evaluation trenches following a 'strip, map and sample' methodology (Carver 2009, 101) have been undertaken thus far, allowing the nature, chronology and extent of archaeological remains to be explored. The main Early Medieval features include three concentric enclosures, a series of internal buildings and postholes, beam settings and pits (Illus 3.3). The outer enclosure consisted of a foundation trench, up to 1.5m deep, that held a wall of huge split oak planks with an internal line of postholes, suggesting an impressive timber wall or box-rampart, perhaps with a raised platform/wall-walk above. There are also two internal ditched enclosures, but any bank material has been truncated; both of the ditches show evidence of infilling and re-cutting over the lifetime of the site. Phasing of these ditches is still tentative. They may represent a successive sequence of earth and timber boundaries or it may be that the internal ditch was replaced after a short period by the larger outer ditch, opening up more space within the interior for buildings and other activities. The Craw Stane appears to stand at the entrance to at least one phase of the ditched enclosures with a complicated timber structure or building opposite it.

In the interior area examined to date, there is at least one square-post-defined rectangular structure measuring c 9m x 5m and a similarly sized oval building. A series

Illustration 3.3 The 2012 evaluation trench showing the Craw Stane (mid left) just outside the trench, entrance structure just to the right, inner and outer ditches and the palisade (top); traces of the internal buildings can also be seen inside. Kite photograph by Oskar Sveinbjarnarson.

Illustration 3.4 The axe-pin from Rhynie. Photography by Oskar Sveinbjarnarson.

of radiocarbon dates from across the main features and Bayesian modelling of the dates indicates a relatively short phase of construction and use from the late fourth to mid-sixth centuries AD for the site.

The character of the site is revealed not only by these impressive timber-built elements, but also by the range of artefactual evidence, recovered largely from a burnt layer that seems to indicate the final occupation of the site. The assemblage, especially given the limited sampling strategy, is exceptional, particularly for northern Britain. Some of the most significant finds are sherds of imported pottery and glass vessels, which are characteristic of high-status forts in Early Medieval Scotland and western Britain. Sherds of eastern Mediterranean Late Roman Amphorae (types LRA1 and LRA2 are both represented, also called B ware in Britain) can be dated to the earlier sixth century and represent the northernmost known findspot of these ceramics (Campbell 2007, 18-24). The glass belongs to a bowl-type drinking vessel (of Group C decorated Atlantic tradition) imported from France in the sixth and seventh centuries (Campbell 2007, 64-69).

Another characteristic of high-status sites in Early Medieval Scotland, non-ferrous metalworking, is also well represented amongst the assemblage from Rhynie. This includes moulds for casting pins and a complete valve of a small Type H penannular brooch (Fowler 1963, 110-11), as well as yellow enamel and a rare pair of fine-metal-working tongs. Access to fine metalwork is also present in the form of bronze pins – one nail headed and two small pins with possible early Anglo-Saxon parallels, and a bronze mount (badly preserved) found in conjunction with amber beads. A remarkable and to date unparalleled object also came from the destruction level above the outer palisade enclosure: an iron pin, its head shaped like an axe with curled beast biting onto its butt-end (Illus 3.4). All of the artefactual and structural evidence from the Craw

Stane complex suggests a site of power and authority with access to trade links and power networks beyond the local and regional.

3.2.3 The cemetery/ritual landscape

The Early Medieval complex sits within a landscape inhabited by several surviving examples of its prehistoric prominence, offering an ancestral backdrop to the fifth-sixth-century occupation of Rhynie. The surrounding landscape is dominated by the impressive large vitrified Iron Age hillfort of Tap O Noth (Illus 3.1). In the field adjacent to the Craw Stane there is a probable Bronze Age burial mound, and several standing stones, stone circles and examples of rock-art in the immediate area (Gannon et al 2007). The location of Early Medieval power centres amongst rich prehistoric landscapes is not unusual in the northern world, as rulers consolidated and legitimised power through memories recreated and embedded within the existing landscape (Bradley 1987; Driscoll 1998; Driscoll 2011, 271-4; see also Campbell et al, this volume). How the pre-existing landscape around Rhynie was actively engaged with is not yet understood as these prehistoric sites have received little investigation to date.

Reports of human remains found south of the village when the turnpike road was built in the nineteenth century and their association with at least two carved Class I stones and two apparently uncarved stones suggested the presence of an Early Medieval cemetery (Fraser and Halliday 2007, 121). To the southeast of the village, aerial photographs by Aberdeenshire Council Archaeology Service also revealed cropmarks of two large square enclosures (Greig 1994) (Illus 3.5). The larger enclosure is c20m across and the smaller is c16m across and both have entrances on the northern side. The two enclosures were identified as potential square barrows (Fraser and Halliday 2007, 121), but their morphology suggested parallels with square enclosures of late Iron Age/ Roman date (Campbell and Gondek 2009, 18; King and Soffe 2013). Evaluation in this field in 2013 sought to clarify the nature and chronology of these enclosures with a minimal intervention targeting key features to obtain preliminary dating evidence (Gondek et al 2013). To date, a basic chronology based on a series of radiocarbon dates can be proposed for activity in this area, beginning with a large ramped posthole or pits dating to the Neolithic, followed by a range of Bronze Age settlement activity (unenclosed) in the form of ring-ditches. The dating of the two enclosures is not entirely clear – the smaller returned Iron Age dates from its ditch fill, but the larger returned a fifth-sixth-century date for an upper fill and for a pit in its centre. The function of the Rhynie enclosures is also unclear as the settlement evidence within them appears to be significantly earlier. The finds assemblage was meager, but two glass beads found in topsoil have a broad Iron Age to Early Medieval range.

Fortunately the evidence for Early Medieval burial activity is clear. Two square barrows were uncovered in the area between the two square enclosures, each containing a central grave (Illus 3.5). The barrows had slight ditches, interrupted at the corners, and surrounded a central burial. The larger barrow contained what appeared to have been a coffin burial and the smaller a well-built cist grave. The latter preserved some skeletal material, which allowed radiocarbon dating. It is the first definitively dated Pictish burial evidence at Rhynie. The burial, dated 420-570 cal AD (95.4%), appears to be contemporary with the Early Medieval activity at the Craw Stane complex.

Illustration 3.5 Kite photographs of the 2013 excavations showing the two large square enclosures (top) and two square barrows with central graves (bottom). Kite photographs by Oskar Sveinbjarnarson.

3.3 Rhynie's reach: European context and contacts

Rhynie provides significant new insights into fifth-sixth-century power centres in Pictland, but it also has parallels with other Early Medieval sites in other regions of Scotland and further afield. The significance of the Rhynie complex comes not only from its well-preserved features, but also its finds assemblage and fifth-sixth-century date, with the finds suggestive of extensive contact across northern Britain, Ireland and probably the North Sea region in an immediate post-Roman context.

The presence of sherds of imported Late Roman amphorae and continental glass vessels (and a sherd of glass at the nearby site of Maiden Castle; Campbell 2012) reveals for the first time that these north-eastern Early Medieval communities were engaged with a strategic high-status exchange network that appears to have been important in allowing elites to promote and display their wealth and standing in the Early Medieval period. This type of material is found almost exclusively in the context of high-status sites, some occasionally associated with documented sites of kingship and until now limited to the Atlantic Sea region of western Scotland, Wales, Ireland and south-western England. The amphorae are likely to have originally held wine, and are probably

Illustration 3.6 The Rhynie Man. Copyright Aberdeen Archaeology Service.

the result of trading links (via western Scotland) with the late Eastern Roman Empire (see Campbell 2007, fig 13 for distribution).

3.3.1 Iconography and intellectual connections

The sculpture at Rhynie, and particularly the two stones carved with single figures, offer potential ways to identify intellectual and ideological connections across the northern world. The Rhynie Man stone (Illus 3.6) was clearly associated with the Craw Stane high-status complex. The incised figure is shown striding forward, wearing a belted long-sleeved tunic and carrying a very thin-shafted axe on his right shoulder (Shepherd and Shepherd 1979). He has a distinctive visage with a slightly enlarged head, sharp teeth, large nose, a strong brow ridge and a pointed beard. The detail and attention given to the head and the Rhynie Man's key attribute – the axe – suggests an emphasis on these characteristics as core aspects of the figure's identity. The figure's axe finds few parallels in contemporary art or in the archaeological record, although its significance is echoed by the iron axe-shaped pin or pendant from the site. The other lone figure from Rhynie, the armed man on no 3, is very worn. He may be carrying a shield in his left hand and in his right a very thin-shafted object with circular butt or ring at its base, most probably a doorknob butted spear (Heald 2001) or a thin staff. Standing at the opposite end of the Early Medieval palimpsest of activity in the Rhynie landscape to the Rhynie Man, this second character may represent a different message or purpose, perhaps associated with the burial zone in this landscape rather than the settlement area around the Craw Stane.

There are a handful of other lone figures in Pictland. These include a figure holding a club from Balblair (Highland) and a large, seemingly naked, figure carrying a spear and shield from Newton of Collessie (Fife). One of the closest parallels for the Rhynie Man is on a stone from Mail (Shetland Isles); this depicts either a human wearing a mask or a part-human/part-animal creature. The Mail figure carries a similar axe to the Rhynie Man, likewise held over its shoulder, but also carries a club or stake. The Mail and Rhynie figures have been interpreted as masked (Kilpatrick 2011, 181-5; Hall 2012, 102), but equally can be read as hybrid figures, human-like, but having other-worldly characteristics.

There are few parallels for the larger lone figures outside Scotland. They include a considerably later eleventh-century rune stone (DK283) from Hunnestad in Sweden (Fuglesang 1998, 206) depicting a lone long-robed/coated, helmeted or capped man walking to the right with an axe on his shoulder; the axe is of a different type to that depicted at Rhynie (Worm 1643). The figure on the Hunnestad stone has not been identified, but another stone from the site (DR 284) depicting a woman riding a wolf has been linked to the Norse myth of the giantess *Hyrrokkin* (Price 2006, 182; Williams 2009, 220) suggesting the Hunnestad axe-carrier may also be a character from myth or legend. A similar mythological background might be posited for the Rhynie Man himself, albeit from a much older, and now lost, story from the Pictish world.

Returning closer to home, the Rhynie Man's axe can be compared with the seventh-century axe-hammer from the Sutton Hoo Mound 1 ship burial: both have similar proportions, a double-ended blade and very thin shaft (Bruce-Mitford 1983, 833-43; Dobat 2006, 881). Recently the axe-hammer has been identified as a symbol of power connected to traditions of animal, particularly cattle, sacrifice (Dobat 2006). Iconographic evidence of the association between an axe-hammer and ritual, although not necessarily animal sacrifice, can also be found in late Roman sculpture. A third-century AD relief from the Gallo-Roman temple at Le Donon, Vosges (Alsace) shows a male figure armed and carrying an axe-hammer in his left hand, standing in front of a stag (Aldhouse-Green 2004, 127-9; Museums of Strasbourg 2013). The representation of the Rhynie Man with his distinctive axe as well as the placement of the Craw Stane at a key entrance to the enclosure suggests the Craw Stane complex not only functioned as a high-status settlement but that activities here also perhaps had a cult element.

3.3.2 Architectures of power

Rhynie exhibits fortified elements, but it is not a hillfort in the conventional sense; it is a lowland site located in the shadow of an Iron Age hillfort at Tap O Noth. Rhynie therefore shows the characteristics of another type of high-status site in Scotland exemplified by Forteviot, Perthshire – a lowland complex of settlement, burial and (in this case later) Christian sculpture and likely monastery (Driscoll 2011, 270-4; Campbell et al, this volume). In the vicinity of Rhynie are more traditionally sited hilltop enclosures, such as the small ringfort at Cairnmore, likely to be contemporary with the lowland site at Rhynie and suggesting the area was relatively well populated in the fifth-sixth century with a range of fortified enclosures.

In northern Pictland more generally, a range of enclosed sites including major hill-forts, promontory forts and ringforts proliferated in the fifth-sixth century (Noble et al 2013), a process mirrored by evidence from Ireland and Scandinavia. In Ireland, Early Medieval settlement enclosures (including ringforts) are largely an architectural tradition of the seventh century and later (Kerr 2007, 98-9; O'Sullivan et al 2014, 32-4, 36-7, 48). The seventh century also saw an increase in crannog construction (O'Sullivan et al 2014, 48). These settlement traditions are historically connected to the emergence of kingship and kingdoms and the increasingly hierarchical nature of Early Medieval Irish society. In southern Scandinavia, the mid-first millennium AD also saw enclosed architecture deployed as a key material manifestation of power (Näsman 1999, 4-5; Fallgren 2009). The evidence from these regions suggests that the construction of enclosed sites around 400-600 was a phenomena deeply intertwined with the formation of new kinds of society and hierarchies that developed in the post-Roman world, albeit with their own trajectories and character in different regions of northern and western Europe. The evidence from Rhynie indicates that northern Pictland was not peripheral to these trends: in contrast to Anglo-Saxon areas to the south, the social and political centralization in Pictland focused on traditions of enclosed settlement and was part of a much wider northern and western tradition that extended from the 'Celtic' west to south Scandinavia. In these regions, the construction of fortified sites was a method of consolidating and marking power over territories as communities developed new and more hierarchical strategies of organisation.

Aspects of the architecture of the buildings and structures at Rhynie also find parallels in other high-status sites across the northern world. The substantial timber palisade of the outer enclosure at Rhynie shares some similarities with the Anglo-Saxon period structures and high-status plank-built architecture found at sites such as Yeavering (Northumberland), documented by Bede as a royal site in the seventh century (Hope-Taylor 1977, 205-9; McClure and Collins 1994, 97, HE II.14). While the Great Enclosure at Yeavering is larger than the Rhynie palisade, the massive plank-built construction is of a similar character to the outer timber enclosure at Rhynie. Yeavering also has Yeavering Bell, a significant regional centre in the Iron Age overlooking the lowland sites, echoing the juxtaposition of Rhynie and Tap O Noth. Tap O Noth's size, complexity and number of associated house platforms (near 100) may indicate that this was an earlier Iron Age tribal centre. At present it is unknown whether the Rhynie complex and Tap O Noth were in contemporary use in the Early Medieval period, but its dominant physical presence in this area cannot be ignored and it is one of a type of Iron Age fort reused elsewhere in Pictland. Tap O Noth provides a key opportunity for investigation of the landscape of power at Rhynie and will be a focus of future work for the project. Based on these analogies, Rhynie can be shown to have some parallels with lowland high-status complexes found in Anglo-Saxon England, but many features at Rhynie also remain unique and earlier in date than those found to the south.

Moreover, neither Yeavering or other Anglo-Saxon high-status secular sites have a contemporary sculptural tradition comparable to that found in northern Britain. Monumental sculpture and imported material are important aspects of the Rhynie complex; given Rhynie's earlier date, this suggests that fruitful comparisons can also be made with fifth-sixth-century complexes found in Scandinavia, such as Gudme and Uppåkra in Sweden. Here, the lowland centres show investment in large timber architecture and material culture very clearly associated with power and ritual authority. The deposition of gold foil figures at halls and more unusual buildings at places such as Gudme and Uppåkra suggest ritual practice and iconographies of power formed an important element of the growing hierarchical and centralising political authority found at these sites (Hedeager 1999, 151; Nielsen et al 1997; Ringtved 1999, 50; Larsson 2007). The presence of special finds at these Scandinavian centres was crucial in detecting the mixed cultic and political nature of these sites, and Rhynie provides close parallels for the ways in which power may have been underpinned by new ways of relating to the gods in a post-Roman context (Noble et al 2013, 1145-7).

3.4 Conclusion

The fifth-sixth centuries were key in the development of first millennium AD polities, but archaeological evidence from this period has traditionally been sparse and difficult to interpret. The re-assessment of the evidence for enclosed settlement in north-east Scotland highlights the importance of this period, one where historical documentation is particularly poorly represented. The work at Rhynie shows the transformations in knowledge that can come from even modest programmes of work on a hitherto under-researched area of Early Medieval Europe. By combining an archaeological approach to monumental carved stones with large-scale evaluative excavation and careful and intensive radiocarbon dating programmes, we are starting to be able to uncover the role of power, symbolism and cult in post-Roman northern Britain. At Rhynie it is now apparent that emerging Pictish polities, like their neighbours to the west and east, were bonded by underlying shared trajectories of change – with defended settlement, cult dimensions and the importation of exotic material culture being key elements of a transition to more hierarchical forms of power than in the later Iron Age. Rhynie is changing our understanding of the contacts, cosmologies and power structures of Pictland and reconfiguring our perceptions of a poorly documented period.

References

Aberdeen Archaeology Surveys 1979 'Aerial reconnaissance', *Discovery and Excavation in Scotland*. Edinburgh: CBA and The Scottish Group.

Alcock, E 1989 'Pictish stones Class I: where and how?', *Glasgow Archaeological Journal* 15, 1-21.

Aldhouse-Green, M 2004 *An archaeology of images: iconology and cosmology in Iron Age and Roman Europe*. London: Routledge.

Allen, J R and Anderson, J 1903 (repr 1993) *The early Christian monuments of Scotland*. Balgavies: The Pinkfook Press.

Bradley, R 1987 'Time regained: the creation of continuity', *Journal of the British Archaeological Association* 140, 1-17.

Brink, S 1996 'Political and social structures in early Scandinavia. A settlement-historical pre-study of the central place', *Tor* 28, 235-81.

Bruce-Mitford, R L S 1983 *The Sutton Hoo ship burial, volume III. Late Roman and Byzantine silver, hanging-bowls, drinking vessels, cauldrons and other containers, textiles, the lyre, pottery bottle and other items*. London: British Museum.

Campbell, E 2007 *Continental and Mediterranean imports to Atlantic Britain and Ireland,* AD *400-800.* Council for British Archaeology Research Report 157. York: Council for British Archaeology.
Campbell, E 2012 'Imported Early Medieval glass from Maiden Castle', unpublished report, University of Glasgow.
Campbell, E and Gondek, M 2009 'Forteviot, Perthshire: excavations of a Pictish cemetery and Iron Age enclosure 2009. Interim and data structure', unpublished report, University of Glasgow.
Carver, M 2009 *Archaeological investigation*. London: Routledge.
Clarke, D V 2007 'Reading the multiple lives of Pictish symbol stones', *Medieval Archaeology* 51, 19-39.
Cook, M 2011 'New evidence for the activities of Pictish potentates in Aberdeenshire: the hillforts of Strathdon', *Proceedings of the Society of Antiquaries of Scotland* 141, 207-30.
Dickinson, T and Griffiths, D (eds) 1999 *The Making of kingdoms. Anglo-Saxon Studies in Archaeology and History* 10. Oxford: Oxford University Press.
Dobat, A S 2006 'The king and his cult: the axe-hammer from Sutton Hoo and its implications for the concept of sacral leadership in Early Medieval Europe', *Antiquity* 80, 880-93.
Driscoll, S T 1988 'Power and authority in Early Historic Scotland, Pictish symbol stones and other documents' *in* Gledhill, J, Bender, B and Larsen, M (eds) *State and society: the emergence and development of social hierarchy and political centralization*, 215-36. London: Taylor and Francis.
Driscoll, S T 1998 'Picts and prehistory: cultural resource management in Early Medieval Scotland', *World Archaeology* 30, 142-58.
Driscoll, S T 2011 'Pictish archaeology: persistent problems and structural solutions', *in* Driscoll, Geddes and Hall, 245-80.
Driscoll, S T, Geddes, J and Hall, M (eds) 2011 *Pictish progress: new studies on northern Britain in the Early Middle Ages.* Leiden: Brill.
Edwards, N 2007 *A corpus of Early Medieval inscribed stones and stone sculpture in Wales: volume II south-west Wales*. Cardiff: University of Wales Press.
Fallgren, J H 2009 'The Ölandic ring-forts and the Iron Age and Medieval agricultural landscapes', *in* Segschneider, M (ed) 2009 *Ringwälle und verwandte Strukturen des ersten Jahrtausends n. Chr. an Nord- und Ostsee: Internationales Symposium Föhr 2005*, 27-50. Neumünster: Wachholtz.
Fowler, E 1963 'Metalwork in the fifth and sixth centuries AD: a reappraisal', *Archaeological Journal* 120, 98-160.
Fraser, I and Halliday, S 2007 'The Early Medieval landscape', *in* RCAHMS *In the shadow of Bennachie: a field archaeology of Donside, Aberdeenshire*, 115-135. Edinburgh: RCAHMS and Society of Antiquaries of Scotland.
Fraser, I (ed) 2008 *The Pictish symbol stones of Scotland.* Edinburgh: RCAHMS.
Fraser, J E 2009 *From Caledonia to Pictland: Scotland to 795*. Edinburgh: Edinburgh University Press.
Fuglesang, S H 1998 'Swedish runestones of the eleventh century: ornament and dating', *in* Düwel, K (ed) *Runeninschriften als Quellen Interdisziplinärer Forschung*, 197-218. Berlin: de Gruyter.

Gannon, A, Halliday, S, Sherriff, J and Welfare, A 2007 'The Neolithic and Bronze Age Landscape', *in* RCAHMS *In the shadow of Bennachie: a field archaeology of Donside, Aberdeenshire*, 45-78. Edinburgh: RCAHMS and Society of Antiquaries of Scotland.

Gondek, M 2006 'Investing in sculpture: power in Early Historic Scotland', *Medieval Archaeology* 50, 105-42.

Gondek, M and Noble, G 2011 'Together as one: the landscape of the symbol stones at Rhynie, Aberdeenshire', *in* Driscoll, Geddes and Hall, 95-110.

Gondek, M, Noble, G and Sveinbjarnarson, O 2013 'REAP 2013: excavation of two square enclosures, square barrows and other features at Rhynie Aberdeenshire, data structure report', unpublished report, University of Aberdeen and University of Chester.

Greig, M 1994 'Sites identified while checking aerial photographs and maps held by GRC, or as the result of an aerial reconnaissance programme', *Discovery and Excavation in Scotland* 1994, 26.

Hall, M 2012 'Performing prehistory in Early Mediaeval Scotland: making sense of the meanings of masks on Pictish sculpture', *in* Meller, H and Maraszek, R (eds) *Masken der Vorzeit in Europa (II)*, 93-110. Halle (Saale): Landesmuseum fur Vorgestchicte.

Handley, M 2003 'The origins of Christian commemoration in late Antique Britain', *Early Medieval Europe* 10, 177-99.

Heald, A 2001 'Knobbed spearbutts of the British and Irish Iron Age: new examples and new thoughts', *Antiquity* 75, 689-96.

Hedeager, L 1999 'Myth and art: a passport to political authority in Scandinavia during the Migration period', *in* Dickinson and Griffiths, 151-56.

Hope-Taylor, B 1977 *Yeavering: an Anglo-British centre of early Northumbria*. London: English Heritage.

Kerr, T 2007 *Early Christian settlement in north-west Ulster*. BAR British Series No 430. Oxford: Archaeopress.

Kilpatrick, K 2011 'The iconography of the Papil Stone: sculptural and literary comparisons with a Pictish motif', *Proceedings of the Society of Antiquaries of Scotland* 141, 159-205.

King, A and Soffe, G 2013 *A sacred island: Iron Age, Roman and Saxon temples and ritual on Hayling Island*. Hampshire: Hayling Island Excavation Project.

Larsson, L 2007 'The Iron Age ritual building at Uppåkra, southern Sweden', *Antiquity* 81, 11-25.

McClure, J and Collins, R (eds) 1994 *Bede: the ecclesiastical history of the English people*. Oxford: Oxford University Press.

Museums of Strasbourg 2013 *Dieu au Cerf*. Available at http://www.musees.strasbourg.eu/index.php?page=l-epoque-gallo-romaine.

Näsman, U 1999 'The ethnogenesis of the Danes and the making of a Danish kingdom', *in* Dickinson and Griffiths, 1-10.

Nielsen, P O, Randsbork, K and Thrane, H (eds) 1997 *The archaeology of Gudme and Lundeborg*. Copenhagen: Akademisk Forlag and Universitetsforlaget i København.

Noble, G and Gondek, M 2011 'Symbol stones in context: excavations at Rhynie, an undocumented Pictish power centre of the sixth-seventh centuries AD?', *Medieval Archaeology* 55, 317-21.

Noble, G, Gondek, M, Campbell, E and Cook, M 2013 'Between prehistory and history: the archaeological detection of social change among the Picts', *Antiquity* 87, 1136-50.

O'Sullivan, A, McCormick, F, Kerr, T R, Harney, L and Kinsella, J 2014 *Early Medieval dwellings and settlements in Ireland,* AD *400-1100.* BAR International Series 2604. Oxford: Archaeopress.

Price, N 2006 'What's in a name? An archaeological identity crisis for the Norse gods (and some of their friends)', *in* Andrén, A, Jennbert, K and Raudvere, C (eds) *Old Norse religion in long term perspectives: origins, changes, and interactions, an international conference in Lund, Sweden, June 3-7, 2004*, 179-83. Lund: Nordic Academic Press.

Ralston, I 2004 *The hill-forts of Pictland since* The problem of the Picts. Rosemarkie: Groam House Museum.

Ringtved, J 1999 'The geography of power: south Scandinavia before the Danish kingdom', *in* Dickinson and Griffiths, 49-64.

Shepherd, I and Shepherd, A 1979 'An incised Pictish figure and a new symbol stone from Barflat, Rhynie, Gordon District', *Proceedings of the Society of Antiquaries of Scotland* 109, 211-22.

Williams, H 2009 'Nordic strategies in missionary times: the case of the rune-stones', *in* Staecker, J (ed) 2009 *The reception of Medieval Europe in the Baltic Sea region: papers of the twelfth Visby symposium held at Gotland University, Visby*, 215-21. Visby: Gotland University Press.

Woolf, A 2006 'Dun Nechtain, Fortriu and the geography of the Picts', *Scottish Historical Review* 85, 182-201.

Worm, O 1643 *Danicorum monumentorum.* Copenhagen.

4

Norrie's Law, Gaulcross and beyond: widening the context of hacksilver hoarding in Scotland

Alice Blackwell and Martin Goldberg

4.1 Introduction

Silver arrived in Scotland from the Roman world and, unlike other parts of Britain and continental Europe, it rapidly became the main material used to create portable prestige objects, a role it maintained across the first millennium AD (Blackwell et al 2017). Gold was used as an embellishment but more often than not it was a thin veneer on a body of silver. Late Roman silver, like the large hoard of hacked objects buried at Traprain Law (East Lothian; Hunter and Painter 2013; Hunter et al forthcoming), appears to have provided the only source of the raw material until new supplies arrived with the Vikings. More than any other type of object, the corpus of massive (also known as 'Pictish') silver chains underlines how much silver was available in Early Medieval Scotland: the existence of eleven chains is documented (Youngs 2013). The largest complete chain weighs around 3kg, and the total weight of the nine that survive (some in a very fragmentary condition) is 11.5kg. These types of objects underpinned the emergence of the Early Medieval kingdoms of Scotland with silver providing a means to create, communicate and contest status and wealth. This paper is part of wider research being conducted through the Glenmorangie Research Project, based at National Museums Scotland, which is examining the role of silver in the first millennium AD. Here we focus on one aspect: hacksilver.

The starting point for this paper is the well-known hoard of silver from Norrie's Law in Fife. The majority of the hoard was lost soon after its discovery in 1819 when it was sold as bullion to silversmiths (Buist 1839; Graham-Campbell 1991a), but around 170 objects and fragments of hacksilver are preserved in the collections of National Museums

in: Blackwell, A.E. (ed.) 2019: *Scotland in Early Medieval Europe*,
Leiden: Sidestone Press, pp. 67-84.

Illustration 4.1 The Norrie's Law hoard, Fife. Copyright Trustees of National Museums of Scotland.

Scotland (see Goldberg and Blackwell 2013).[2] The 1839 estimate of the total hoard's weight put it at nearly 12.5kg (Buist 1839), though this, and the nature of the lost portion of silver, must be treated with care (Graham-Campbell 1991a; Youngs 2013, 414);[3] something closer to 750g survives today. The circumstances surrounding the discovery are clouded by a 20-year lapse between the find and any kind of publication. The surviving hoard material was recovered in 1819 by the landowner and quietly kept at his estate; 20 years later a local antiquarian and journalist George Buist learned of it whilst visiting and began to investigate, publishing the results in 1839. There is no full published (or unpublished) catalogue or detailed academic study of the whole of the surviving hoard. This is currently being prepared and specifics concerning the identification and dating of objects will be discussed in detail elsewhere. This paper instead sets out some of the broad directions of research currently being pursued, and has several main aims. First, to shift emphasis to the surviving hacksilver component of the Norrie's Law hoard, and second,

2 A small box containing fragments of silver and marked with a NMS accession number linked to the Norrie's Law hoard was discovered during recent research. The fragments are clearly part of the hoard but have never been displayed as such or included in previous discussions of the material. All are very small fragments of silver sheet; further details will be published in a forthcoming catalogue of the hoard. Their discovery increased the total number of fragments in NMS collections from 114 to 171.

3 Particularly since this information was from Robert Robertson, the jeweller who seems likely to have misled George Buist vis à vis 'recovery' of objects which we now know were nineteenth-century copies; see below, and Goldberg and Blackwell 2013 and Foster et al 2014. The amount and nature of the lost portion of the hoard has a significant bearing on the discussion of the surviving silver; there is, however, no way of advancing our understanding of it.

to highlight a new discovery that closely parallels it. Finally, to begin to situate this newly recognised Scottish post-Roman/pre-Viking hacksilver phenomenon in the context of hacksilver hoarding in northern Europe during the first millennium AD.

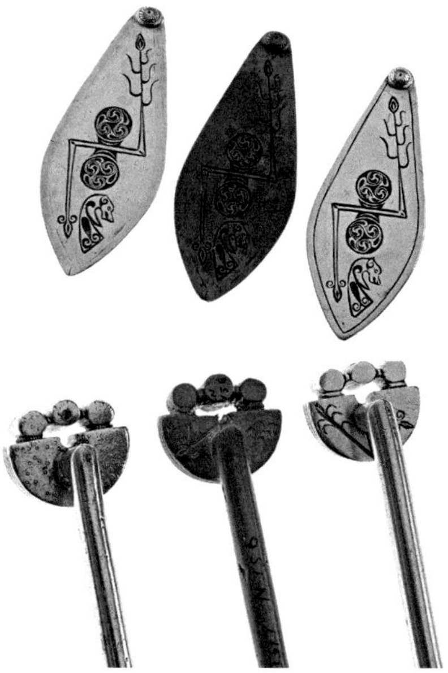

Illustration 4.2 Symbol-decorated plaques and handpins associated with the Norrie's Law hoard: left, Early Medieval; middle, nineteenth-century pewter facsimile; right, nineteenth-century silver copy. Copyright Trustees of National Museums of Scotland.

4.2 The Norrie's Law hacksilver hoard

The silver hoard as it survives today is comprised of four complete objects and 166 partial objects or fragments at varying stages of being cut down (Illus 4.1). Earlier research demonstrates that two of the objects from the hoard – a silver handpin decorated with a Pictish z-rod symbol and one of a pair of silver Pictish symbol-decorated plaques – can be excluded from the Early Medieval material; both are nineteenth-century copies (Goldberg and Blackwell 2013). In 1839 George Buist commissioned pewter facsimiles of some of the Early Medieval hoard in order to encourage recovery of the portion that had been sold for bullion in 1819. It seems likely that the silver copies were also made at the same time (and perhaps from the same moulds) (Illus 4.2). Buist published them as a sign of the success of using facsimiles to raise awareness of the loss of original material (Foster et al 2014) and ever since they have been generally accepted as belonging to the Early Medieval hoard. It now appears that Buist was misled (Goldberg and Blackwell 2013). This leaves only one legitimate symbol-bearing object amongst the genuine Early Medieval silver and significantly reduces the distinctively Pictish component within the hoard.

In addition to the single genuine Pictish symbol-decorated plaque, and a large silver handpin (which has been repaired), the other complete objects are a ribbed spiral finger ring, and a plain penannular brooch with twisted hoop (missing its pin). Amongst the incomplete objects are fragments of a further twisted penannular brooch, broken in two pieces and repaired with a nineteenth-century silver sleeve, at least one more spiral finger ring, and part of another, miniature, handpin. Two circular objects, one clearly folded and unfolded, are likely to be mounts of some kind, removed from whatever they originally adorned. A large thick silver sheet of unknown function, decorated with three high-relief repoussé spirals, shows clear evidence of being cut down. The rest of the material is very fragmentary, being pieces of: wire, beaded-vessel rim,[4] bangle (body and terminals), fragments decorated with punched and incised motifs,

4 Described occasionally in the past as decorative mounting for a shield (Graham-Campbell 1991a, 247).

and unidentifiable sheet. Some of the fragments were made into parcels (attested by clear fold marks) but all have been unfolded, presumably since discovery. Unfolding the parcels evidently caused some to break: although cut edges are apparent amongst the fragments, many are breaks along fold lines.

Only one fragment in the Norrie's Law hoard is typologically identifiable as a Late Roman object – a spoon fragment inscribed with Roman letters. Scientific analysis (using PIXE, or proton induced x-ray emission) of 12 pieces of Norrie's Law silver together with a larger sample of the Late Roman hacksilver hoard from Traprain Law demonstrated clear compositional differences between the two hoards (not limited to silver purity but also levels of tin, zinc and gold: Tate and Troalen 2009, currently being prepared for publication). This work revealed another piece of silver with an apparently Late Roman-composition amongst the Norrie's Law material. Subsequent surface XRF (x-ray fluorescence) analysis of the whole of the Norrie's Law hoard has demonstrated that there are more undiagnostic fragments than expected that have a composition suggestive of Late Roman silver (Susanna Kirk pers comm; in preparation for publication).[5]

In addition, Roman coins were mentioned in early accounts (Wilson 1863, 260) but subsequently lost;[6] a newly recognised illustration (dated 1832-8) of some of the lost coins (Illus 4.3) allows them to be identified as typical late fourth-/early fifth-century siliquae, small late Roman silver coins (Bland et al 2013, 132). The illustration of the Norrie's Law coins is detailed enough to show various degrees of clipping, whereby the edge of a coin is carefully trimmed whilst leaving the imperial portrait intact. The clipping of siliquae is a British phenomenon, resulting from the need to manage increasingly limited supplies of coinage in the fifth century, perhaps in order to manufacture new coins (Guest 2013, 96-8) or jewellery, tableware or ingots (ibid, 100).[7] The corpus of siliquae found in Scotland is small: in addition to the three recorded amongst the Norrie's Law hoard there are four from the Traprain Law hoard and another from the site, as well as two single finds (Bland et al 2013, 132),[8] and eight new finds from Gaulcross, Aberdeenshire (identifications Nicholas Holmes pers comm). The latest of the three Norrie's Law coins, heavily clipped, gives a *terminus post quem* for the hoard of after AD 397-402 (Bland et al 2013, 132). It is not possible to gauge how long these coins were circulating, though the phenomenon of clipping had ceased by the time new silver coinage became available in Britain from the 470s (Guest 2013, 101).

---

5 Surface analysis can give a misleading picture of the silver:copper ratio because of surface enrichment. However, Tate and Troalen (2009) demonstrated that Late Roman silver has a characteristic composition in terms of minor elements, specifically tin, zinc and gold; these are not significantly affected by surface enrichment, and so surface analysis with XRF remains a reliable technique. Low levels of zinc were one of the characteristics that distinguished the Traprain Law silver from the majority of Norrie's Law; similar levels have been found in other Late Roman silver analysed, including the Hoxne treasure (Cowell and Hook 2010).

6 An apparently separate discovery from the find spot of the Norrie's Law hoard of two brass coins, from the first century AD (Roman) and sixth/seventh century (Byzantine), has been regarded as dubious; summarised in Graham-Campbell 1991a, 243.

7 Clipping small amounts of silver from large numbers of coins could yield significant amounts of silver, for example an estimated 7kg in the case of the 14,000 *siliquae* from the Hoxne hoard (Guest 2013, 98).

8 The two single finds are: one 'dredged from the Clyde'; and one from the Parish of Clatt, Aberdeenshire (Bland et al 2013, 132).

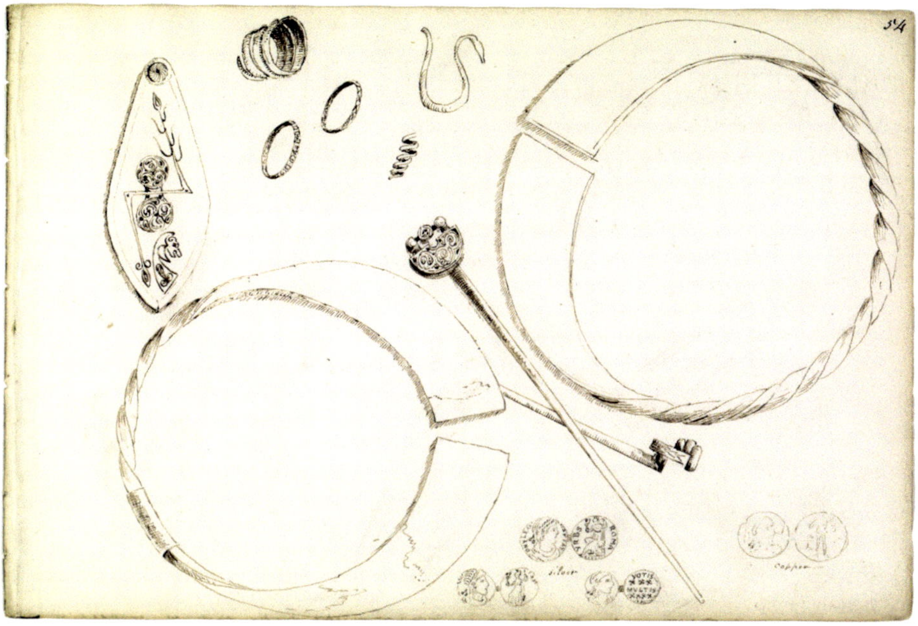

Illustration 4.3 An illustration from the Society of Antiquaries of Scotland archive (SAS 464, held by RCAHMS: catalogue number FID 405/1) dated 1832-8 showing lost late fourth- / early fifth-century siliquae from Norrie's Law. Only the genuine handpin and symbol-decorated plaque are illustrated here as the image predates the creation of the pewter facsimiles and silver copies in 1839. Image SC 730304, copyright courtesy of Historic Environment Scotland (Society of Antiquaries of Scotland Collection). Licensor canmore.org.uk.

The small corpus of portable objects bearing Pictish symbols (Fraser 2008, Appendix) is both important in its own right and relevant to the far larger corpus of carved stones that carry symbols. For this reason the symbol-bearing (one genuinely Early Medieval, two nineteenth century) objects associated with Norrie's Law have often provided a starting point for discussion of the hoard's significance or interpretation in wider narratives of Early Medieval Scotland. The symbol-plaque(s) have also been central to most discussions of the hoard because (supposed) stylistic similarities between the beast-head symbol and a dog's-head motif in the Lindisfarne Gospels have been used to date the hoard's deposition. This art-historical comparison of motifs (representing different types of beasts, on very different types of objects, from different parts of northern Britain) has led some to place the Norrie's Law plaques somewhere in the seventh century, others as late as the eighth (summarised by Graham-Campbell 1991a; based on Stevenson 1955; Stevenson and Emery 1964; Henderson 1967; most recent appraisal in Henderson and Henderson 2004). The plaques have been regarded as the latest objects in the hoard, with the fragment of Late Roman spoon at the other end of the spectrum (Stevenson 1955). Identifying the rest of the material has proved elusive: for instance, attempts at dating the spiral-decorated plate vary, on stylistic grounds, between the Iron Age and seventh century (Stevenson 1976, 249).

Discussion of prominent individual components, particularly those bearing symbols, has overshadowed the fact that Norrie's Law is primarily a hacksilver hoard – as it survives today the vast majority is composed of cut or broken fragments of silver, some of which had been folded into parcels. Partly, this blind spot must be due to the lack of a published catalogue,[9] but another significant factor has been the unique nature of the hoard: until 2013 no similar hoards were recognised from Scotland (see below), and no hacksilver has been recognised from excavated sites (though Clatchard Craig, Fife, produced a silver ingot; Close-Brooks 1986, 167, cat no 121). Hacksilver has not been a recognised phenomenon of Early Medieval (pre-Viking) Scotland; hoarding is well represented amongst surviving material, but examples like those from St Ninian's Isle (Shetland) or Talnotrie (Dumfries and Galloway) are composed of whole objects (albeit some broken) rather than deliberately fragmented pieces of bullion. Norrie's Law as a hoard of hacked silver has rarely been integrated into interpretations of Early Medieval Scotland, despite the fact that it poses interesting questions about the sources, circulation and access to silver, which constitutes the raw material for making prestige objects between AD 400-800, casting light on wider economic and political structures. Excavation assemblages from nucleated forts such as Dunadd (Argyll; Lane and Campbell 2000), Mote of Mark (Dumfries and Galloway; Laing and Longley 2006), Clatchard Craig (Close-Brooks 1986) and Trusty's Hill (Dumfries and Galloway; Toolis and Bowles 2017) are most often used in narratives of kingship, gift exchange and hierarchies of supply and control, but hacksilver provides another source of evidence that has rarely been utilised for Scotland.

Until recently, only one other hoard of pre-Viking hacksilver was known from Scotland: the Late Roman Traprain Law treasure. Lloyd Laing made a direct comparison with the Traprain Law hoard, and deviated from the accepted seventh-/eighth-century dating of Norrie's Law by arguing that some objects were significantly earlier than had previously been accepted (1994). Laing suggested the Norrie's Law material was 'a bullion hoard of silver, looted from elsewhere and hammered down for ease of transport, concealment and remelting' (Laing 1994, 35), using Late Roman hoards from Britain and Ireland – Traprain Law, Balline (Co Limerick) and Coleraine (Co Londonderry) – for comparison. In his opinion there was 'no evidence to suggest that any of these objects [in the Norrie's Law hoard] was produced later than the end of the fourth century, or possibly early in the fifth, and indeed there is nothing in the composition of the hoard that need indicate a later date for any of the objects' (Laing 1994, 35). Laing's case included parallels for the spiral-decorated plate dated by him to the second century AD; re-identification of the penannular brooches as torcs worn in a Roman Iron Age manner on the chest; placement of the handpin(s) significantly earlier in the series, circa fourth-fifth centuries; and interpretation of the symbol-plaque(s) as native versions of Roman-style votive objects.

Many of the objects within the Norrie's Law hoard are either unique or find parallel only with objects of equally uncertain date, and consequently Laing's line of investigation has not generally been accepted by later commentators. For instance, James Graham-Campbell rejected Laing's interpretation of Traprain Law and Norrie's Law as 'a similar kind of cache' on the grounds that the Traprain Law silver is 'massive and ornate' rather than 'generally slight and largely plain' and that it contains no 'native' types of object (Graham-Campbell 1991a, 251). In fact Laing did recognise this fundamental difference between the Norrie's Law and Late Roman hoards – that

9 The catalogue in Laing 1994 features 'the most notable items' only.

the latter are entirely composed of (mainly fragmented) Roman objects, whereas the former contains parts of both native and Roman types,[10] but for him it did not negate the usefulness of his comparison. Ongoing artefact analysis of both hoards provides new evidence with which to approach this debate, and for different reasons to Laing we too prioritise their shared identification as hacksilver hoards over their different (Roman versus native) contents.

Latest research demonstrates that the Traprain Law hoard was likely to have been buried during the first half of the fifth century (Kaufmann-Heinmann 2013, 259), two or three hundred years before the art-historically-derived date for the Norrie's Law hoard. This chronological gap has overshadowed the connection between the two hoards that Laing rightly pointed to – they are both silver hacked into bullion and until recently were the only two such hoards from pre-Viking Scotland. But this is not the limit of Traprain Law's relevance, for the site has also produced non-hoard material that has a bearing on the production and use of material within the Norrie's Law hoard. This includes a silver proto-handpin (NMS x.GVM 120),[11] two tinned copper-alloy (ie imitation silver) proto-handpins (x.GVM 118 and 119; Kirk 2011), proto-handpin moulds (x.GVM 552-4), one whole and another partial ribbed silver spiral finger ring (x.GVM 147 and x.GVM 149), as well as some of the earliest evidence for silver-working in Scotland (Hunter 2013) and a massive silver chain. The date of the latter remains uncertain; the type as a whole has tended to be dated to the sixth-seventh centuries (post-650 in Youngs 2013, 403), largely due to two examples that carry Pictish symbols. As noted above, the chains utilise significant quantities of silver and production closer to the time of maximum availability, in the fifth century, should be considered (Blackwell et al 2017, 101-4). A decorated thin bronze leaf-shaped plaque from Traprain Law also provides one of the closest parallels for the form of the silver plaque from Norrie's Law (Curle 1920 fig 8, no 6; x.GVM 270). As a site, therefore, Traprain Law has the combination of quantities of Late Roman silver buried during the fifth century and the presence and manufacture of native object types that were also made in this high-status material.

4.3 Post-Roman hacksilver in Scotland

Our understanding of the Norrie's Law hoard has been altered dramatically since the Scotland in Early Medieval Europe conference by a new discovery made in 2013 at Gaulcross, Aberdeenshire (Goldberg et al 2015). Three pieces of silver – a handpin, a piece of chain, and a spiral bangle – were found there around 1838, along with 'other pins and brooches' that no longer survive (Illus 4.4; Stuart 1867, 75, pl 9; Stevenson and Emery 1964) and a silver chain 'about 4 feet long' which may be a more complete incarnation of the surviving chain (Coles 1906, 188). Reconstruction and investigation of the find spot (a collaboration between the Northern Picts project at University of Aberdeen led by Gordon Noble, and the Glenmorangie Research Project at National

10 There is insufficient evidence to support Laing's suggestion that Norrie's Law is a collection of material removed from a shrine: 1994, 35.

11 The NMS accession numbers for the metal and mould finds from Traprain Law comprise a site code (x.GVM) followed by Burley's 1956 catalogue number, ie Burley catalogue number 120 = x.GVM 120.

Illustration 4.4 A silver handpin, bangle and chain, the only surviving items from the nineteenth-century discovery of silver at Gaulcross. Copyright Trustees of National Museums of Scotland.

Illustration 4.5 Fragments of silver found at Gaulcross during 2013-2014. Copyright Trustees of National Museums of Scotland.

Museums Scotland) demonstrated that these pieces were part of a much larger hoard with a significant hacksilver component. Dispersed remnants of this hoard were recovered by metal detector survey (Goldberg et al 2015; Noble et al 2016). Full study of these eighty newly discovered fragments of silver (Illus 4.5) is in progress and will include analysis of the metal composition, identification of objects, and investigation of hacking strategies, but ahead of this some preliminary observations can be made.

Gaulcross has always been linked to Norrie's Law because of the presence of a large silver handpin in each hoard (Stuart 1867, 45; Youngs 2013) and the newly recovered material serves to strengthen this link dramatically. Both hoards are a mixture of hacked pieces from Late Roman and native types of object, and both contain a similar range of Late Roman clipped siliquae, with eight recovered at Gaulcross. Gaulcross has also produced new parallels for the plain silver penannular brooches with twisted hoops and the repoussé bangles with defined, round-ended terminals that were previously only known from Norrie's Law (though the nineteenth-century discovery at Gaulcross produced an intact silver bangle with tapered terminals). Both hoards contained parcels made from pieces of bangle; while all the Norrie's Law parcels are fragmented, those from Gaulcross survive intact, and several incorporate Late Roman silver coins within the bundles (Illus 4.6). This survival is significant because of the opportunity it provides for assessing whether the weights of hacksilver pieces and parcels conform to a (Roman or alternative) standard of measurement and early findings do suggest some relationship with divisions of the Roman ounce. There are also differences between the two hoards. Ingots are present amongst the Gaulcross hoard (and make up 36% of the weight of the 2013 silver) but there are none amongst the surviving Norrie's Law material (though they might have been an obvious choice for the nineteenth-century silversmiths' crucible). Generally, there is a greater proportion of typologically-identifiable fragments of Late Roman silver amongst the Gaulcross hoard and more may be identified through scientific analysis of the silver composition, as was the case for the Norrie's Law hoard. Amongst the typologically Late Roman Gaulcross material are spoon fragments and militaria in the form of a strap fitting (the latter absent from amongst the surviving Late Roman fragments from Norrie's Law) (Illus 4.7).

The types of objects present in the Gaulcross and Norrie's Law hoards have very different distributions, suggesting a range of contacts or mechanisms resulted in their arrival. Silver handpins (and proto-handpins) are found across central and south-western England, Scotland and Ireland, as well as a single continental example from Hallum Terp in the Netherlands.[12] This widespread distribution points to intriguing but poorly understood elite networks across Britain and Ireland around the mid-first millennium AD; known manufacturing evidence is restricted to the Northern and Western Isles, but the extent to which this is a product of the survival of evidence is uncertain.[13]

Establishing when the hoards were accumulated or deposited is not straightforward: as has been long recognised for Norrie's Law, many of the objects, besides being fragmentary, are rare or unique and those objects which are paralleled elsewhere (such

---

12 A further example from an unknown location recently came up at auction, Anon 2014, 73, lot 392, in addition to another known from auction only, Youngs pers comm.

13 Upper Scalloway, Mainland Shetland; Gurness broch, Mainland Orkney; Loch na Beirgh broch, Lewis, Western Isles; Eilean Olabhat, North Uist, Western Isles; Armit et al 2008, 86-7.

Illustration 4.6 Hacksilver parcels, many made from pieces of bangle, some incorporating coins, from the Gaulcross hoard. Copyright Trustees of National Museums of Scotland.

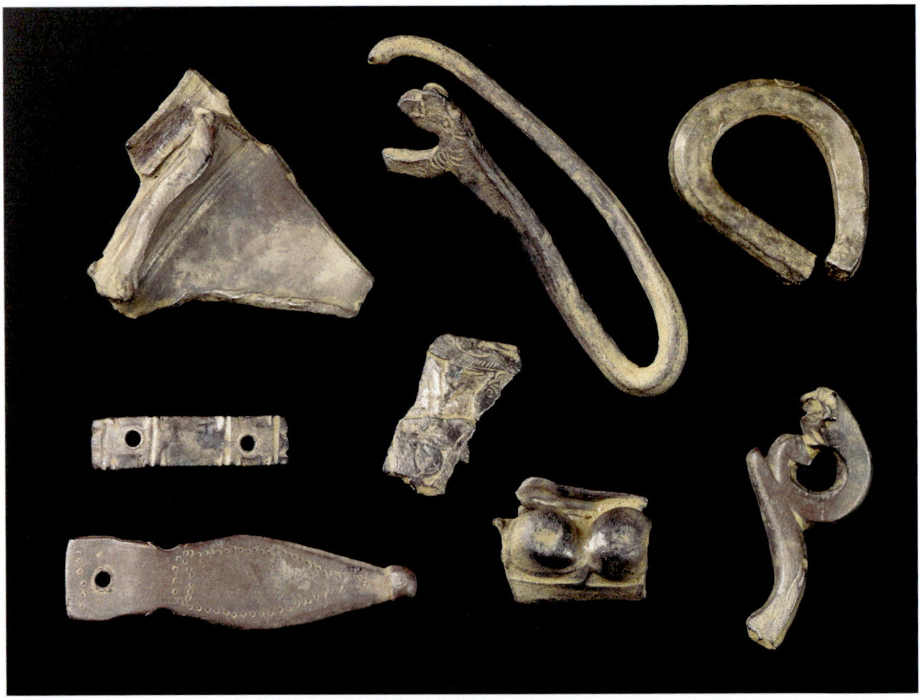

Illustration 4.7 Some pieces of typologically-identifiable Late Roman silver amongst the Gaulcross hoard. Copyright Trustees of National Museums of Scotland.

as spiral finger rings) tend to be matched by examples that themselves lack firm dating evidence. There are now, however, indications of an increased amount of circa fifth-century material amongst the surviving portions of both hoards. As mentioned above, there are both fourth-/fifth-century coins from each of the hoards and a greater amount of silver consistent with a Late Roman origin; this is a significant change from recognition of a single 'heirloom' spoon in Norrie's Law and suggests accumulation during a period where Late Roman silver was still circulating in hacked but (compositionally) unadulterated pieces, some of which appear to conform to Roman weight standards. Changes to the established chronology of handpins means the three (two large and one miniature) silver examples from Norrie's Law and Gaulcross should now be regarded as closer to fifth (rather than sixth or seventh) century in date (Youngs 2005, 253), and as part of a wider Insular participation in fourth- to fifth-century Late Roman Military Style metalwork (Gavin 2013a; Gavin and Newman 2007). Part of a zoomorphic brooch from Gaulcross (Fowler's Type F, 1960; 1963; Kilbride-Jones's Initial Form, 1980; or Class 1 after Graham-Campbell 1991b and Youngs 1995; Booth 2014), a rare survival in silver, can be dated to the fourth to fifth, or at the latest, the early sixth century AD. And although neither hoard is complete, the absences are also telling: there are no objects decorated in seventh- and eighth-century Insular style, nor any of the seventh- to eighth-century penannular brooch types. The very fact that the best potentially datable types discussed above are from the fourth/fifth centuries, a period often problematic to define in material terms, is a strong indication that these are not seventh-century hoards.

Both Gaulcross and Norrie's Law are clearly very closely related, part of the same phenomenon of bullion hoarding and accumulated around the same period, which seems likely on the basis of present evidence to be closer to the fifth or perhaps early sixth century AD than the eighth. Both are partial survivals and neither of the collections are likely to be representative of the whole. However, viewed together they can give us a much fuller picture of hacksilver hoarding and thus the accumulation and circulation of the primary material used to display power and status in post-Roman Scotland. Post-Roman hacksilver hoarding is not, however, a phenomenon limited to Scotland. The Norrie's Law and Gaulcross hoards are part of a bigger story, of strategies employed towards the powerful resource of precious metals along the fringes of the crumbling Empire. In order to understand them fully we need to look beyond Britain and Ireland.

4.4 Hacksilver hoarding in Europe

Hacksilver hoarding beyond the imperial boundaries is a phenomenon limited to the mid-fourth to the sixth centuries (Rau 2013b, 339). Within this material Andreas Rau has recognised three groups of hacksilver hoards: I, those containing only Late Roman hacked silver; II, mixed hoards containing both Late Roman and Early Medieval (Migration Period) material; and III, those only containing Early Medieval material (Rau 2013a). This approach sees hoards such as Traprain Law and Norrie's Law as related phenomena, whilst recognising their important differences. Group I Roman-only hoards are found in Scotland (Traprain Law), Ireland, across central Europe and perhaps at the Gudme-Uhrenholt site in Denmark. Mixed (Group II) hoards known to Rau were limited to southern Scandinavia, particularly Denmark (Rau 2013a, 193; Dyhrfjeld-Johnsen 2013). The Norrie's Law and Gaulcross hacksilver hoards can now be added to this distribution, meaning Group II hoards are now recognised in Scotland and Denmark. Group II hoards can be characterised as comprising: 'loaf-shaped or rectangular ingots, fragments of Roman silver tableware, various small rods, wire and sheet metal as well as fragmented jewellery of local provenance' (Rau 2013a, 189). This description is a good reflection of the established range of surviving silver from the Norrie's Law and Gaulcross hoards, especially as both types of ingot are present at Gaulcross.

Study of the Danish material, in common with the Scottish hacksilver, has been hampered by lack of analysis and full publication of the contents of the hoards (Dyhrfjeld-Johnsen 2013; Rau 2013a). There has been a significant increase in this material in recent years, principally due to metal detecting activity (Rau 2013a, 189; 2013b, 242); interestingly central European Barbaricum has not seen such an increase in finds (Rau 2013b, 341). This material has been summarised by Mads Dyhrfjeld-Johnsen who profiled 17 hoards, the majority of which include both whole and fragmentary objects of Late Roman and Early Medieval origin; stray finds of hacksilver are also known (Dyhrfjeld-Johnsen 2013). The ratio of Roman to native objects in the Danish hoards varies considerably. Rau has attempted to characterise this variation by drawing a further distinction within his Group II Late Roman/post-Roman hoards based on the proportion of Roman vessels represented amongst the hacked fragments. His Group IIa hoards are comprised of at least two-thirds fragmented Roman vessels; coins are common, and the distribution is primarily in Jutland and Funen. Rau suggests this type of hoarding dates to AD 360-460. Group IIb hoards are made up of a greater proportion of ingots (at least a third), with less than 40% from Roman vessels; coins are less common and Germanic Style I objects can feature. Rau notes that these hoards, found in Zealand and elsewhere in Denmark, could be deposited as late as AD 540. There are indications that the contents of Danish hacksilver hoards could be accumulated over a long period, more than 100 years in the case of the Høstentorp hoard (Rau 2013a, 192).

Neither Norrie's Law nor Gaulcross (as they survive) are predominately made up of Roman vessels and therefore they do not fit the picture of Rau's Group IIa hoards; spoon fragments are present in both and there is at least one fragment of Late Roman vessel amongst the Gaulcross silver, but overall these make up a small proportion of the weight. Taken together, Gaulcross and Norrie's Law have more in common with Rau's Group IIb hoards: a small proportion of Late Roman vessels/sheet silver fragments, local objects, ingots (but not Roman stamped ingots) and a small proportion of Late Roman coins.

Another similarity might rest in the degree of fragmentation, though again the limitations of interpreting only partially surviving hoards comes into play. Danish hacksilver hoards usually only contain small proportions of individual vessels, in contrast to, for example, the Irish hoards from Coleraine, Balline and that from Grossbodungen (Thuringia, Germany) (Rau 2013b, 349). Possible interpretations of this fragmentation, and perhaps also of that within the Scottish hacksilver hoards, include: later deposition, allowing more time for objects to be fragmented; direct transformation into a weight system based on small units leading to immediate fragmentation; and arrival in

Denmark as already fragmented hacksilver rather than complete vessels (Rau 2013b, 251). Amongst the Traprain Law hacksilver are both substantial portions of single objects, and objects represented only by single fragments (and indeed folded parcels); fragmentation before the silver reached Britain has been suggested as likely, perhaps in several stages (Kaufmann-Heinmann 2013, 257; Painter 2013, 226-7). Levels of fragmentation similar to those found in the Danish hoards are also known from within the Empire, for instance in the Patching (West Sussex) and Whorlton (Yorkshire) hoards (Painter 2013, 226).

Late Roman siliquae provide a further parallel between the Scottish and Danish Group IIb hoards. The Scottish finds of siliquae show variable evidence of clipping. This has been regarded as a distinctly British practice, only rarely encountered in continental Europe, and yet an unusual concentration of around 400 clipped siliquae is also found amongst the Danish hacksilver hoards (Guest 2013, 103-4). They have been seen as most likely to have been clipped in Britain before being exported, perhaps via Frisia – this has raised the possibility that the Late Roman silver plate in the Danish hoards likewise was fragmented in Britain and shipped abroad (Guest 2013, 104). The Danish finds of clipped siliquae attest 'previously unnoticed evidence of contacts between Britain and the Germanic continent during the fifth century AD' (Rau 2013a, 198). Clipped siliquae found in the region between the lower Weser and Elbe rivers have been interpreted as indicating an economic relationship between post-Roman England and the Saxon homeland (Rau 2013b, 348), and southern Jutland (which has produced hoards such as that from Nydam) is an area that has been associated with the Anglii or Angles (ibid, 339). The place of Scottish hacksilver hoards in these material connections between the continent and Britain during the fifth century remains to be explored but the common occurrence of clipped siliquae in Danish and Scottish hoards is particularly interesting given these two areas appear to be the only two in which mixed Roman/post-Roman hacksilver hoards were deposited beyond the imperial frontiers.

Interpretation of the Danish hacksilver hoards has in the past tended to see them as metalworkers' caches (eg Vang Petersen 1994), but Rau has pointed to the lack of closely associated metalworking evidence and the number of hoards found in contexts associated with settlements, such as close to fences, house walls or interior post holes (Rau 2013a, 191). Of the Late Roman hacksilver hoards from Britain, only one, the second-century hoard from Snettisham (Norfolk) has been interpreted as a jeweller's cache; as well as hacksilver, 110 denarii coins and a small quantity of gold, a quartz blade which had been used for burnishing gold was included. Rau has suggested that the Danish hacksilver hoards should be seen as family valuables, deposited in a safe place, and repeatedly accessed (Rau 2013a, 192), though several hoards have been discovered from sites with non-ferrous metalworking evidence (such as Lundeborg and Seden; Dyhrfjeld-Johnsen 2013, 324, 327). In contrast, both the Norrie's Law and Gaulcross hoards were deposited at prehistoric monuments: inserted within a (probable) Bronze-Age cairn at Norrie's Law, and adjacent to one of two stone circles at Gaulcross. This appears to be a significant difference to the Danish hoards, but whether a ritual or symbolic motive lay behind the selection of these deposition sites or something more practical – their function as landmarks, for instance – remains unclear.

The density of hacksilver hoards in Denmark is not paralleled in the surrounding regions that had a more direct relationship with the Roman administration: the Saxon German North Sea coast, the Frankish lower and middle Rhine, and the Alamannic region by the Upper Rhine have not produced equivalent hacksilver hoards. The reasons behind this concentration around the fringe of the empire in southern Scandinavia may well have a bearing on interpreting the Scottish hacksilver finds. It has been suggested that the Danish hacksilver was operating beyond, and taking the place of, the circulation of small units of silver in the form of denarii and other systems of imperial reward in the form of the distribution of Roman belt fittings and fibulae (Rau 2013b, 351-3). Rau's conclusion (ibid, 353-4) that 'in the Germanic area hacksilber hoards are typical of those regions that lay just outside the zone of direct influence of late Roman civilisation in the sense of economic, military and interpersonal relations' also applies to those hacksilver hoards from Scotland.

4.5 Conclusion

Gaulcross and Norrie's Law should be seen as post-Roman hacksilver hoards – a new area of study for Scotland. Objects from within both hoards can tell us about attitudes towards silver as a relatively new prestige material that came to be the preeminent medium for portable symbols of power across the Early Medieval period in Scotland. British hacksilver hoards are part of 'an Atlantic/North Sea tradition of silver deposition after c 400 that extended from Ireland in the west to southern Scandinavia and the Baltic in the east' (Guest 2013, 104). European hacksilver hoarding, and particularly the mixed hoards from Denmark, opens a very promising direction for further study: there will be plenty to compare and contrast in the make-up, accumulation and deposition of the Scottish mixed hoards. The significance of the shared phenomenon of post-Roman hacksilver hoarding and the common inclusion of clipped siliquae in both areas will require further study and collaboration with colleagues abroad. Approaching Scottish hacksilver hoarding as a continuum embracing hoards that contain only Late Roman material, those with mixed Late Roman and Early Medieval silver, and those comprised only of Early Medieval hacksilver is an important advance. Such an approach encourages us to draw Late Roman hacksilver hoards like Traprain Law into our thinking about Norrie's Law, but in a way that does not require us to argue Norrie's Law is Late Roman nor tie us to a binary distinction between Late Roman : Early Medieval. A hoard's chronological place on this spectrum is not the only factor that will have affected its makeup – access to various types of hacksilver (and the motivation to deposit them) will have depended on (difficult to reconstruct) short-term circumstances as well as long-term trends. Understanding the relationships represented by the hoard deposited on Traprain Law and the material produced there (in silver and coated in tin to imitate silver) will be key to future analysis, as some of these objects were found in the Norrie's Law and Gaulcross hoards. Considering all the Scottish hacksilver hoards together, and looking beyond Britain means this material can be used to explore the various strategies of forming elite identities across Europe during the centuries following the end of the Western Roman Empire.

Addendum

During the preparation of this paper, a further hacksilver hoard was discovered by metal detectorists in Fife. It is comprised parts of four third-century Roman silver vessels (Fraser Hunter pers comm); evidence of hacking is clearly apparent, but the material has also been significantly fragmented by the plough and now consists of over 350 fragments of silver. No non-Roman silver was found during subsequent excavation and systematic metal-detector survey of the findspot.

Acknowledgements

We would like to thank Fraser Hunter, Andreas Rau and our anonymous referee for insightful comments on a previous draft of this paper, and we are deeply indebted to Susy Kirk for her work on analysis of the Norrie's Law hoard. MG would like to thank Gordon Noble for joining him on the trail to Gaulcross and AB would like to thank Sally Foster for acting as Editor for this submission.

References

Anon, 2014 'TimeLine auctions catalogue, Sale 2-4 December 2014'.

Armit, I, Campbell, E and Dunwell, A 2008 'Excavation of an Iron Age, Early Historic and Medieval settlement and metalworking site at Eilean Olabhat, North Uist', *Proceedings of the Society of Antiquaries of Scotland* 138, 27-104.

Blackwell, A, Hunter, F and Goldberg, M 2017 *Scotland's early silver*. Edinburgh: National Museums Scotland.

Bland, R, Moorhead, S and Walton, P 2013 'Finds of late Roman silver coins from Britain: the contribution of the Portable Antiquities Scheme', *in* Hunter and Painter, 117-66.

Booth, A 2014 'Reassessing the long chronology of the penannular brooch in Britain: exploring changing styles, use and meaning across a millennium', unpublished PhD thesis, University of Leicester.

Buist, G 1839 *Report on the silver fragments in the possession of General Durham, Largo, commonly called the silver armour of Norrie's Law*. Cupar.

Burley, E 1956 'A catalogue and survey of the metalwork from Traprain Law', *Proceedings of the Society of Antiquaries of Scotland* 89, 118-226.

Close-Brooks, J 1986 'Excavations at Clatchard Craig, Fife', *Proceedings of the Society of Antiquaries of Scotland* 116, 117-84.

Coles, F R 1906 'Report on stone circles surveyed in the north-east of Scotland, chiefly in Banffshire, with measured plan and drawing, obtained under the Gunning Fellowship', *Proceedings of the Society of Antiquaries of Scotland* 40, 164-206.

Cowell, M R and Hook, D R 2010 'The analysis of the metal artefacts' *in* Johns, C *The Hoxne Late Roman treasure*, 175-83. London: British Museum.

Curle, A O 1920 'Report of the Excavation on Traprain Law', *Proceedings of the Society of Antiquaries of Scotland* 54, 54-124.

Dyhrfjeld-Johnsen, M D 2013 'Danish Hacksilber hoards: a status report', *in* Hunter and Painter, 321-38.

Foster, S M, Blackwell, A and Goldberg, M 2014 'The legacy of nineteenth-century replicas for object cultural biographies: lessons in duplication from 1830s Fife', *Journal of Victorian Culture* 19(2), 137-60.

Fowler, E 1960 'The origins and development of the penannular brooch in Europe', *Proceedings of the Prehistoric Society* 26, 149-77.

Fowler, E 1963 'Celtic metalwork of the fifth and sixth centuries AD: a reappraisal', *Archaeological Journal* 20, 98-106.

Fraser, I 2008 *The Pictish symbol stones of Scotland*. Edinburgh: RCAHMS.

Gavin, F 2013a 'Insular Military-Style silver pins in late Iron Age Ireland', *in* Hunter and Painter, 427-39.

Gavin, F 2013b 'Symbolism and mimesis: new perspectives on Late Iron Age pins from Ireland', in Hawkes, 187-200.

Gavin, F and Newman, C 2007 'Notes on Insular silver in the "Military Style"', *Journal of Irish Archaeology* 16, 1-10.

Goldberg, M and Blackwell, A 2013 'The different histories of the Norrie's Law hoard', *in* Hawkes, 326-38.

Goldberg, M, Noble, G, Mcpherson, A and Sveinbjarnarson, Ó 2015 'Rediscovering the Gaulcross hoard', *British Archaeology* 143, 38-43.

Graham-Campbell, J 1991a 'Norrie's Law, Fife: on the nature and dating of the silver hoard', *Proceedings of the Society of Antiquaries of Scotland* 121, 241-59.

Graham-Campbell, J 1991b 'Dinas Powys metalwork and the dating of enamelled zoomorphic brooches', *The Bulletin of the Board of Celtic Studies* 38, 220-32.

Guest, P 2013 'Siliquae from the Traprain Law treasure: silver and society in later fourth- and fifth-century Britain', *in* Hunter and Painter, 93-106.

Hawkes, J (ed) 2013 *Making histories: proceedings of the sixth international conference on Insular art 2011*. Donnington: Shaun Tyas.

Henderson, G and Henderson, I 2004 *The art of the Picts. Sculpture and metalwork in Early Medieval Scotland*. London: Thames and Hudson.

Henderson, I 1967 *The Picts*. London: Thames and Hudson.

Hunter, F 2013 'Hillfort and hacksilber: Traprain Law in the late Roman Iron Age and Early Historic period', *in* Hunter and Painter, 3-10.

Hunter, F and Painter, K (eds) 2013 *Late Roman silver: the Traprain Treasure in context*. Edinburgh: Society of Antiquaries of Scotland.

Hunter, F, Kaufmann-Heinimann, A and Painter, K forthcoming *The Late Roman silver treasure from Traprain Law*. Edinburgh: National Museums Scotland.

Kaufmann-Heinmann, A 2013 'The Traprain Treasure: survey and perspectives', *in* Hunter and Painter, 243-61.

Kilbride-Jones, H E 1980 *Zoomorphic penannular brooches*. London: Society of Antiquaries of London.

Kirk, S 2011 'Analysis of non-hoard silver and other metals from Traprain Law', unpublished report, AR 2011/14, National Museums Scotland.

Laing, L 1994 'The hoard of Pictish silver from Norrie's Law, Fife', *Studia Celtica* 28, 11-38.

Laing, L and Longley, D 2006 *The Mote of Mark: a Dark Age hillfort in south-west Scotland*. Oxford: Oxbow.

Lane, A and Campbell, E 2000 *Dunadd: an early Dalriadic capital*. Oxford: Oxbow.

Noble, G, Goldberg, M and Sveinbjarnarson, O 2016 '(Re)discovering the Gaulcross hoard', *Antiquity* 90, 726-41.

Painter, K 2013 'Hacksilber: a means of exchange?', *in* Hunter and Painter, 215-42.

Rau, A 2013a 'Some observations on Migration Period 'Hacksilber' hoards with Roman components', in Ludowici, B (ed) *Individual and individuality? Approaches towards an archaeology of personhood in the first millennium* AD, 189-203. Hannover: Niedersächsisches Landesmuseum.

Rau, A 2013b 'Where did the late empire end? Hacksilver and coins in continental and northern Barbaricum c 340-500', *in* Hunter and Painter, 339-57.

Stevenson, R B K 1955 'Pictish art', *in* Wainwright, FT (ed) *The problem of the Picts*, 97-128. Edinburgh: Greenwood.

Stevenson, R B K 1976 'The earlier metalwork of Pictland' *in* Megaw, J V S (ed) *To illustrate the monuments: essays on archaeology presented to Stuart Piggott*, 246-51. London: Thames and Hudson.

Stevenson, R B K and Emery, J 1964 'The Gaulcross hoard of Pictish silver', *Proceedings of the Society of Antiquaries of Scotland* 97, 206-11.

Stuart, J 1867 *The sculptured stones of Scotland*. Edinburgh: Spalding Club.

Tate, J and Troalen, L 2009 'Investigating the Traprain Law Roman Treasure', Technical Report, Eu-Artech.

Toolis, R and Bowles, C 2017 *The lost Dark Age kingdom of Rheged: the discovery of a royal stronghold at Trusty's Hill, Dumfries and Galloway*. Oxford: Oxbow.

Vang Petersen, P 1994 'Excavations at the site of Treasure Trove finds at Gudme', *in* Nielsen, P O, Randsborg, K and Thrane, H (eds) *The archaeology of Gudme and Lundeborg. Papers presented at a conference at Svendborg, October 1991*, 30-40. Copenhagen: Akademisk.

Wilson, D 1863 *The prehistoric annals of Scotland*. Volume 2. London: Macmillan.

Youngs, S 1995 'A penannular brooch from near Calne, Wiltshire', *Wiltshire Archaeological and Natural History Magazine* 88, 127-31.

Youngs, S 2005 'After Oldcroft: a British silver pin from Welton le Wold, Lincolnshire', *in* Crummy, N (ed) *Image, craft and the Classical world. Essays in honour of Donald Bailey and Catherine Johns*, 249-54. Monographies Instrumentum 29. Montagnac: Éditions Monique Mergoil.

Youngs, S 2013 'From chains to brooches: the uses and hoarding of silver in northern Britain in the Early Historic period', *in* Hunter and Painter, 403-25.

5

An Early Medieval and prehistoric nexus: the Strathearn Environs and Royal Forteviot project

Ewan Campbell, Stephen Driscoll, Meggen Gondek and Adrián Maldonado

5.1 Introduction

The lower valley of the River Earn (Perthshire) is one of the most significant areas in Scottish archaeology. It holds one of the country's densest concentrations of early prehistoric ceremonial monuments, as well as being at the centre of the development of the early Scottish kingdom. Forteviot is documented as the site of the ninth-century *palacio* of Cináed son of Alpín (Kenneth MacAlpin), one of the first kings of a united Scotland, who died there in AD 858. The site remained an important royal centre until the twelfth century, though it diminished in importance in relation to the nearby royal inauguration site at Scone (Duncan 2003; Driscoll 2004). The ninth century was a pivotal period in Scottish history, as the Gaelic west and Pictish east coalesced into the newly-imagined kingdom of Alba (Broun 2005; Woolf 2007), so the siting of a royal palace there is of great significance to understanding the process of kingdom formation. The Forteviot area also has an outstanding collection of Early Medieval sculptured stone monuments, and there is an early Christian copper-alloy hand-bell in the parish church, one of only six in Scotland. The stone monuments include the Dupplin cross, a large free-standing highly-decorated cross which has an inscription dedicated to Constantin I, king of Picts, who died around AD 820 (Forsyth 1995) (Illus 5.1). The Strathearn Environs and Royal Forteviot (SERF) project at the University of Glasgow was set up in 2006 to investigate this remarkable concurrence of Early Medieval royal and prehistoric ceremonial centres, along with the landscape which moulded human activity there over a period of at least five millennia. Excavations and surveys around

in: Blackwell, A.E. (ed.) 2019: *Scotland in Early Medieval Europe*,
Leiden: Sidestone Press, pp. 85-102.

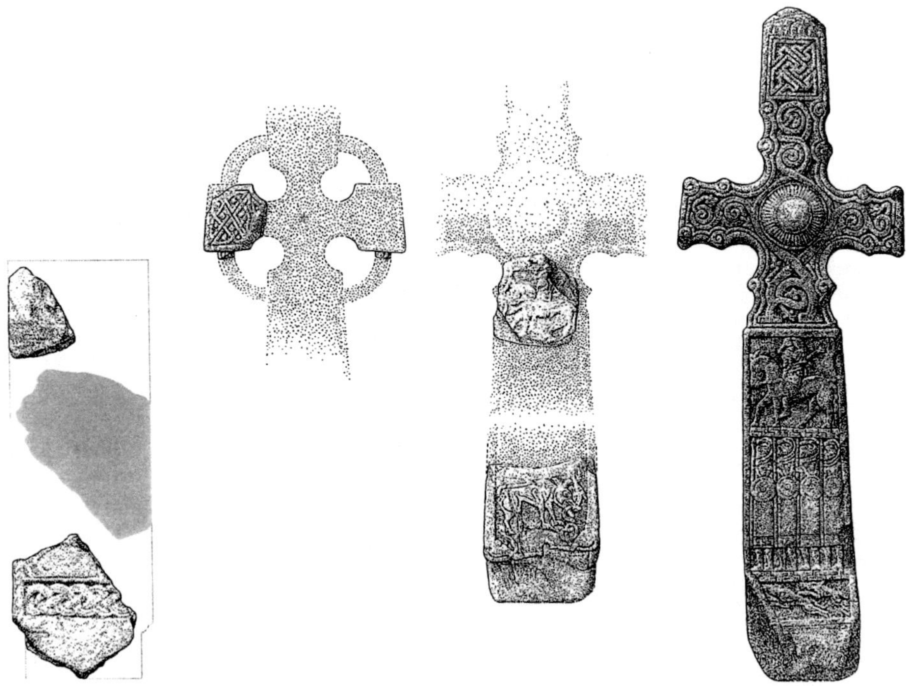

Illustration 5.1 The Dupplin cross and other Early Medieval sculpture from Forteviot, drawn by Ian Scott. Dupplin cross height: 2.92m.

Forteviot were carried out by SERF over a five-year programme from 2007-11, after which the focus of the investigations moved to the adjacent small town of Dunning, which has a similar large complex of ceremonial prehistoric monuments. Interim reports on all the excavations are available online (SERF Project), and the full excavation reports will be published in a series of monographs. This paper gives summary results of the Early Medieval excavations with a discussion of the main issues raised, focussing on three areas: the barrow cemeteries, the church, and the Early Medieval interventions in prehistoric monuments. The excavated sites lie mainly within two cropmark complexes; the Western Complex which consists mainly of early prehistoric burial and ceremonial monuments; and the Eastern Complex, which includes dug-grave cemeteries along with round and square barrows (Illus 5.2). These two foci lie immediately south of the modern village of Forteviot (National Grid Reference NO 052175).

5.2 The barrow cemeteries

The Eastern Complex was first recognised by Leslie Alcock (1980; 1982) to have examples of what were then considered to be distinctively 'Pictish' types of burial monument. These included both square and round barrows, alongside areas of dug graves in rows, as well as a large square enclosure of uncertain date and an apparent boundary ditch to the north. The cemeteries were investigated in two places, Sites K and J, the boundary ditch in Site M, and the square enclosure also in Site K (Illus 5.3). A further pair of square barrows was excavated on the southern edge of the Western Complex at

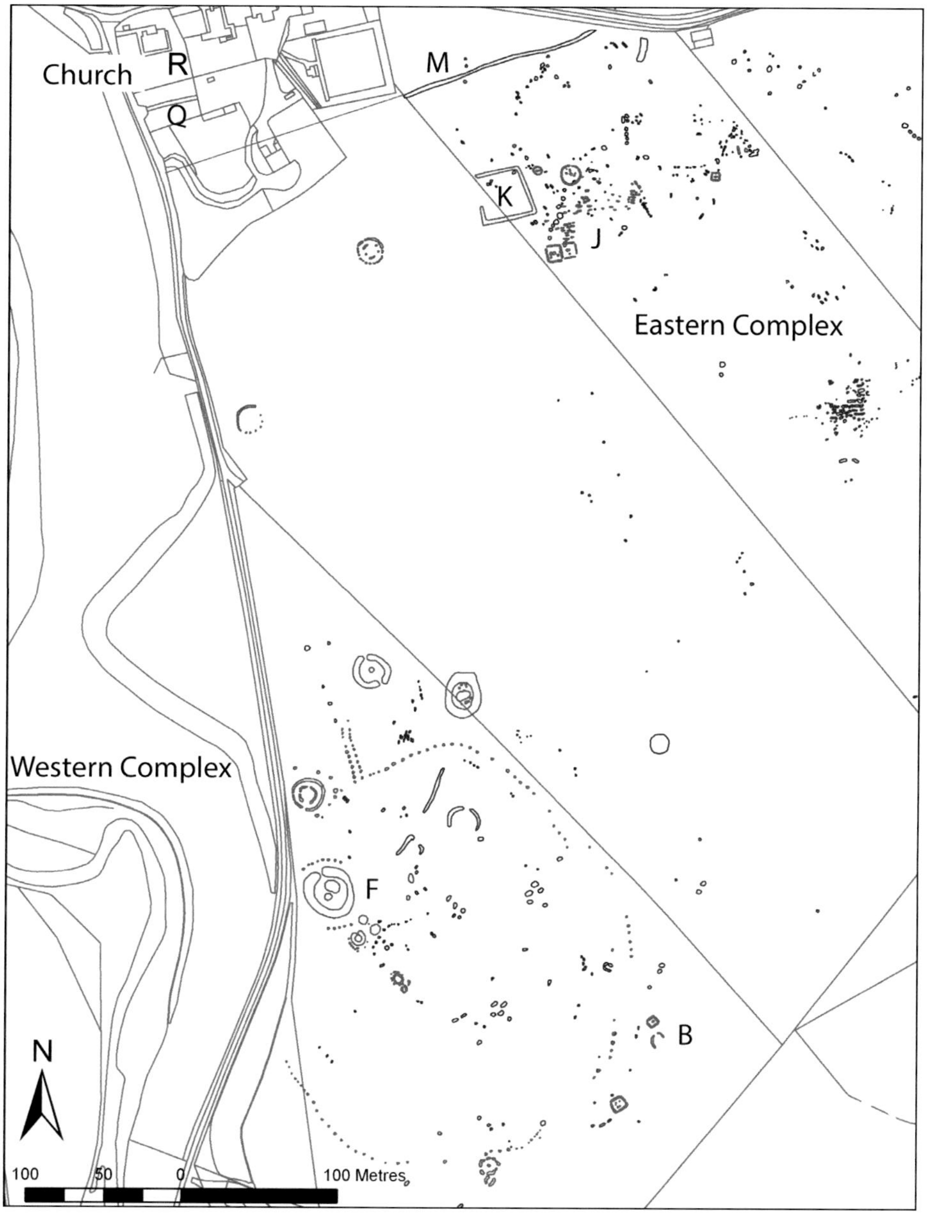

Illustration 5.2 Forteviot cropmark complexes, with excavated areas referred to in the text.

site B. All the cemeteries were badly affected by plough damage, but the evidence suggested that the monuments may have been upstanding until the agricultural improvements of the eighteenth century. The gravel subsoil resulted in very poor preservation of organic material, and skeletons in particular only survived as occasional fragments of dental enamel, making dating difficult.

The square barrows on Sites B and J both consisted of conjoined pairs, a common feature of this period, and three had interrupted corners. Although square barrows and cairns have long been considered to be a characteristic feature of Pictish burial

Illustration 5.3 Aerial view of Site K under excavation, showing a round barrow and part of the square enclosure.

practice, they are now recognised as occurring in many other areas of contemporary Britain and Ireland (Maldonado 2011; 2013). Many of these barrows are small low mounds, rather than the larger 'monumental barrows' often associated with rich burials which are widespread in northern Europe (Carver 2002). Both joined pairs of barrows had the western barrow as the original, with the eastern one added later, suggesting a possible family relationship between the inhumations, and a deliberate remembrance of this family significance (Williams 2007a, 159). Significant features included four-post structures around the two central barrow burials on Site J, and a stone lining to a log burial in another central burial on Site B. One of the row graves on Site K was also a log burial, in this case charred on the interior before burial. Log burials have become increasingly recognised in Early Medieval Scotland, with large numbers at Whithorn (Dumfries and Galloway) (Hill 1997) and Thornybank (Midlothian) (Rees 2002), and they are also a feature in some Anglo-Saxon, Welsh and Irish cemeteries (Maldonado, this volume). It has been suggested they are associated with high-status graves and contemporary literary references suggest that burial in 'a withered oak' may have a symbolic aspect (Maldonado 2011, 103-5; Williams 2007b, 234). The practice is first recorded in the Bronze Age and is widespread, as Early Medieval log coffins, sometimes decorated, survive intact at sites such as Landevennec (Finistère, France) and Oberflacht (Baden-Württemberg, Germany; Williams 2007b, 234, fig 2). The Forteviot round barrow on Site J had a central grave with charred branches deposited in the fill, again a practice attested elsewhere, in Anglo-Saxon England and in northern France (Halsall 1995, 6-9; Williams 2006, 129). The four-post structures on Site J could be interpreted as mortuary structures or an enclosure like the one at Thornybank (Rees 2002). Again there are parallels in other areas of Britain: at several sites in Kent (Hogarth 1973; O'Brien 1999, 139-41), Apple Down (Sussex; Down and Welch 1990) and Castledyke South, Barton-on-Humber (North Lincolnshire; Drinkall and Foreman 1998). There is also an example on the continent at München-Aubing (Dannheimer 1967). The mis-alignment of the four-post structure with the central burial may indicate that it post-dates the actual interment of the body. The charred log burial is very unusual but is paralleled by a charred coffin at Snape (Suffolk; Filmer-Sankey and Pestell 2001). Apart from the charred branches mentioned above, the only finds within the graves were small groups of quartz pebbles at the head and foot of the western barrow burial on Site B, a feature seen in several other Early Medieval burials in Scotland such as at Whithorn and the Isle of May (Maldonado 2011, 230). However, a Bronze Age flint barbed and tanged arrowhead from the fill of Unenclosed Grave 8 on Site J seemed to be a deliberate deposition. Both the central barrow graves on this site also had flint artefacts in the fill, and given the lack of flint lithics in the topsoil of this site, these may also have been deliberate depositions. In total these burial practices give an interesting insight into both burial rites and ongoing commemorative practices around the graves. Rather than being distinctively Pictish, these seem part of a nexus of practices which developed in late prehistoric society in Britain and beyond, but with regional differences in adoption.

Whether these burials are Christian is debateable, particularly given the lack of clarity in the process of adoption of Christianity in Scotland (Maldonado 2013, 6-7). The burials are generally supine inhumations aligned west – east with head to west, they respect other burials, and do not contain grave goods, but none of these features are now considered sufficient to characterise specifically Christian burials in the Early Medieval period (O'Brien 2009). Although none of the burials could be dated directly as insufficient bone material survived, a range of dates were obtained from the grave fills which cover the period from the fifth to ninth centuries. No coherent pattern could be resolved, but the burial in the round barrow and the charred log burial were the earliest, dating to the fourth to sixth century (SUERC-29209, 1580 ± 30; SUERC-29214, 1635 ± 30); while Unenclosed Grave2 on Site K gave a date in the eighth to ninth centuries (SUERC-22856, 1210 ± 30). The earlier dates fall within the normal range for barrow cemeteries and unenclosed field graves in Scotland (Maldonado 2011), but the later run into the period when the Church was taking an active interest in promoting burial within consecrated ground and discouraging the use of ancestral burial sites (O'Brien 2009). It may be that the importance of the Forteviot prehistoric monument complex exerted a strong pull to retain burial close to it. As we shall see below, burial was also taking place at Forteviot within the area of the Medieval (and putative Early Medieval) churchyard, suggesting a range of practices were tolerated.

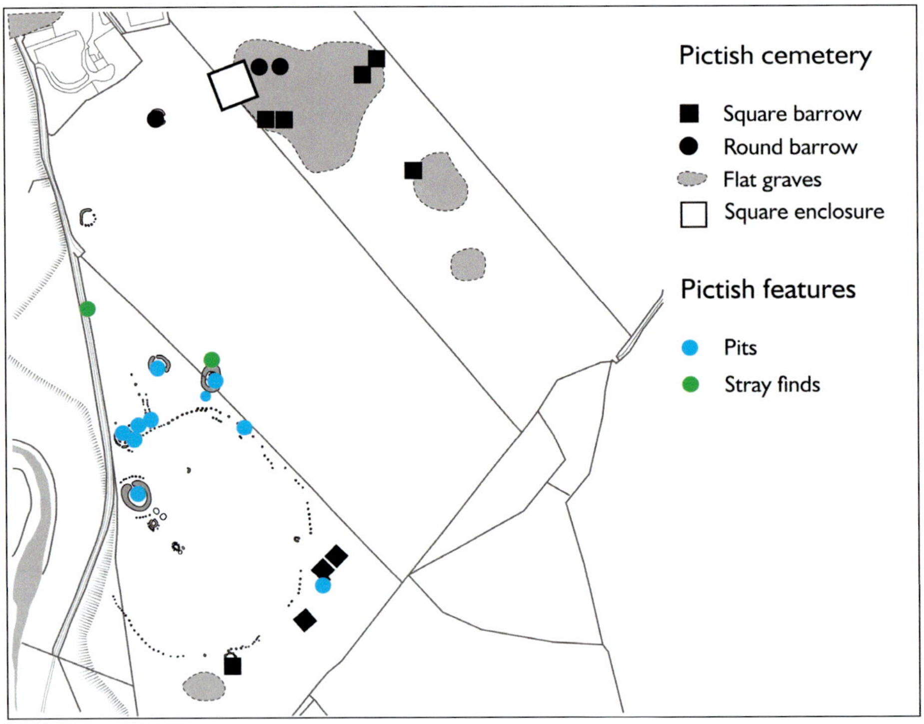

Illustration 5.4 Early Medieval cemeteries and interventions in prehistoric monuments.

The layout of the cemeteries is very unusual, being spread over a large area with a number of different foci (Illus 5.4), something not seen on other Pictish sites (cf Alexander 2005, illus 32). The aerial photographic evidence shows that there were at least 10 square barrows, 3-4 round barrows and at least 40 dug graves within the wider Forteviot cropmark complexes, spread over a distance of some 800m. There are two other noticeable features of this layout: firstly, a concentration around but not within the large square enclosure on Site K; and secondly, that no burials were within the area of the prehistoric monuments in the Western Complex, despite the evidence presented below for extensive Early Medieval interventions in these monuments. The northern boundary ditch of the complex in Site M gave radiocarbon dates in the seventh/ninth century, and its situation suggests that there was a rectilinear enclosure around the area of the modern village of Forteviot, separating a neck of land between the floodplains of the River Earn and the Water of May from the adjoining terraces. This enclosure may have been monastic, or the inner bounds of the documented royal palace. It has been postulated that the outer bounds of the royal estate were marked by the positions of the Dupplin and Invermay Crosses on opposite sides of the River Earn (Aitchison 2006, fig 17). These prominently marked the entry points to the royal estate and can be regarded as comparable to threshold markers in continental royal palaces such as Aachen and Ingelheim which had high symbolic importance (Airlie 2014).

The square enclosure (site K) measured an exact 30.5m square externally, and excavation confirmed that the 2m-wide ditches were remarkably regular in their line and form, showing they had been precisely laid out. In excavation, the ditches were

V-shaped with flat bottoms, again very regular in profile. No internal features contemporary with the ditch were identified in excavation or on aerial photographs, and the ditch fills were remarkably clean and free of any occupation evidence. Unfortunately this meant no direct dating evidence was recovered, but did illustrate that this was not a normal settlement enclosure. Roughly square enclosures of approximately this size are a feature of Iron Age settlement in eastern Lowland Scotland (eg Haselgrove 2009), but none of these share the precision of layout and construction of the Forteviot example. The clustering of the Early Medieval burials around the enclosure, but not within it, suggests it was contemporary with or earlier than these burials, and that it had some significance for Early Medieval society. Some Early Medieval barrows have outer enclosures similar in size to Forteviot. The only excavated example is at Beverly Field, Rhynie (Aberdeenshire), which has two similar large square enclosures with square barrows outside of them, but initial results are inconclusive as to the date of construction (G Noble pers comm). The closest formal parallel is at Cuiltburn (Perthshire), 16 kilometres to the east of Forteviot (Wooliscroft and Hoffman 2001), situated at the side of the Roman road along the Gask Ridge. This site was dated to the first century AD, but its function was enigmatic. Both the Cuiltburn and Forteviot sites have features which are reminiscent of the temenos sanctuary enclosures of Roman-Celtic temples, though these often have double enclosures (Lewis 1965). Further afield, single-ditched enclosures of this size and shape are found in Germany (Viereckschanzen), The Netherlands and northern France (enclose cultuels) associated with important later Iron Age sites (Collis 1984; Gerritsen 2001, 162-73). These appear to be sanctuary sites for ritual assemblies, possibly associated with the creation or commemoration of ancestors. Several excavated examples in The Netherlands date to the first century AD (Gerritsen 2001, 162). The dimensions and shapes of these enclosures closely resemble the Forteviot enclosure, and two of them are surrounded by later square burial monuments much as at Forteviot, though there the burials also date to the first century AD. One of the most interesting of these is at Nijmegen-Kops Plateau, where the cult site is linked to an early prehistoric complex, and has been suggested to be a staging place in burial rituals, a liminal place where ancestors were created (Gerittson 2001, 168-9; Fontijn 2003). It may be that the Forteviot enclosure is a similar cult site, constructed by the Roman soldiers familiar with such sites from their Batavian homeland (the nearby Gask Ridge Roman forces were Batavian), and deliberately situated at Forteviot as this was still a major cultic or assembly site of the region associated with the major prehistoric monument complex. A scatter of Roman period finds have come from the topsoil in and around Forteviot.

5.3 The Early Medieval church

The Forteviot arch, dating to the ninth century, is one of the most significant pieces of sculpture from Early Medieval Scotland (Illus 5.5). Its form shows that it is from part of a large stone-built structure, but there has been debate as to whether this was a church, a chapel-royal, or a secular palace, and other possibilities include a baptistery or a burial monument. Pre-Romanesque stone-built churches are extremely rare in Scotland (see Foster, this volume), and secular stone buildings unknown, so the presence of the arch re-enforces Forteviot's position as an important royal centre in the

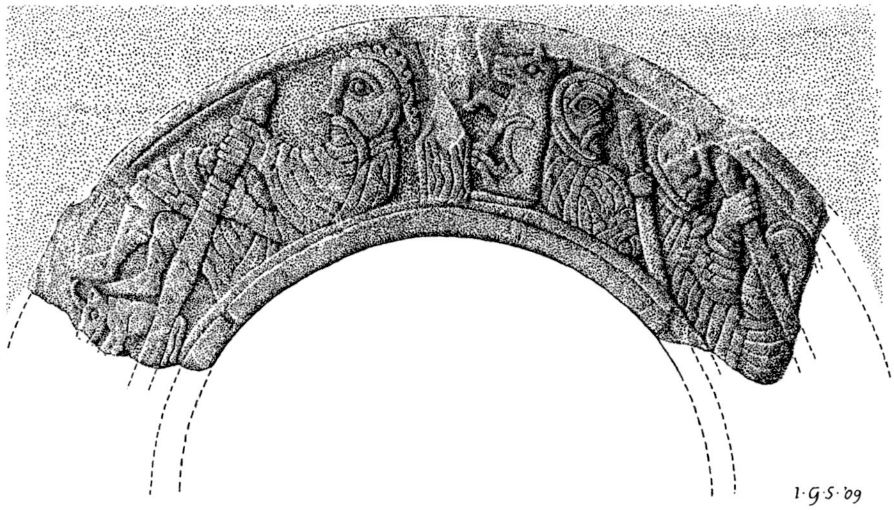

Illustration 5.5 The Forteviot arch, drawn by Ian Scott.

ninth century, whatever the exact nature of the building it came from. Excavations in 2011 around the present parish church revealed that this eighteenth-century building was constructed on the remains of a Medieval predecessor, probably in the thirteenth century. The northern part of the east wall was underlain by burials dated to the eleventh/twelfth century, showing that an earlier church must have stood on the site. An early boulder foundation on a slightly different alignment may represent this earlier, narrower church building, but the evidence is not strong and it may be part of the thirteenth-century foundations.

Excavations on Site Q, immediately to the south of the Medieval churchyard, revealed a series of dug graves in rows, similar to those found in the barrow cemeteries, and with similarly poor bone preservation, which contrasted with the good preservation of the eleventh-/twelfth-century burials described above. Associated with these burials were the remains of a wooden structure or structures which included a row of post-holes and a beam-slot for a sill-beam (Illus 5.6). This seems likely to have been either an early wooden church or shrine, given that the graves respected its position. Similar simple wooden structures are known from a number of Scottish and Irish early Christian sites (Thomas 1971; Ó Carragáin 2010, 15-26). Unfortunately no dating evidence was recovered, and no other area was available for excavation due to an extension of the modern cemetery, but the form and preservation of the graves differs from the Medieval burials under the church, and is similar to the graves in the field cemeteries of Site J and K. It seems that there was an early burial focus in the area of the Medieval church, and that this may have functioned alongside the field cemeteries to the south.

The Forteviot arch is unweathered, despite being found in an abandoned channel of the Water of May, near the parish church, around 1800 (Jamieson 1830, 207). It is clear that it had always been inside a building, forming part of a doorway, chancel arch or altar screen. Antiquarian accounts of palace ruins being washed away by floods from the Water of May (Aitchison 2006, 37-48) clearly refer to much later buildings, but have

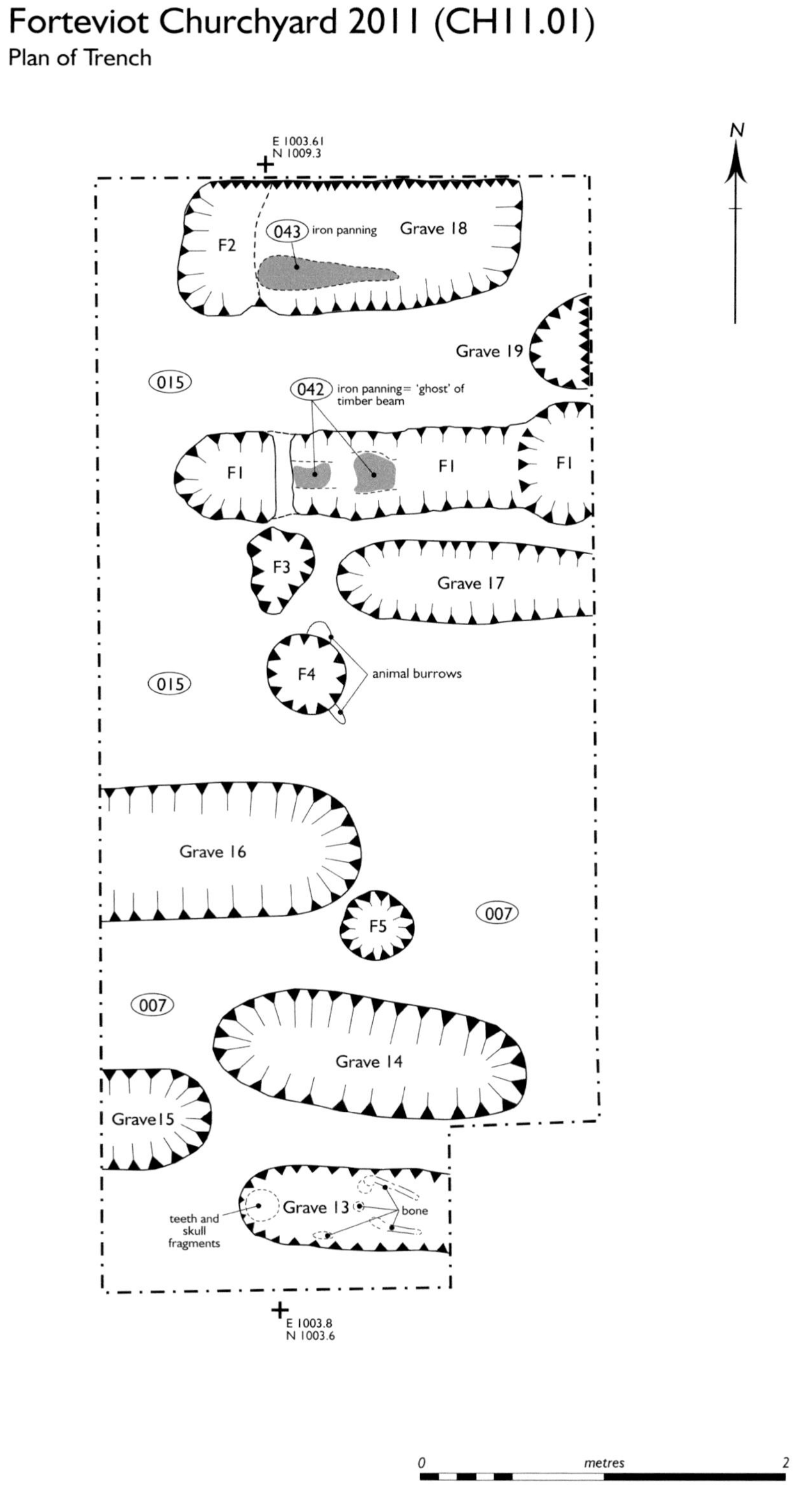

Illustration 5.6 Early Medieval structures and graves on Site Q, Forteviot parish church.

caused some commentators to assume the early royal church/chapel was destroyed and the arch washed into the river. The unworn condition and placement of the arch suggest a different scenario. The arch was part of a royal complex of buildings on the site, bounded by the boundary ditch seen on aerial photographs and excavated on Site M. The arch was incorporated into the Medieval church in the thirteenth century, when the original stone building was demolished, possibly as part of a shrine associated with the tenth-century handbell relic, or the royal tomb of Cináed. During the Reformation, the arch was preserved from destruction by burial in an abandoned meander of the river, much as the Ruthwell Cross (Dumfries and Galloway) was saved from destruction by the actions of a local minister (Farrell and Karkov 1992). This may have happened during one of the periods of rebuilding of the east wall of the church in the seventeenth century recorded in documentary sources (Meldrum 1926, 279), and evidenced in the 2011 excavations where a doorway into an added eastern chamber was blocked up.

5.4 Interventions in early prehistoric monuments

The prehistoric monuments in the Western Complex include at least three large henge monuments, one mini-henge, a timber circle, a cremation cemetery, a double-ditched enclosure with central triple cist, several standing stones, and numerous pits, all situated within or around a massive palisaded enclosure. This large enclosure is one of only five in Scotland, but similar monuments occur in Ireland and Scandinavia (Noble and Brophy 2011a; 2014). Numerous radiocarbon dates show a striking pattern of use of the two complexes (Illus 5.7). The prehistoric use begins in the middle Neolithic and continues into the later Bronze Age, and consists of burial and other ceremonial activities. The absence of dates throughout most of the first millennium BC initially suggests that the monuments were completely abandoned before becoming the focus for Early Medieval burial practices around and outside the decayed monuments.

One of the most surprising results of the excavations in the prehistoric monument complex was the discovery of numerous Early Medieval interventions in the prehistoric monuments. Each of the three henge monuments had a massive central pit dug into it – these pits had no obvious function, but their location suggests early attempts to discover tombs such as the impressive Early Bronze Age dagger burial uncovered in Henge 1 in 2009 (Noble and Brophy 2011b). Even more surprising was the fact that another pit contained cremated human bone dated to the seventh/ninth centuries, an exceptionally late date for cremation practices. It may be that the disposal of the bone within the prehistoric complex reflected a deviance from normal burial practices. In this context it is interesting that some of the other examples of late cremation in Scotland have also involved utilisation of prehistoric monuments or artefacts such as Bronze Age urns (Maldonado 2013, 12). Further evidence of unusual activities was found in the central cist of the double-ditched enclosure on Site F. Although initially the site of a Bronze Age burial, the cist had been uncovered and filled with burnt material in the fifth/sixth century. It is possible that the barbed-and-tanged arrowhead found in the Early Medieval grave on Site J was obtained from this cist, and may have gained cultic significance from its association with the ancient site. In another case, the upper part of one of the massive post-holes of the palisaded enclosure had been reused in the Early Medieval period for the disposal of burnt material, showing both

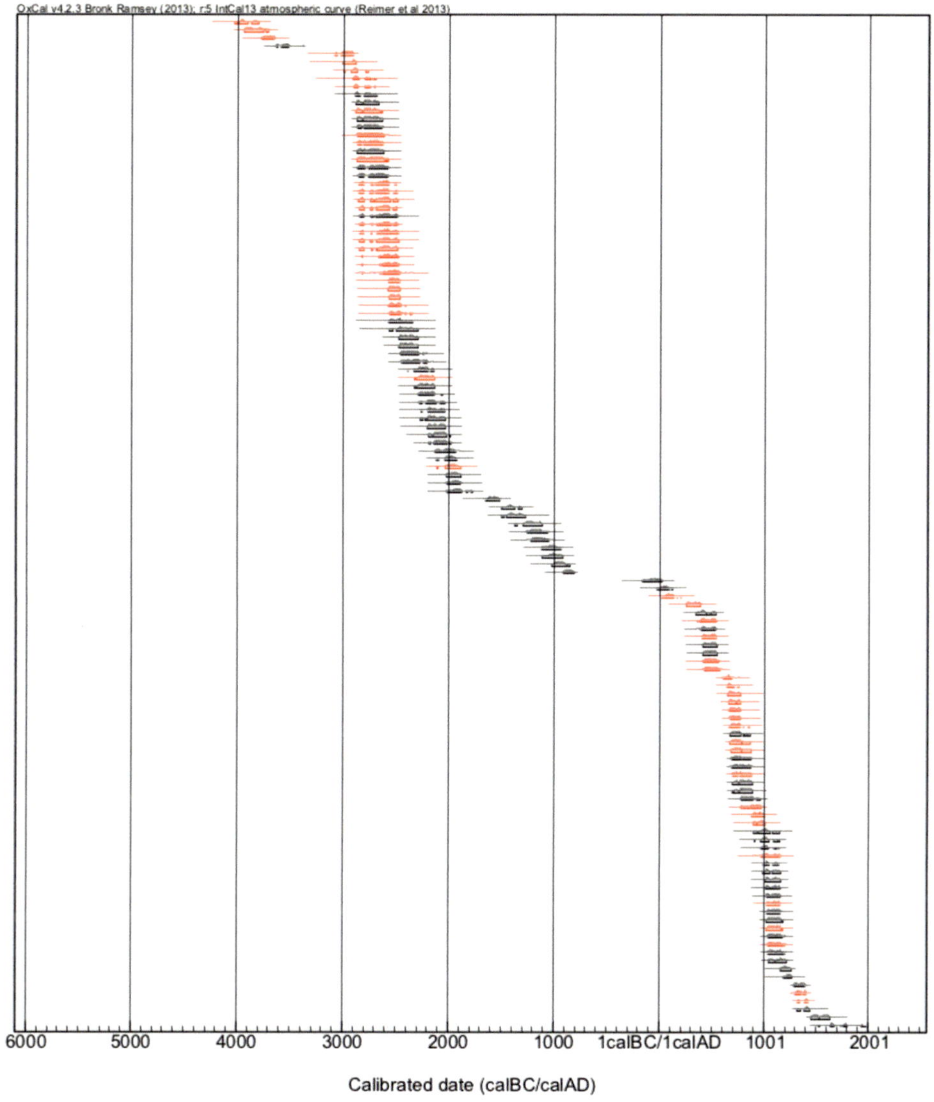

Illustration 5.7 All radiocarbon dates from Forteviot excavations, burning episodes in red.

that the post-holes were still visible as hollows in the landscape, and that they were seen as special places for the disposal of certain types of material. In all, at least twelve of these interventions were discovered, all only recognised due to an intensive radiocarbon dating programme, as no Early Medieval artefacts were found within the features (Table 5.1). A recurring feature of these pits is the presence of burnt material, often including cereals. While some of these are the result of cremation activities others are more puzzling, and cannot be explained as domestic refuse, as there is no settlement evidence anywhere within the complexes at any period. However, it is noticeable that many of the other dates from the Forteviot excavations are also from burnt deposits (Illus 5.7), suggesting some type of continuity of assembly practices over long periods of time which involved burning rituals, even if the burial practices were discontinuous.

Site	feature	size (m)	Depth (m)	dates Cal AD (2 σ)	charcoal	grain
B	Small pit	1.5 x 0.7	0.1	610-690 (660-790)	Ash, hazel	Barley, oats
C	Small pit	0.4 x 0.2	0.3	410-540 (390-540)	Hazel	
Henge 1 D	Massive pit	10.5 x 10.7	1.5	650-780 (680-790)	Heather, willow, ash, oak, hazel	
F	Large pit	3.1 x 1.9	0.6	420-580 (420-570)	Alder, hazel	Barley, oats
F	Cist	1.0 x 0.4	0.7	400-550 (380-540)	Oak, hazel	Oats, barley
F	Large pit	2.5 x 1.9	0.6	640-720 (670-830)	Alder, hazel	
F	Large pit	3.5 x 2.4	0.6	890-1020 (810-980)	Oak, heather, birch, hazel	Barley
G	Pit	1.7 x 0.8	0.4	640-780	Alder, hazel	Barley, ?wheat
G	Pit and paving	0.8 x >0.3	0.3	40BC – AD120 (10-170)	Hazel, alder, willow	
Henge 2 G	Massive pit	12.0 x 5.0	2.2		Oak	
K	Small pit	0.4 x 0.4	0.2	1310-1440 (1290-1420)	Ash, oak	Wheat
Henge 3	Massive pit	10.0 x 5.0		Unexcavated		

Table 5.1 Details of Early Medieval interventions in prehistoric monuments.

5.5 Discussion

The Forteviot excavations have shown that the prehistoric monument complex was an important focus for ceremonial and burial activity, not just in the early prehistoric period, but also in the Early Medieval period (cf Driscoll 1998). The co-location of prehistoric and Late Iron Age/Early Medieval cultic sites is known from other areas of Europe, for example in Ireland at sites such as Tara (Co Meath) and Navan (Co Armagh). However, unlike at these sites, at Forteviot the Early Medieval burials all lie outside of the prehistoric monuments, and indeed have one focus around a possible Roman-period enclosure. Also in contrast to the sites of continental royal palaces, elite dominance is mainly not articulated through very large building complexes such as Charlemagne's palace at Aachen (North Rhine-Westphalia), but through monumental sculpture set in the landscape. The other unusual aspect of the Forteviot evidence is the active digging into, and re-use of, the earlier monuments in the Early Medieval period for a variety of purposes, some of which may have had pagan overtones linked to fire festivals.

The archaeological evidence from Forteviot invites comparison with other Early Medieval royal sites in Britain in Ireland, where there are instructive similarities and striking contrasts. The greatest resonances are seen in the Gaelic world, where prehistoric ritual monuments are frequently associated with locations linked to kingship ceremonies in the Middle Ages. Such connections between the Early Medieval era and the more ancient past are rarer in England and southern Britain, but this is not the only contrast. In Ireland it is rare for royal sites to have a church, while the early ecclesiastic presence at Forteviot is one of its most distinctive features, one that it shares with sites in Francia (Airlie 1994).

In recent years there has been a lively interest in the archaeology of royal ceremonial sites and places of popular assembly in Ireland, where the rich historical evidence allows sites to be identified with confidence and for their religious and cosmological significance to be appreciated (Wailes 1982; Warner 2004; FitzPatrick 2004; Schot et al 2011). The most famous of these sites is undoubtedly the Hill of Tara, with its particularly rich mythological and historical evidence and a great density of monuments (Newman 1997; Bhreathnach 2005), but it is far from unique. Studies of the provincial royal centres Emain Macha (Co Armagh; Lynn 2003), Dun Alinnie (Co Kildare; Johnson and Wailes 2007), Rathcroghan (Co Roscommon; Waddell et al 2009) and Cashel (Co Tipperary; Gleeson 2012), all reveal links with an ancient past and as well as the construction of Early Medieval structures for kingship and assembly. At a local level it is possible to identify places of assembly and ceremony which were used by lesser rulers to govern their realms well into the Middle Ages drawing upon on similar cosmological traditions. Taken as a whole this material is diverse, but nevertheless it is possible to identify a number of traits which are shared by many of the sites (Waddell 2011). These features include topographical situations which provide expansive views, prehistoric burial mounds, large artificial enclosures, mounds for assembly and processional ways leading to structures with a figure-of-eight plan. For purposes of comparison with Forteviot, the key features are the large enclosure and the burial mounds. At Tara and Emain Macha, where the enclosure ditch is on the interior of the boundary bank, it has been argued that not only are they intended to mark out a sacred space, but they are designed to contain things with in the enclosure (Newman 2011). At Forteviot the sacred boundary was originally defined by hundreds of massive oak posts, which long after their decay continued to define a sacred space. A long sequence of burials dating from the middle Neolithic through to the late Bronze Age, and the construction of several henge monuments, show continuing reinvention and remodelling of this ceremonial space (Brophy and Noble 2012; Noble and Brophy 2014). Most remarkably, given the long span of time between the Neolithic and the Iron Age, is the positioning of burials of Iron Age or Early Medieval form just outside the Neolithic post-defined enclosure. We believe that an enclosing bank must have remained visible until it was removed by modern agriculture. The prehistoric burial mounds and earthworks were also of great interest to the Picts, judging from the efforts expended excavating, reusing and recycling material from them.

Reasonable people have been sceptical of the possibility of transmission of sacred knowledge over millennia, but archaeological evidence, particularly radiocarbon dates, have revived interest in the possible continuity of at least interest in, and awareness of, the sacred nature of some special places from the early prehistoric through to the Early Medieval periods (Waddell 2014). The key point in this context is the notion that burial mounds served as portals to the otherworld and as such were potential sources of sacred knowledge and power. The excavation of deep pits within prehistoric monuments during Pictish times is perhaps best interpreted as an effort to engage with the Otherworld, in mythological terms, the ultimate source of legitimacy.

The other relevant feature at Forteviot which is characteristic of the Irish ritual landscape is the use of fire rituals to mark season festivals (Samhain, Imbolc, Beltane and Lughnasadh). Although in modern times popular attention focuses on Beltane (1 May), the widespread occurrence of burnt grain in these deposits make it more likely that the burning at Forteviot was associated with Samhain (1 November), which was not only a harvest festival, but also associated with popular assembly. The large number of burning episodes at Forteviot is one the site's most striking features, but was only revealed as a result of digging extensively and a comprehensive programme of radiocarbon dating funded by Historic Scotland.

The Irish material also throws up a number of contrasts with Forteviot. Permanent residences are not an essential or frequent feature of the majority of Irish 'Royal' sites. The most conspicuous exceptions, Knowth, Brú na Bóinne (Co Meath; Byrne et al 2008) and Clogher (Co Tyrone; Warner 1988), are unusual in many respects and neither was a provincial royal place. Churches are also a rarity at Irish royal sites, again Clogher with its nearby monastery is an exception, but so too is Cashel, a royal site crowned by a later great church. However, it is much more characteristic for important churches to be located at some distance from the royal sites, which were presumably centres of pagan religious practice at the time of conversion.

When looking south for comparative material on royal centres, the main analogy is with the residence, assembly place and cult centre at Yeavering (Northumbria), which some now consider to be a hybrid British/Anglo-Saxon site (Hope-Taylor 1977; Frodsham and O'Brien 2005; O'Brien 2011; Noble et al 2013, 1146). However, more examples of close relationships of Anglo-Saxon royal sites with prehistoric monuments are being recognised, for example at Sutton Courtney (Oxfordshire) and Grateley (Hampshire), though in England more often the relationship with prehistoric sites is to assembly places, burial and particularly execution sites (Semple 2013, 194-222).

Forteviot appears to acquire permeant royal residence, probably linked to or within a monastery, but certainly with a church. It seems to reflect some elements of a continental concept of a palace, as a permanent establishment, suitable for the holding of a royal court, blessed and in some way protected by the presence of the church (Airlie 1994). However, it has its own unique Scottish twist, as it is located at, and respects, a site of great antiquity, marked by many prehistoric burial monuments, and is demarcated in the landscape by massive stone crosses. Thus it reflects a particular local fusion of elements combined from continental and Celtic approaches to the expression of royal power, deliberately forged as part of the process of creating a new political entity, the nascent kingdom of the Scots.

Acknowledgements

The project was partly sponsored by the British Academy (LRG: 45610); Historic Scotland (Archaeology Funding Programme) and the University of Glasgow. The research of SERF has benefited from partnerships with the University of Aberdeen, the University of Chester, the Royal Commission on the Ancient and Historical Monuments of Scotland, Perth and Kinross Heritage Trust, and Dunning Historical Society.

References

Airlie, S 1994 'The view from Maastricht', *in* Crawford B E (ed) *Scotland in Dark Age Europe*, 33-46. St Andrews: University of St Andrews.

Airlie, S 2014 'The palace complex', *in* Hudson, J and Rodriguez, A (eds) *Diverging paths? The shapes of power and institutions in Medieval Christendom and Islam*. Leiden: Brill.

Aitchison, N 2006 *Forteviot: a Pictish and Scottish royal centre*. Stroud: Tempus.

Alcock, L 1980 'Populi Bestialis Pictorum feroci anime…: a survey of Pictish settlement archaeology', *in* Hanson, W S and Keppie, L (eds) *Roman Frontier Studies 1979*. BAR International Series 71, 61-95. Oxford: Archaeopress.

Alcock, L 1982 'Forteviot: a Pictish and Scottish royal church and palace', *in* Pearce, S (ed) *The early Church in western Britain and Ireland: studies presented to C A Ralegh Radford*. BAR British Series 102, 211-39. Oxford: Archaeopress.

Alexander, D 2005 'Redcastle, Lunan Bay, Angus: the excavation of an Iron Age timber-lined souterrain and a Pictish barrow cemetery', *Proceedings of the Society of Antiquaries of Scotland* 135, 41-118.

Bhreathnach, E (ed) 2005 *The kingship and landscape of Tara, Dublin: the Discovery Programme*. Dublin: Four Courts Press.

Brophy, K and Noble, G 2012 'Henging, mounding, blocking: the Forteviot henge group', *in* Gibson, A (ed) *Enclosing the Neolithic: recent studies in Britain and Europe*, 21-35. Archaeopress: Oxford.

Broun, D 2005 'Alba: Pictish homeland or Irish offshoot?', *in* O'Neill, P (ed) *Exile and homecoming: papers from the Fifth Australian Conference of Celtic Studies*, 234-75. Sydney: University of Sydney.

Byrne, F J, Jenkins, W, Kenny, G and Swift, C 2008 *Historical Knowth and its hinterland*. Dublin: Royal Irish Academy.

Carver, M 2002 'Reflections on the meanings of monumental barrows in Anglo-Saxon England', *in* Lucy, S and Reynolds, A (eds) *Burial in Early Medieval England and Wales*, 132-43. London: Society for Medieval Archaeology.

Collis, J 1984 *The European Iron Age*. London: Batsford.

Dannheimer, H 1967 'Der Holzbau am Rande des Reihengräberfeldes von München-Aubing', *Germania* 44, 326-38.

Down, A and Welch, M 1990 *The Chichester excavations 7: Apple Down and the Mardens*. Chichester: Chichester District Council.

Drinkall, G and Foreman, M 1998 *The Anglo-Saxon cemetery at Castledyke South, Barton-on-Humber*. Sheffield: Sheffield Academic Press.

Driscoll, S T 1998 'Picts and prehistory: cultural resource management in Early Medieval Scotland', *World Archaeology* 30, 142-58.

Driscoll, S T 2004 'The archaeological context of assembly in Early Medieval Scotland – Scone and its comparanda', *in* Pantos, A and Semple, S (eds) *Early Medieval assembly places*, 73-94. Dublin: Four Courts Press.

Duncan, A A M 2003 'Before coronation: making a king at Scone in the thirteenth century', *in* Welander, R, Breeze, D and Clancy, T (eds) *The Stone of Destiny: artefact and icon*, 139-68. Edinburgh: Society of Antiquaries of Scotland Monograph.

Farrell, R and Karkov, C 1992 'The construction, deconstruction and reconstruction of the Ruthwell cross: some caveats', *in* Cassidy, B (ed) *The Ruthwell Cross*, 35-47. Princeton: Princeton University Press.

Filmer-Sankey, W and Pestell, T 2001 *Snape Anglo-Saxon cemetery: excavations and surveys 1824-1992*. Ipswich: East Anglian Archaeology Report 95.

FitzPatrick, E 2004 *Royal inauguration in Gaelic Ireland, c1100-1600: a cultural landscape study*. Woodbridge: Boydell.

Fontijn D R 2003 *Sacrificial landscapes. Cultural biographies of person, objects and 'natural' places in the Bronze Age of the southern Netherlands, c2300-600* BC. Leiden: Leiden University.

Forsyth, K 1995 'The inscription on the Dupplin Cross', *in* Bourke, C (ed) *From the isles of the north: Medieval art in Ireland and Britain*, 237-44. Belfast: HMSO.

Frodsham, P and O'Brien, C (eds) 2005 *Yeavering. People, power and place*. Stroud: Tempus.

Gerritsen, F 2002 *Local identities: landscape and community in the late prehistoric Meuse-Demer-Scheldt region*. Amsterdam: Vrije Universiteit.

Gleeson, P 2012 'Constructing kingship in Early Medieval Ireland: power, place and ideology', *Medieval Archaeology* 56, 1-33.

Halsall, G 1995 *Early Medieval cemeteries: an introduction to burial in the post-Roman west*. Glasgow: Cruithne Press.

Haselgrove, C 2009 *The Traprain Law environs project: fieldwork and excavations 2000-2004*. Edinburgh: Society of Antiquaries of Scotland Monograph.

Hill, P 1997 *Whithorn and St Ninian. The excavation of a monastic town, 1984-91*. Stroud: Sutton Publishing.

Hogarth, A C 1973 'Structural features in Anglo-Saxon graves', *Archaeological Journal* 130, 104-19.

Hope-Taylor, B 1977 *Yeavering: an Anglo-British centre of early Northumbria*. London: HMSO.

Jamieson, J 1830 *Select views of the royal palaces of Scotland, from drawings by William Brown, Glasgow; with illustrative descriptions of their local situation, present appearance, and antiquities*. Edinburgh: Cadell and Co.

Johnson, S A and Wailes, B (eds) 2007 *Dún Ailinne: excavations at an Irish Royal site, 1968-1975*. Philadelphia: Penn Press.

Lewis, J 1965 *Temples in Roman Britain*. Cambridge: Cambridge University Press.

Lynn, C 2003 *Navan Fort: archaeology and myth*. Bray: Wordwell.

Maldonado, A 2011 'Christianity and burial in late Iron Age Scotland, AD 400-650', unpublished PhD thesis, University of Glasgow.

Maldonado, A 2013 'Burial in Early Medieval Scotland: new questions', *Medieval Archaeology* 57, 1-34.

Meldrum, N 1926 *Forteviot: the history of a Strathearn parish*. Paisley: Alexander Gardener.

Newman, C 1997 *Tara and archaeological survey*. Dublin: Discovery Programme.

Newman, C 2011 'The sacral landscape of Tara: a preliminary exploration', *in* Schot, R, Newman, C and Bhreathnach, E (eds) *Landscapes of cult and kingship*, 22-43. Dublin: Four Courts Press.

Noble, G and Brophy, K 2011a 'Ritual and remembrance at a prehistoric ceremonial complex in central Scotland: excavations at Forteviot, Perth and Kinross', *Antiquity* 85 (329), 787-804.

Noble, G and Brophy, K 2011b 'Big enclosures: the later Neolithic palisaded enclosures of Scotland in their northwestern European context', *European Journal of Archaeology* 14, 60-87.

Noble, G and Brophy, K 2014 'Construction, process, environment: altering the landscape in Neolithic lowland Scotland', *in* Furholt, M, Mischka, D, Noble, G and Olausson, D (eds), *Landscapes, histories and societies in the northern European Neolithic*, 65-77. German Research Foundation: Frühe Monumentalität u. soziale Differenzierung, 4.

Noble, G, Gondek, M, Campbell, E, and Cook, M 2013 'Between prehistory and history: the archaeological detection of social change among the Picts', *Antiquity* 87 (338), 1136-50.

O'Brien, C 2011 'Yeavering and Bernician kingship: a review of debate on the hybrid culture thesis', *in* Petts, D and Turner, S (eds) *Early Medieval Northumbria: kingdoms and communities, 450-1100*, 207-20. Turnhout: Brepols.

O'Brien, E 1999 *Post-Roman Britain to Anglo-Saxon England: burial practices reviewed.* BAR British Series 289. Oxford: Archaeopress.

O'Brien, E 2009 'Pagan or Christian? Burial in Ireland during the fifth to eighth centuries AD', *in* Edwards, N (ed) *The archaeology of the Early Medieval Celtic churches*, 135-54. Leeds: Maney Publishing.

Ó Carragáin, T 2010 *The archaeology of the early Irish Church*. New Haven: Yale University Press.

Rees, A R 2002 'A first millennium AD cemetery, rectangular Bronze Age structure and late prehistoric settlement at Thornybank, Midlothian', *Proceedings of the Society of Antiquaries of Scotland* 132, 313-56.

Schot, R, Newman, C and Bhreathnach, E (eds) 2011 *Landscape of cult and kingship*. Dublin: Four Courts Press.

Semple, S 2013 *Perceptions of the prehistoric in Anglo-Saxon England: religion, ritual and rulership in the landscape*. Oxford: Oxford University Press.

SERF Project: http://www.gla.ac.uk/schools/humanities/research/archaeologyresearch/projects/serf/furtherinformation/#reports [accessed 23/2/16].

Thomas, C 1971 *The early Christian archaeology of north Britain*. Oxford: Oxford University Press.

Waddell, J, Fenwick, J and Barton, K 2009 *Rathcroghan: archaeological and geophysical survey in a ritual landscape*. Dublin: Wordwell.

Waddell, J 2011 'Continuity, cult and conquest', *in* Schot, R, Newman, C and Bhreathnach, E (eds) *Landscapes of cult and kingship*, 192-212. Dublin: Four Courts Press.

Waddell, J 2014 *Archaeology and Celtic myth: an exploration*. Dublin: Four Courts Press.

Wailes, B 1982, 'The Irish "royal sites" in history and archaeology', *Cambridge Medieval Celtic Studies* 3, 1-29.

Warner, R B 1988 'The archaeology of Early Historic Irish kingship', *in* Driscoll, S T and Nieke, M (eds), *Power and politics in Early Medieval Britain and Ireland*, 47-68. Edinburgh: Edinburgh University Press.

Warner, R B 2004 'Notes on the inception and early development of the royal mound in Ireland', *in* Pantos, A and Semple, S (eds) *Assembly places and practices in Medieval Europe*, 27-43. Dublin: Four Courts Press.

Williams, H 2006 *Death and memory in Early Medieval Britain*. Cambridge: Cambridge University Press.

Williams, H 2007a 'Depicting the dead: commemoration through cists, cairns and symbols in Early Medieval Britain', *Cambridge Archaeological Journal* 17, 145-64.

Williams, H 2007b '"Burnt Germans", Alemannic graves and the origins of Anglo-Saxon archaeology', *in* Burmeister, S, Derks, H and von Richthofen, J (eds) *Zweiundvierzig. Festschrift für Michael Gebühr zum 65*, 229-38. Rahden: Geburtstag, Internationale Archäologie – Studia honoraria 25.

Woolf, A 2007 *From Pictland to Alba 789-1070*. Edinburgh: Edinburgh University Press.

Woolliscroft, D J and Hoffmann, B 2001 'Excavations at Cuiltburn on the Roman Gask System, Perth and Kinross', *Proceedings of the Society of Antiquaries of Scotland* 131, 149-66.

6

Political transition at Portmahomack: the European context

Martin Carver

6.1 Introduction

The Tarbat project began in 1994, fieldwork was completed in 2007 and was published in 2016 (Carver et al 2016; Carver 2016). Twenty-two years is a barely adequate period to devote to a great archaeological site, but to the modern academic it can appear lengthy: the research community would expect to generate four or five new paradigms in that time. It is therefore unsurprising that, in conceptual terms, the outcome of a field project is often hard to match against the objectives of two decades earlier, and it can take longer still to assess its impact. The objectives in this case sought the origins of a northern Pictish kingdom and its conversion, and hoped that the Portmahomack site would be informative in these matters. In fact neither kingdom nor conversion were manifested directly. The high point of the site's development – and the one with the most European connections – proved to be a monastery, the first definition of a Pictish Christian establishment that was promptly celebrated in print (Carver 2008a, 2008b). But the outcome of the subsequent analysis has been to enlarge the significance of the sequence as a whole, which has captured change over the course of a millennium (AD 550-1550). Chameleon-like, the site changed its character every 150 years or so, experiencing transformations in layout and materiality that were quite emphatic. Attempts to read the meaning of these changes using the historical framework were only partly successful; the search for evolutionary processes, such as state formation or even Christianisation, was still less revealing. The approach that worked best was to regard the material package of each stage as representing the expression of a political agenda. Part drawn from prehistoric antecedents, part aligned with influential neighbours, and part local invention, these packages are held to show where a particular region of Scotland stood at a given moment in time, the social emphasis of its power, its economic strategy and the connections (or lack of connections) exercised over a hin-

in: Blackwell, A.E. (ed.) 2019: *Scotland in Early Medieval Europe*, Leiden: Sidestone Press, pp. 103-116.

Illustration 6.1 View of St Colman's church (the white building), with the Dornoch Firth and the hills of Sutherland in the background.

terland or across the sea. The hope is that episodes so defined will be able to contribute to new historical syntheses.

The design for the Tarbat project included a large-scale excavation in and around St Colman's Church at Portmahomack, a survey over the Tarbat peninsula and a comparative study of the Early Medieval Moray Firth region (Illus 6.1). In the event, resources were concentrated on the excavation and the work on the peninsula was restricted to the search for the portage (implied by the Tarbat place name; Watson 1986, 505) and selected site surveys at Hilton, Shandwick and Nigg (Illus 6.2). The sequence that emerged at Portmahomack was divided by stratigraphy and radiocarbon-dating into four periods, summarised below and in Illus 6.3.

It should be stressed that the purpose of this summary article is to highlight certain general aspects of the Tarbat research project that might be relevant to the theme of the present volume, leaving more curious readers to consult the detailed report (Carver et al 2016).

6.2 Period 1 (c550-c680) – an estate centre

Burials have taken place on the Tarbat peninsula since the Bronze Age, and by the first millennium AD they appear to cluster in three places: at Balintore/Shandwick, Nigg and Portmahomack. These represent nodal points providing seamarks and access. Portmahomack has the best sheltered landing place on the Tarbat peninsula, and the cemetery there took the form of long-cist graves spread along the ridge

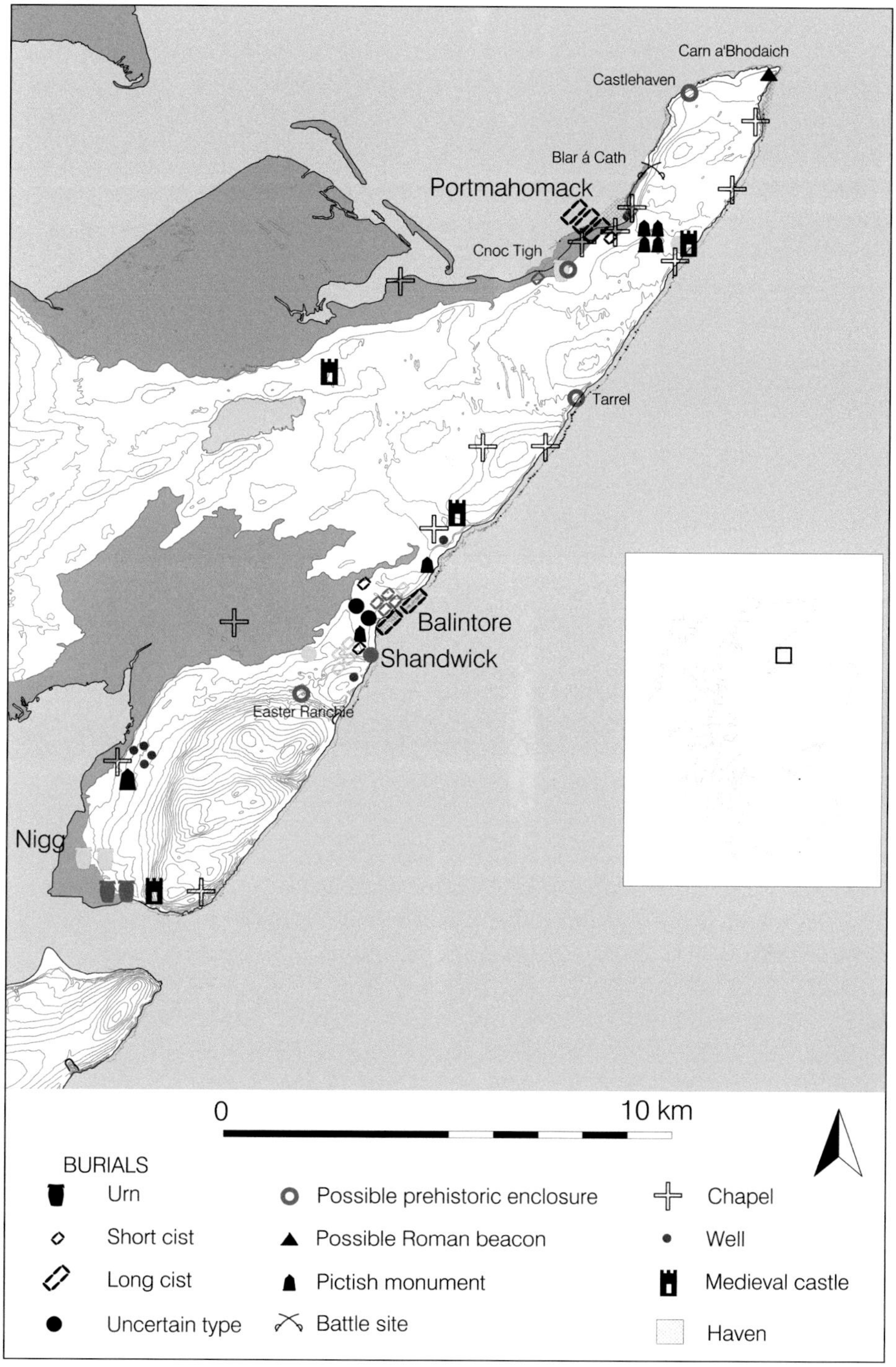

Illustration 6.2 The Tarbat peninsula, showing prehistoric and Medieval sites known up to 2012. Research on the peninsula has been continued and amplified by the University of Aberdeen, whose interim results can be found at http://www.abdn.ac.uk/geosciences/departments/archaeology/the-northern-picts-project-259.php.

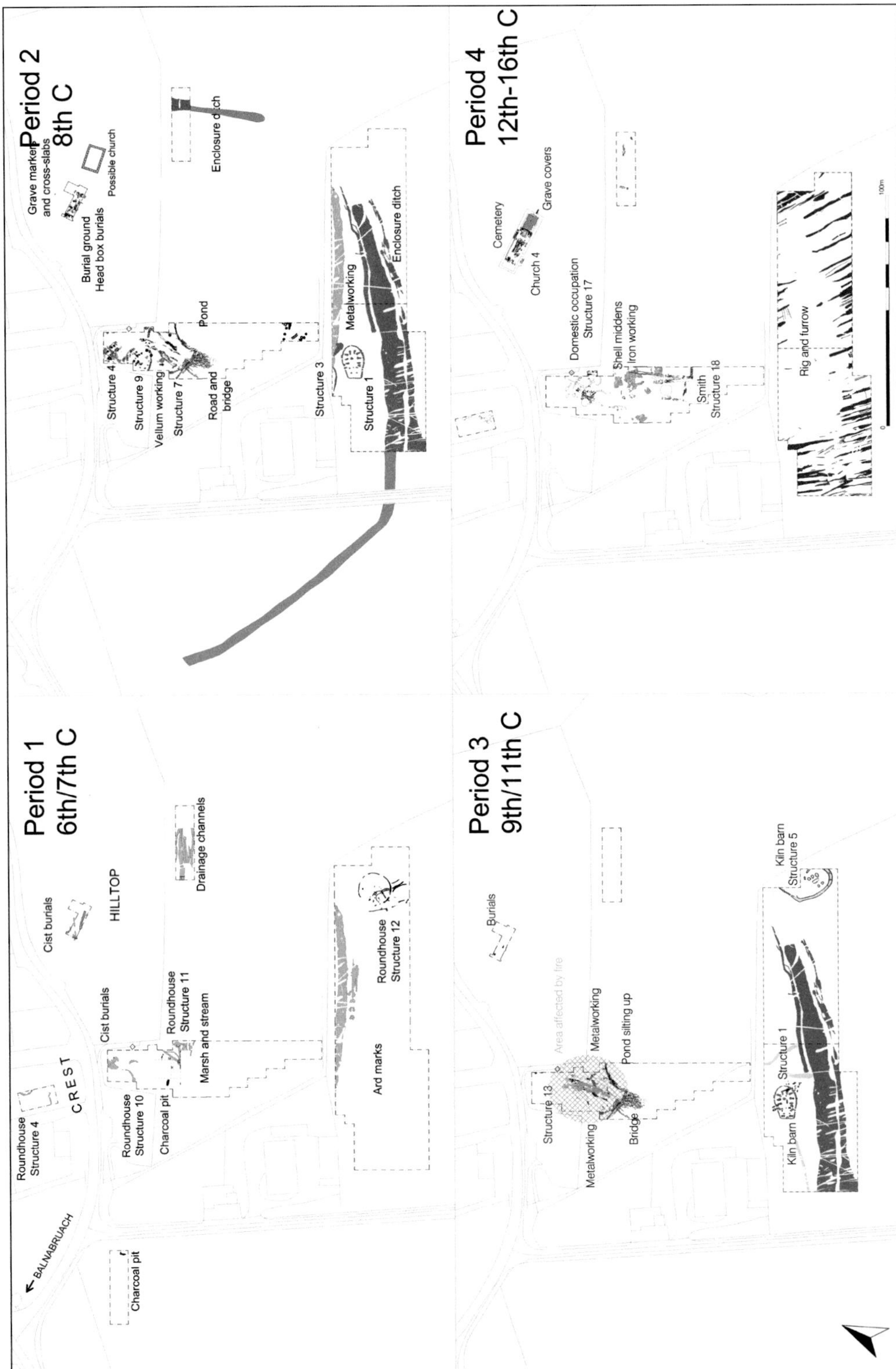

Illustration 6.3 Summary period plans for the Portmahomack excavations.

overlooking the beach and the Dornoch Firth beyond. Some of these are known from antiquarian encounters, but 19 were excavated during the current project and the group dated fifth to seventh century AD by radiocarbon. An aerial photograph of 1947 (RCAHMS 106G/UK751 flown 31 Aug 1945) showed a number of ring ditches along the ridge next to St Colman's Church, which, taken together with the excavated features, suggested that some of the long cists were originally topped by round barrows. Bordering the cemetery on the ridge was a gulley containing burnt grain (wheat and barley), displaced plough pebbles gathered in the valley and in the fields to the south were extensive sets of plough marks that should belong to this phase. On the slopes of the marshy valley behind was a round structure with a hearth where smithing took place, served by an elaborate system of gullies connecting a well and a cistern. Significant finds include a group of four iron dress pins and a gilded copper-alloy disk from a horse harness, the nearest parallel for which is found on the Mound 17 bridle at Sutton Hoo (Carver 2005, 490; Illus 6.4a). The co-location of equestrian patrons in an agricultural setting has led to a proposed classification of this stage of the site as an 'elite farm' or 'estate centre'. Stylistic and radiocarbon dates for all these activities converge in the late sixth/seventh century, and the site can find a parallel in the 'cemetery-settlements' excavated in advance of Ireland's national road schemes (eg Kinsella 2010, 124; Ó Carragáin 2009; O'Sullivan and Nicholl 2010; O'Sullivan et al 2014, 306-12). As well as having both cemeteries and settlements in the same place, these sites feature iron-working and crop-processing as principal activities. However, they show few signs of religious affiliation and have been characterised as family establishments 'engaging with the new religion on their own terms' (Ó Carragáin 2009, 219). This is a description that might also be a fit for Portmahomack in its first period of existence, when it has little reason to claim a function that is recognisably monastic. While the parallel site of Whithorn is classed as a *monasterium* in the fifth to seventh century (Hill 1997, Period I, 29-33), it has been interpreted by others, notably Ewan Campbell, as being at that stage a high-status settlement rather than a monastery in the sense of a specialist religious centre (Campbell 1991, 172; Campbell 2007; Toop 2005, 279-86; Maldonado 2011, 183).

Illustration 6.4
a: mercury-gilded, leaded bronze Style II harness mount from Period 1; b: corbel with convex chamfer and head modelled in the round: conjoining fragments TR217, 223, 263 recovered from late eighth-/ early ninth-century contexts (Period 2).

Although the changes that were to occur in the next phase were drastic, the new cemetery was a continuation of the old, and stable isotopes indicate that the population in this period and the one that followed was mainly local. The explanation offered is that while the Period 1 settlement was not itself a monastery, its owners may have given the land adjacent to the ancestral burial ground to found one (Carver et al 2016, Ch 4).

6.3 Period 2 (c680-c810) – a monastery

In the next period the site was reconstructed to offer a wide range of significant features and facilities: the area of the marshy stream was landscaped and a massive infrastructure put in place: the stream was dammed, forming a pool; a road led down to it from the hill and over a bridge to the fields beyond. A C-shaped ditched enclosure embraced the whole, up to the beach with the open edge of the firth beyond. Cattle appeared to be the principal economic asset, meat and dairy products providing subsistence and it is proposed that the hides were stored as capital (McCormick and Murray 2007, 105, 181; Campbell 2009, 52). On the east side of the road, cattle were slaughtered, and on its west side were a washing tank, a bag-shaped building and a yard littered with debris associated with the preparation of vellum. In the south fields, a workshop was established, dedicated to the making of church plate, as evidenced by crucibles and moulds and an inlaid glass stud. The craft was served by an architecturally innovative bag-shaped building, in this case well-preserved.

In the developed cemetery on the hill the bodies were laid in rows and marked by incised stone grave-markers, several having head-support stones. By the late eighth century a church is argued to have stood in this place: the best evidence for its existence is circumstantial: the panels and post of a shrine or *cancellum* and a remarkable corbel with protruding human head carved in the round deposited in three conjoining pieces in well-stratified eighth-/ninth-century contexts (Illus 6.4b).

6.4 Period 3 (c810-c900) – a trading farm

The change between the monastery and its successor, like that between the estate centre and the monastery, was an episode of ruthless physical disruption that nevertheless allowed an underlying continuity. The disruption involved the burning down of the northern workshops and violence visited on the sculpture but aimed mainly at the large monuments. These were broken up into fist-sized pieces and distributed over the smouldering remains. The find of the corbel, one of the few indicators of a stone church, among this rubble suggests that the church building had also been subject to damage if not demolition.

Over this strongly marked, but chronologically brief, stratigraphic horizon work resumed immediately with the installation of a metal workshop, its smiths using the same techniques as the monastery but (as determined from the moulds) making different things: pins, rings, mounts, and a brooch, as opposed to chalices, patterns and reliquaries. Among the most telling of the new products indicated by the moulds were bronze weights, seen as facilitators of trade. The old workshops of the monastic metal-workers in the south field were now redundant; their building was converted into a kiln barn, probably of two storeys and equipped with a flue. Another grain dryer was erected nearby, strengthening the impression that cereal production had returned as the principal staple. On the hill, burial using the monastic rite dwindled in small numbers until the tenth century. After this the cemetery was gradually abandoned. The metal-working and the ordered use of the cemetery are reckoned to have ended together no later than CAD900.

This stage has therefore been dubbed a 'trading farm'. It lasted barely a century. From its materiality, the site was not apparently absorbed into the Norse cultural zone in the manner of Birsay on Orkney (Curle 1982). Less is known of the Scottish (as opposed to the Pictish) signature either here or further west, but the Scots would seem the more probable clients of the new workshop. In the first post-monastic century it would seem that the same people remained in residence, but had radically altered their way of life. The subsequent period (900-1050) was bleak at Portmahomack. The documentation is sparse but it seems that the Tarbat peninsula lay at the centre of a war zone in which Scots and Norse competed for dominance, and the Picts lost to both. This was an era that parallels the Viking wars in England, 500 miles further south. Less celebrated, but equally significant, the Moray Mormaers under Macbeth fought just such a fight and won just such a victory as did Alfred and the house of Wessex in their struggle against the Danes.

6.5 Period 4 (twelfth-sixteenth century) – a Parish church

It was a not until the eleventh or twelfth century that Portmahomack revived under the new Christian governance of King David I and his mother (Oram 2004). The site of the former monastery was remembered or could still be recognised, since there were large pieces of broken cross slabs in the graveyard. A parish church was built over the site of the former Pictish church and cemetery, scooping up the grave markers and incorporating them in the Medieval foundations. In the thirteenth century, the church was lengthened and provided with a crypt. The monastic enclosure was finally filled in and over-ploughed with rig and furrow. A village with numerous shell and fish bone middens was established over the workshops of the post-monastic metalworkers. Further development followed in the fifteenth century with the establishment of an iron-working facility covering many acres, energetic activity mirrored in the church by a surge in burial up to the Reformation. Four more phases of church building were recorded after the Reformation, but that is another story.

6.6 Import and outreach

From the period of its earliest occupation (fifth to seventh century), the Portmahomack settlement shows an awareness of island-wide elite British culture in the form of a decorated harness disc, paralleled at Dunadd, Mote of Mark and Sutton Hoo (Mound 17), and a set of flat-headed iron pins paralleled (in copper-alloy) at Chalton, in Hampshire. By contrast the materials used in the rich monastic phase (late seventh to early ninth century) were predominately local, and reflect both the ingenuity of the local Picts and also probably a stage of north British monasticism that was relatively late and short-lived. The new prescription seems to have arrived as know-how rather than as a material package, a know-how constructed from components both exotic and

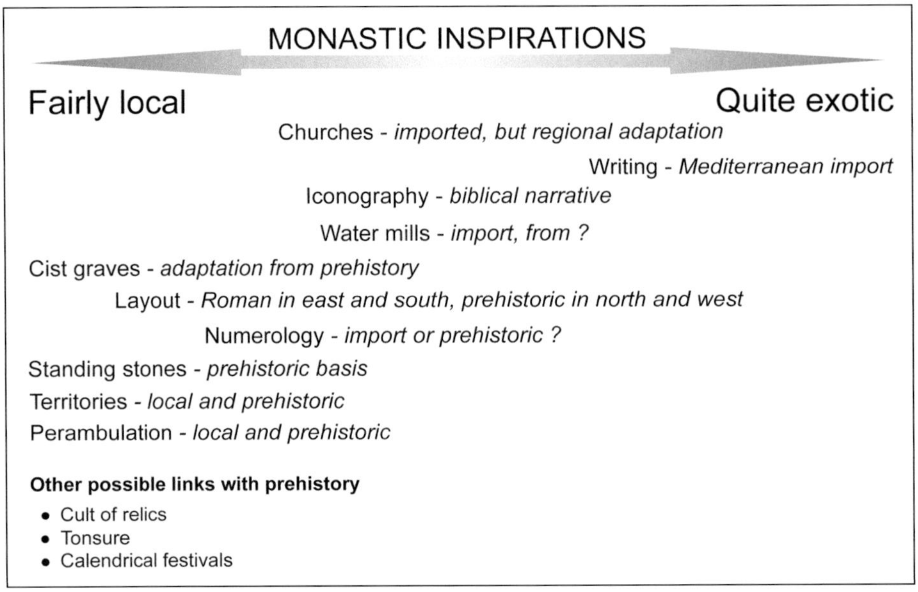

Illustration 6.5 Diagram showing the likely sources of inspiration in early Pictish monasticism.

home-grown (Illus 6.5). Writing is a Mediterranean import, but at Portmahomack the technology of vellum-production was mediated through local exigency: metapodial pegs and white pebbles for stretcher frames, and burnt seaweed and shells to produce an astringent in the absence of lime. Iron could be obtained locally as bog-iron, but copper and silver must have been imported in some form, perhaps as ingots or objects for recycling. There was one fragment of a reticella glass sherd of twisted opaque yellow and self-coloured glass, of a type distributed in Scandinavia and around the North Sea coasts. A blue glass stud was thought to have been recycled from Roman glass. Other pieces of glass were either not certainly imported or not certainly Early Medieval (Campbell, Peake and Freestone in Carver et al 2016, D6.7, D6.8). Pumice used for vellum working was floated in from Iceland (Newton in Carver et al 2016, D6.11). But of 98 working stones used in vellum and metal-working, there were none from a source that was certainly exotic (Portmahomack online archive, ADS, 7.1.3.3). In half a hectare of sieved excavation there were no sherds of Mediterranean, North African or Aquitanian pottery such as was reaching Dunadd, Rhynie or even Craig Phadraig by Inverness (Foster 2014, 87). However, this type of pottery is generally dated earlier than the monastic phase at Portmahomack and the site in Period 1 was perhaps insufficiently important to attract this type of import. There were a few other tenuous material links: an example of the Frisian sceattas that reached East Anglia and Dunbar now arrived at Portmahomack, the most northerly find to date (Blackburn in Carver et al 2016, D6.2).

The bag-shaped building at Portmahomack is unique at present – a plan that joins a semi-circle to a trapezium. It has a particular design and metrology that may be either a learned import or a prehistoric inheritance. However, long distance inspiration should not be excluded. The byre-houses defined at Pitcarmick in Perthshire, recalling those built across the North Sea in Jutland and the Netherlands, have opened another line of possible interaction between Pictland and the continent (Carver et al 2012, 191-5).

The sculpture, comprising 264 pieces derived from grave markers, a sarcophagus lid and four large cross-slabs, offers a natural medium in which to discover intellectual and technical connections, and many were referenced (Henderson and Henderson 2004, passim; Carver et al 2016, Ch 5.3, D5.1). But stylistically there is little indication of a particular axis of supply: the carving is insular in its ornament, Pictish in its symbols and Mediterranean in at least some of its iconography. As expected, the ornament looks to Ireland, the Scottish west coast and Northumbria, but links have also been observed with the British areas of Strathclyde, Cumbria and south west, reminding us that the relationship between the Picts and their fellow Britons, the two senior peoples on the island, probably deserves fuller exploration. This puts the spotlight back onto the local Pictish workshop, one of the few to have left us a sculptor's chisel. All the stone for carving was obtained from the Tarbat area with one exception: the small portable grave marker TR21 was imported onto the peninsula from an unknown source (Ruckley in Carver et al 2016, D6.10).

Architectural pieces sent us looking for exotic origins: the corbel is currently unique, but its criss-cross hair and almond eyes allow it a home in the company of Pictish carving, albeit with Irish and Mediterranean inspiration. Ninth-century parallels relatively close in form are known at the Alpine church of Malles, and echoed in a twelfth-century version guarding the doorway to the cloister at Bobbio (pers comm Eleonora Destefanis). Plain corbels are known from Early Medieval Irish churches, externally on the gable and less frequently internally (Ó Carragáin 2010, 88). Another Irish connection is offered by a stray fragment at Portmahomack that appears to have derived from a butterfly finial, typically sited on a gable end (Ó Carragáin 2010, 42).

While the iconography draws on biblical characters and narratives (King David, St Paul and St Anthony at Nigg), the labelling of the great stones at Portmahomack, Nigg, Shandwick and Hilton with Pictish symbols hint that local persons, and arguably local saints, are being celebrated (Carver 2008a, 187-8). The erection of large monoliths in the landscape is itself a prehistoric tradition. The use of stones and burial places to mark territories and itineraries is also prehistoric in origin and present on the Tarbat peninsula. There are other adaptations of the Christian period that have also been claimed as having prehistoric antecedents: the cult of relics, the tonsure and the date of seasonal festivals (Carver 2009). The implication is that the Tarbat sculpture is the work of local Pictish masters, combining local knowledge and spiritual inheritance with themes of up-to-date orthodoxy drawn from a wider European catchment.

In Period 3, the expected Norse cultural signature was weak: there was a single cylindrical lead weight from the surface, of a type found in the Scar ship burial (Maleska in Carver et al 2016, D6.13). There were some indications of recycling: a fragment of Roman fretwork mount and a lone carnelian gem, with three spalls showing it had been levered out of a second-century Roman ring. A gaming board, its lines incompletely drawn, was in found in the debris after the raid. A small hoard was deposited north of the church in c1000 AD, probably marking a moment of increased insecurity (Graham-Campbell 1995, 143-4). Its contents of Norse ring-silver and English and French coins show something of the economic activity that, war or no war, had enlivened the Moray Firth in the ninth/tenth century. In Period 4, Medieval but still relevant to the wider story, the first pottery appears at Portmahomack in the thirteenth century and is from Yorkshire (Hall in Carver et al 2016, D6.18.1).

Stable isotope analysis suggests that human mobility varied with each phase: in Period 1 (fifth-seventh century), out of four measurable people, two were local or east Britain, one from west Britain and one from Britain more generally; in Period 2 (the monastic phase) five were local or from east Britain and two of Scandinavian extraction; in Period 3 (after the raid) three were from east Britain, and one from west Britain. Only in Period 4 (and specifically in the fifteenth century) was there a marked immigration from the west: out of 11 assessed, eight were from west Britain, three local or east Britain (Carver et al, 2016, 60, Table 3.5).

This information, very compressed here, serves to show that at Portmahomack the changes of direction were acute and the cultural and geographical awareness of their significance was considerable. By contrast, material evidence of actual cultural intrusion was of a minor order. This draws us to the conclusion that the changes observed were powered by local agency standing on a platform of extensive knowledge of the European theatre. The prompt for these moments of change may have been mediated through known centres, Iona or Jarrow, or through the Vikings. But they become more comprehensible if viewed as part of successive political trends affecting Europe as a whole.

6.7 European context

The Portmahomack sequence portrays an estate centre changing direction to become a monastery and a monastery turning its attention to secular production. Such a trajectory has been noted before in Scotland, at Whithorn, although here the transmogrifications were deemed less radical, and all stages from the fifth century to the eleventh were defined as monastic – a monastic farm, a Northumbrian monastery, a monastic town (Hill 1997), descriptions argued as less applicable here (Carver 2016). In Ireland too, related trajectories have been noted: a change from arable to cattle and back, an increased output of manufacture. At Clonmacnoise, the early settlement of the seventh-eighth century was reorganized and expanded between the ninth and eleventh centuries, with the industrial working of antler, bone, stone, lignite, bronze, glass, silver possibly gold (King 2009, 333). While the seventh-/eighth-century phase had an emphasis on mature cattle (McCormick and Murray 2007, 213), the ninth-century expansion was reflected in an increased exploitation of red deer. The exploitation of antler and output of metal products resembles that of Dublin and has accordingly been declared 'urban' (King 2009, 338). In Ireland they erected High Crosses after the period of the Viking raids and the establishments concerned were still termed 'monasteries'. In England, the workshops of Building D at Jarrow remained in use and their occupants continued to handle coins there into the ninth century (Cramp 2005, 219-29). They were now making or using strapends and hooked tags (Cramp 2006, 230, 234) but Professor Cramp reads this is as the continuation of the monastery in straightened circumstances (Cramp 2005, 360). At Portmahomack, there is no more sculpture or vellum and the metal-workers have a different order book. Since the Period 3 settlement has few monastic attributes it seems reasonable to suppose that it is no longer a functioning monastic institution. Nevertheless it need not be supposed

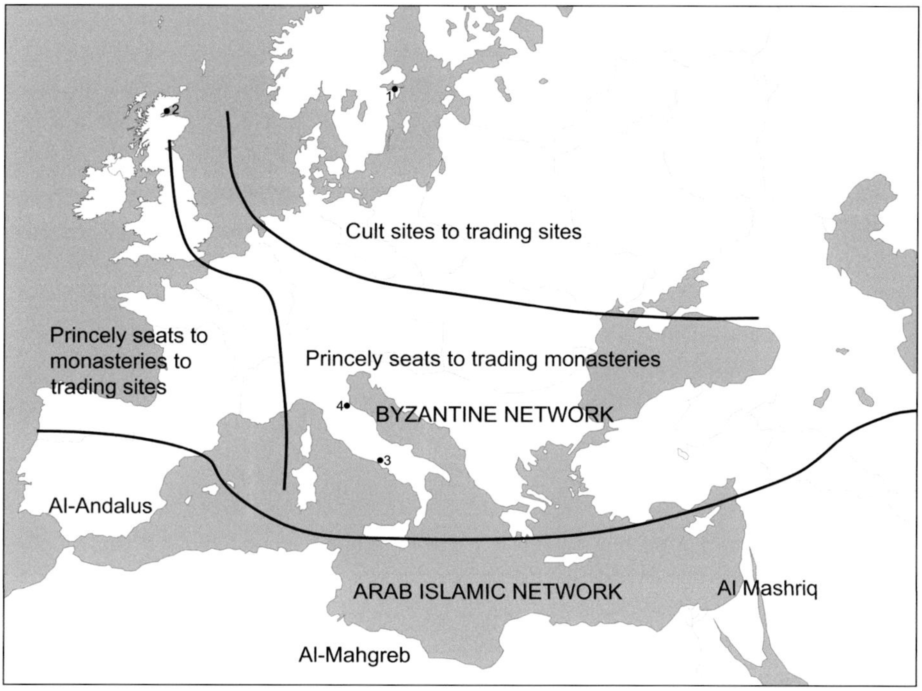

Illustration 6.6 A sketch of ideological trends in sixth- to ninth-century Europe (Carver 2015, figure 1 ; the sites compared there are (1) Helgo (2) Portmahomack (3) San Vincenzo and (4) Comacchio).

that the community was exterminated or dispersed. Monks are people, and people who work; it may be that there are obstinate monks, adaptable monks and pliable monks, but there is little doubt that the zeitgeist is channelling them down a new road. What is being suggested here is a matter of policy and its performance a matter of degree.

These changing emphases of allegiance, to an aristocracy, to a deity or to the market, can be observed on the wider European stage (Carver 2015, figure 1; Illus 6.6). In the Scandinavian areas, sites such as Gudme on Fyn in Denmark and Uppåkra in Sweden feature votive deposits, putative temples and apparently secular halls (Skre 2012, 52-3; Larsson 2007). This combination of implied functions has earned the sites the working title of 'central places' (Fabech and Näsman 2013, 58-9), but it may be argued that the different political strategies actually appear in sequence. At Tissø, for example, swords were thrown into the lake in the sixth-/seventh-century phase, but later developments included a magnate hall and shrine (Jørgensen 2010). At Helgö, the latest interpretation shows the site to have been receiving pilgrim-type visitors, with provision for healing and acquiring souvenirs (Arrhenius and O'Meadhra 2011). As a working hypothesis, ritual properties attract a 'congregation' to a natural place (a lake), votive deposits follow, a spiritual authority emerges which collects the offerings of visitors converting them into wealth, the visitors are sold souvenirs and by the eighth century the aristocracy have captured the 'salvation industry' (Carver 2015). To take advantage of wider catchment, the trade element subsequently transfers to a seaport, culminating in the first true towns, Hedeby, Birka, Ribe II and Kaupang (Skre 2012, 57). In France, the monasteries less affected by pressure from the north become power-houses of the economy, capturing, retaining and monetarising a large part of the salvation industry to themselves (Lebecq 2000). For Joachim Henning this amounts to a monopoly, a restrictive practice, impeding the development of the market and delaying the re-emergence of towns (Henning 2007, 15, 20).

It can be argued that monastic Britain and Ireland follow related trajectories. Led by the Celtic lands (Ireland, Scotland, Pictland, Wales and Northumbria), in the late seventh century the elite running the family businesses of their numerous polities entrusted a large part of the political agenda to the spiritual leadership of campaigning Christians. The monastic network so created represents one of Europe's most revolutionary movements prior to socialism. In the ninth century, the Norse raids ushered in a change of thought. But it can be seen that this was at least partly the result of the political stage reached in Scandinavia: a 'reformation' of the votive places in favour of wealth-creation. This does not have be a hostile ideology, enforced on the raided islands. The zeitgeist appears to encourage the church too to turn its hand to amassing wealth as a prescription at least as effective as prayer.

This necessarily abbreviated account hopefully offers entry to an area worthy of further exploration. The ideology of monasticism, in which things are made and wealth is amassed for the greater glory of God and the saving of souls, is always in competition with the equally self-assured dominance of the elite and the market, with first one, and then the next in the ascendant. The material anthologies of excavated archaeological sites like Portmahomack are manifestations of local political thinking, barometers of the wider political weather. Naturally, the changes that occur are owed in part to local circumstances and events. But in some measure they may be seen as participating in an ever-restless European debate, and, on occasion, leading it.

Acknowledgements

The Tarbat Discovery Programme was co-directed by the author with Justin Garner-Lahire and Cecily Spall of FAS-Heritage, and a large proportion of the field results and their interpretation is owed to them. The project was hosted by Tarbat Historic Trust who run the museum and visitor centre now installed in St Colman's Church. Fieldwork was funded primarily by Highland Council, Heritage Lottery (Scotland) and National Museums Scotland; analysis and publication by Historic Scotland. The summary account of the project was published by Edinburgh University press in 2016, the research report by the Society of Antiquaries of Scotland in the same year and the Online Archive is hosted by ADS. While pressure of space has necessarily condensed the arguments and limited the references given here, the reader will hopefully find the assertions given here supported in this tier of detailed publications.

References

Arrhenius, B and O'Meadhra, U (eds) 2011 *Excavations at Helgö XVIII: conclusions and new aspects.* Kungl. Vitterhets Historie och Antikvitets Akademien, Stockholm.

Campbell, E 1991 'Imported goods in the Early Medieval Celtic west', unpublished PhD thesis, University of Wales Cardiff.

Campbell, E 2007 *Continental and Mediterranean imports to Atlantic Britain and Ireland,* AD*400-800.* CBA Research Report. York: Council for British Archaeology.

Campbell, J 2009 'Archipelagic thoughts: comparing Early Medieval polities in Britain and Ireland', *in* Baxter, S, Karkov, C, Nelson, J L and Pelteret, D (eds) *Early Medieval studies in memory of Patrick Wormald*, 47-61. Farnham: Ashgate.

Carver, M O H 2005 *Sutton Hoo. A seventh century princely burial ground and its context.* London: British Museum Press.

Carver, M O H 2008a *Portmahomack Monastery of the Picts.* Edinburgh: Edinburgh University Press.

Carver, M O H 2008b *The Pictish Monastery at Portmahomack.* Jarrow Lecture for 2008.

Carver, M O H 2009 'Early Scottish monasteries and prehistory: a preliminary dialogue', *The Scottish Historical Review* 88, 332-51.

Carver, M O H 2015 'Commerce and cult. Confronted ideologies in sixth-ninth century Europe', *Medieval Archaeology* 59, 1-23.

Carver, M O H 2016 *Portmahomack Monastery of the Picts.* Second edition. Edinburgh: Edinburgh University Press.

Carver, M O H, Barrett, J, Downes, J and Hooper, J 2012 'Pictish-period byre-houses at Pitcarmick and their landscape: investigations 1993-5', *Proceedings of the Society of Antiquaries of Scotland* 142, 145-200.

Carver, M O H, Garner-Lahire, J and Spall, C 2016 *Portmahomack on Tarbat Ness. Changing ideologies in north-east Scotland, sixth to the sixteenth century.* Edinburgh: Society of Antiquaries of Scotland.

Cramp, R 2005 *Wearmouth and Jarrow monastic sites volume 1.* Swindon: English Heritage.

Cramp, R 2006 *Wearmouth and Jarrow monastic sites volume 2.* Swindon: English Heritage.

Curle, C L 1982 *Pictish and Norse finds from the Brough of Birsay 1934-74.* Edinburgh: Society of Antiquaries of Scotland.

Fabech, C and Näsman, U 2013 'Ritual landscapes and sacral places in the first millennium AD in South Scandinavia', *in* Walaker Nordeide, S and Brink, S (eds) *Sacred sites and holy places. Exploring the sacralization of landscape through time and space*, 53-110. Turnhout: Brepols.

Foster, S M 2014 *Picts, Gaels and Scots. Early Historic Scotland.* Edinburgh: Birlinn.

Graham-Campbell, J 1995 *The Viking-age gold and silver of Scotland (*AD *850-1100).* Edinburgh: National Museums of Scotland.

Henderson, I and Henderson, G 2004 *The art of the Picts. Sculpture and metalwork in Early Medieval Scotland.* London and New York: Thames and Hudson.

Henning, J 2007 'Early European towns: the way of the economy in the Frankish area between dynamism and deceleration 500-1000AD', *in* Henning, J (ed) *Post-Roman towns, trade and settlement in Europe and Byzantium. Vol 1 The Heirs of the Roman West,* 3-40. Walter de Gruyter: Berlin.

Hill, P 1997 *Whithorn and Saint Ninian*. Stroud: Sutton.

Jørgensen, L 2010 'Gudme and Tissø. Two magnate complexes in Denmark from the third to the eleventh century', *Neue Studien zur Sachsenforschung* 1, 273-86.

King, H 2009 'The economy and industry of Early Medieval Clonmacnoise: a preliminary view', *in* Edwards, N (ed) *The archaeology of the Early Medieval Celtic churches*, 333-49. Society for Medieval Archaeology Monograph 29, Society for Church Archaeology Monograph 1. Leeds: Maney Publishing.

Kinsella, J 2010 'A new Irish Early Medieval site type? Exploring the recent archaeological evidence for non-circular enclosed settlement and burial sites', *Proceedings of the Royal Irish Academy* 110C, 89-132.

Larsson, L 2007 'The Iron Age ritual building at Uppåkra, southern Sweden', *Antiquity* 81, 11-25.

Lebecq, S 2000 'The role of the monasteries in the systems of production and exchange of the Frankish world between the seventh and the beginning of the ninth centuries', *in* Hansen, I L and Wickham, C (eds) *The long eighth century*, 121-48. Turnhout: Brill.

Maldonado, A 2011 'Christianity and burial in late Iron Age Scotland, AD 400-650', unpublished PhD thesis, University of Glasgow.

McCormick, F and Murray, E 2007 *Excavations at Knowth 3. Knowth and the zooarchaeology of Early Christian Ireland.* Dublin: Royal Irish Academy.

Ó Carragáin, T 2009 'Cemetery settlements and local churches in pre-Viking Ireland in light of comparisons with England and Wales', *in* Graham-Campbell, J and Ryan, M (eds) *Anglo-Saxon/Irish relations before the Vikings. Proceedings of the British Academy* 157, 329-66.

Ó Carragáin, T 2010 *Churches in Early Medieval Ireland. Architecture, ritual and memory.* New Haven: Yale University Press.

Oram, R 2004 *David I. The king who made Scotland.* Stroud: Tempus.

O'Sullivan, A and Nicholl, T 2010 'Early Medieval settlement enclosures in Ireland', *Proceedings of the Royal Irish Academy* 111C, 59-90.

O'Sullivan, A, McCormick, F, Kerr, T and Harney, L 2014 *Early Medieval Ireland, AD 400-1100: the evidence from archaeological excavations.* Dublin: Royal Irish Academy.

Portmahomack online archive, ADS. Available at: https://archaeologydataservice.ac.uk/archives/view/portmahomack_2015/index.cfm

Skre, D 2012 'Markets, towns and currencies in Scandinavia ca AD 200-1000', *in* Gelichi, S and Hodges, R (eds) *From one sea to another. Trading places in the European and Mediterranean Early Middle Ages*, 47-64. Turnhout: Brepols.

Toop, N 2005 'Dialogues of power: Early Christian monumentality around the northern Irish Sea area AD400-1000', unpublished PhD thesis, University of York.

Watson, W J 1986 [1926] *The Celtic placenames of Scotland.* Reprinted, Edinburgh: Birlinn.

7

Early Medieval burial in European context: log coffins in Scotland

Adrián Maldonado

Is annamh,
iar mbeith i rríghe thuaithe,
ceppán caue crínn dara
im mac rígh Ala Cluathi.

It is an unaccustomed fate,
for one who held the sovereignty of a kingdom,
that an old hollow oak-trunk
should enclose the son of the king of Ail Chluaithe.

Thus goes a tenth-century elegy for a Pictish king, Bridei son of Bili, victor of the Battle of Nechtansmere in AD 685, who was supposedly buried in the monastery of Iona, Argyll and Bute upon his death in 692 (Herbert and Ó Riain 1988, 58-9). Regardless of the historicity of this lament, it is notable that a famous Pictish king was remembered as being buried in a coffin made from an oak tree trunk. It is a rare contemporary commentary on a form of burial that is archaeologically attested in the area it is describing.

Burial in a log coffin was hardly an 'unaccustomed fate' in Scotland and across Europe at the time of Bridei's death. Indeed, there is a single excavated example of a log coffin from outside St Columba's Shrine at Iona, described further below. The evidence for log coffin burial in Scotland is thus already ambiguous – on the one hand, it is portrayed as a lowly, even demeaning form of burial. On the other, it was remembered as an appropriate receptacle for a king, and can be found in a privileged position at the heart of a major monastery.

The ambiguity of this passage is an apt metaphor for the position of mortuary archaeology in narratives of Early Medieval Scotland. Mortuary archaeology is essential

in: Blackwell, A.E. (ed.) 2019: *Scotland in Early Medieval Europe*, Leiden: Sidestone Press, pp. 117-134.

to the understanding of Early Medieval Scotland, as the existing settlement, economic and documentary evidence is comparatively slight. Inhumation burial comprises the largest coherent body of data for the period, with well-dated finds from controlled excavation covering the full extent of the mainland and its islands (Maldonado 2011; 2013). This data is also readily comparable with trends across Britain, Ireland and the continent as they are part of the wider phenomenon of burial in cemeteries that characterises the first millennium AD. Despite all these advantages, the lack of grave goods or surviving accoutrements such as sarcophagi or inscribed grave markers has meant that the Scottish evidence has rarely been seen in its wider Insular or European context.

Log coffins provide a unique opportunity to cut across the divide. Over a hundred log coffins, or hollowed tree-trunk burials, are now known from six Early Medieval sites in Scotland, summarised in the current essay. These represent a fraction of the 3657 excavated Early Medieval burials from 188 sites based on the author's doctoral work (Maldonado 2011), but poor preservation and lack of recognition means this is likely to underestimate their actual occurrence. Even so they comprise a significant addition to a wider body of evidence for log coffin burial across northern and central Europe in the first millennium AD (Päffgen and Hoeke 2004; Zimmermann 1992). As with their portrayal in the elegy for Bridei, they have been seen as uncommon, requiring extraordinary circumstances to explain their occurrence. Yet there are parallels in the chronology and context of log coffins in Scotland which open up new questions about how we read the evidence for Early Medieval death and burial more widely. To get there, this chapter will first define the log coffin burial rite as it occurs across Europe, then summarise the evidence from Scotland with a view to exploring new interpretive possibilities that can be pursued through comparative study.

7.1 Log coffins in Europe

The log coffin has a long pedigree in Europe, originating in the Neolithic but flourishing in the Bronze Age (Päffgen and Hoeke 2004; Parker Pearson et al 2013). Around the fourth century AD, log coffins began to reappear in large numbers along with the growing spread of large inhumation cemeteries. In light of their frequent discovery in south-west Germany at sites like Oberflacht, Baden-Württemberg (Schiek 1992), Salin's authoritative review of the practice linked log coffins to 'Alamannic' burial customs, their spread across Europe explained by the migrations of Germanic peoples (Salin 1952, 125-6). This interpretation has seen deconstruction in more recent years. Zimmermann (1992, 100-1) has identified three broad phases of Medieval log coffin use, deeming them Merovingian (fourth to seventh centuries), Carolingian (eighth to eleventh centuries) and High Medieval (twelfth century and later). It is clear that not only were log coffins used after the conversion to Christianity, in some areas they were strongly associated with early converts and church founders (eg Nordeide 2011, 195-8, 209-15). Overall, their widespread occurrence across time and space, and their discontinuous appearance at any given site, militates against any specific ethnic or religious meaning to the log coffin grave type (Bärenfänger 1988, 173-6). However, the weight of the existing evidence still tends to skew interpretation towards the log coffin as an aspect of a shared 'Germanic' or, in Britain, 'foreign' burial practice (eg Scull 2011).

The evidence from Britain has largely been secondary to the discussion around log coffins. In Wales, log coffins occur alongside other wooden funerary structures such as post-defined grave markers and wooden chambers, but are generally poorly dated (Longley 2009).The most high-profile examples are from Anglo-Saxon contexts. For instance, the late sixth- and early seventh-century royal burial ground at Sutton Hoo, East Anglia is best known for its opulent boat burials, but the form of the graves in mounds 1 and 17 suggest a rare form of log coffin with iron clasps (Carver 2005, 132-4, 192-4). Boat burials and wooden coffins which may either be hollowed logs or dugout boats occur at Snape, Suffolk (Filmer-Sankey and Pestell 2001, 240), suggesting an interesting metaphorical potential for the log coffin as a vessel in both senses of the word. The issue of preservation in the interpretation of log coffins comes to the fore at Mucking, Essex in which half of 345 burials across two cemeteries were in organic linings represented primarily by soil stains; in cemetery 1 alone, 21 (or 33%) could be identified as 'dugouts' by the shape and size of the stain (Hirst and Clark 2009, 468, 646-52). Even these came in a wide range of shapes, from wooden 'biers' represented by the bottom half of a hollowed trunk, to 'troughs' with protruding ends for carrying, to full coffins with lids in rare cases. Identification was only possible from careful recording in plan and section, and the excavators argue that coffins and tree trunks were more common in the early Anglo-Saxon period than is generally assumed; on this basis, they go on to re-interpret several older excavations to identify more possible examples (Hirst and Clark 2009, 468-76). The same presumably applies far beyond south-east England. In light of this, we can turn to the Scottish material.

7.2 Log coffins in Scotland

There are up to 105 recorded log coffins from six Early Medieval cemeteries in Scotland, plus one more dated to the later Iron Age at Boysack Mills (Illus 7.1). In two cases, Whithorn, Dumfries and Galloway (53 instances) and Thornybank, Midlothian (45 instances), the number of excavated log coffins is comparable to some of the most well-known sites in Europe, including 74 at Slusegård (Andersen et al 1991) and 60 at Oberflacht (Schiek 1992). As such, the evidence is a major addition to the study of log coffin burial more generally, though as the above discussion makes clear, there are issues of interpretation that still need to be addressed (Illus 7.2). Identification remains the biggest issue: in only two cases, from Iona and Forteviot, was there any preserved wood. There is thus a very real possibility that other forms of organic lining or wrapping have been mistaken for log coffins in some cases, as acknowledged by the excavators themselves. The discussion will return to this issue.

The following presentation is in broadly chronological order, beginning with one that is most likely Iron Age but occurring in a square barrow grave, a form of monument strongly associated with Early Medieval 'Pictish' burial practices. In all cases, the orientation is cited with the position of head first (ie, W – E if the head is to west).

7.2.1 Boysack Mills, Angus

Two 6m square barrows outside a Neolithic enclosure were identified as cropmarks and excavated in 1977 (Murray and Ralston 1997). One of these contained a central grave pit with vertical sides 1.5m deep, oriented E – W. This was marked by a posthole at

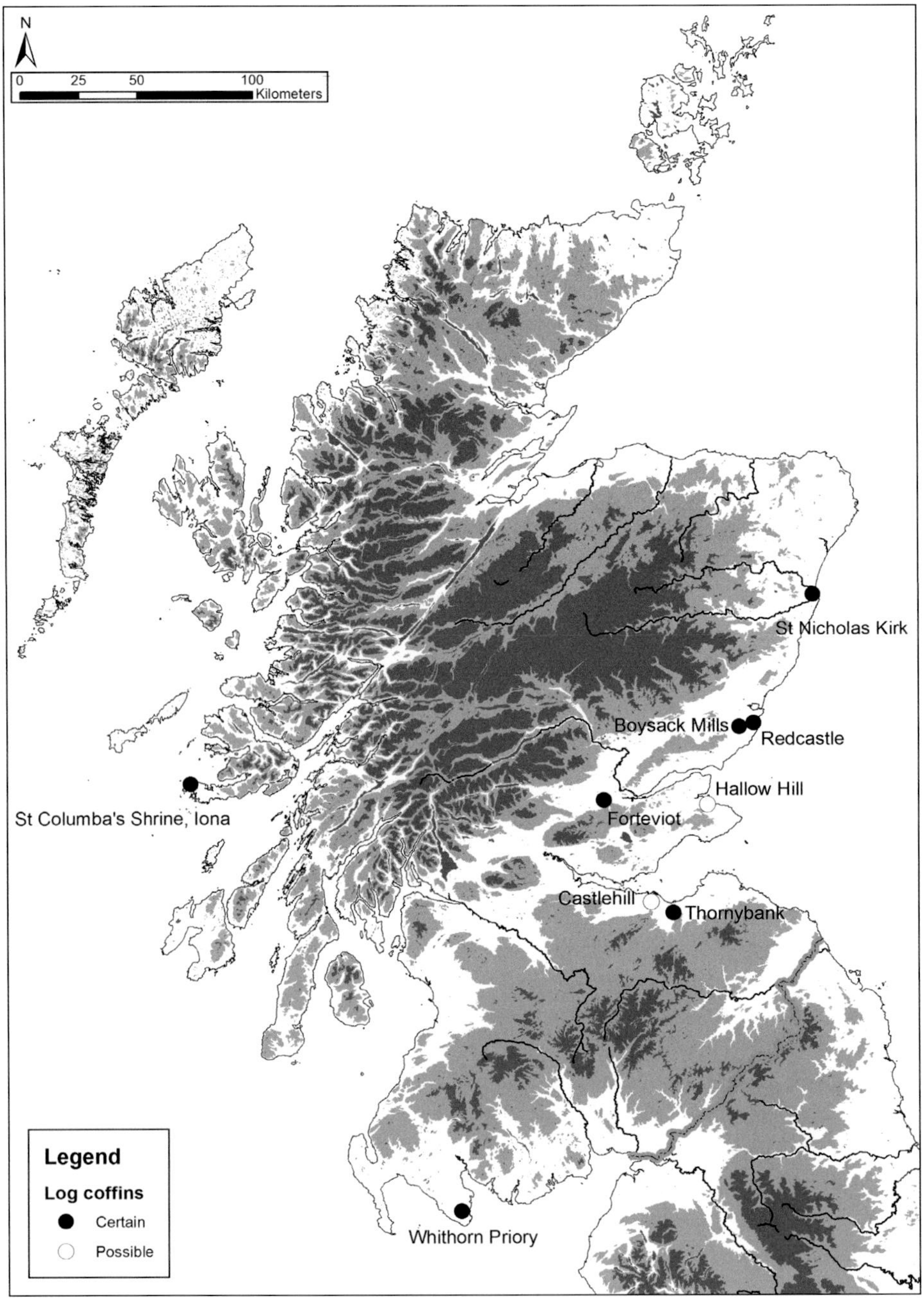

Illustration 7.1 Location map of sites mentioned in the text.

the head end and another to the southwest of the grave. The recording was incomplete due to the rescue conditions in advance of gravel quarrying, but the excavators noted the round-bottomed profile of the coffin stain and the survival of wood fragments over the body stain suggesting a lid. The body survived as a stain, and the only find was a ring-headed iron pin dated to the first or second century AD. The upper fill of the grave

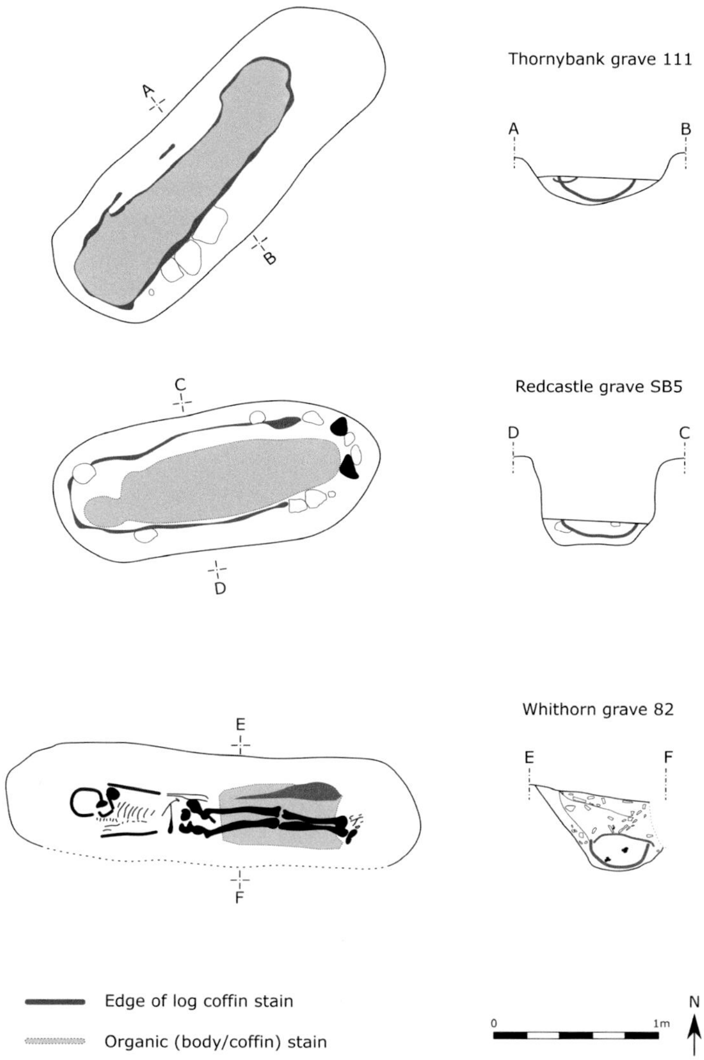

Illustration 7.2 Sections and profiles of selected log coffin graves. Redrawn by the author.

contained charcoal and fire-cracked stone, interpreted as a slighted megalithic grave marker, which would be very out of place in an Early Medieval context. The form of the square barrow, enclosed by a continuous ditch with rounded corners and no causeways unlike later square barrows, is also indicative of an Iron Age date (cf Stead 1991), but an Early Medieval date cannot be ruled out.

7.2.2 Whithorn, Dumfries and Galloway

The Glebe Field excavations south of the Medieval Whithorn Priory revealed a cemetery of 118 graves stratigraphically dated to the sixth to eighth centuries, overlain by graves associated with a Northumbrian timber church and stone chapel of the eighth/ninth century, all sealed by a tenth-century Hiberno-Norse occupation layer (Hill 1997). While there is some debate over the phasing and interpretation of the pre-Northumbrian site (Maldonado 2011, 182-9, 203-6; Toop 2005, 279-86), this was clearly a Latinate Christian community with links to western

British and Irish power centres, as evidenced by inscribed stones and imported Byzantine and Gaulish ceramic and glass vessels, all dated to the fifth to seventh centuries (Campbell 2007; Forsyth 2009).

Overall there were 53 log coffins found on site. These were identified by their distinctive rounded shape and profile, and deeper grave cuts, but not by preserved wood. However, the occurrence of long cists and timber plank-lined graves allowed the excavators to perceive a real difference in approach to those graves identified as log coffins, which also had the best-preserved skeletons, although bone preservation was generally very poor. The excavator also noted the awkward position of some skeletons in these graves, perhaps due to the limited available space in hollowed logs or due to tumbling while moving the heavy coffin; one example was also buried 'backwards', with head to east, perhaps by accident (Hill 1997, 70-3).

The complicated burial sequence proposed by the excavator has been disputed on stratigraphic grounds, and the following discussion refers to the author's revised phasing (Hill 1997, 70-117; cf Maldonado 2011, 182-9; a programme of radiocarbon dating of this assemblage is in progress at the time of writing). It is clear from the intercutting of graves that there were at least three phases in the Whithorn Glebe Field cemetery, marked by changes in orientation and layout. The earliest graves were oriented SW – NE and were spread widely across the site. These were primarily in long cists, although log coffins were also used, while a few graves used a combination of stone flags and timber planks to enclose the cadaver. It seems there was no prescriptive difference between the use of wood or stone lining in this phase. Around the start of the seventh century, the scattered early graves were overlain by a larger cemetery of evenly-spaced rows of graves oriented W – E to either side of a cobbled road running N – S across the trench. Log coffins predominated in this phase, clustering on the west side of the road, and cutting earlier graves. Whether the road was intended as a boundary between users and non-users of log coffins, the spatial imbalance suggests it was by then being seen as a social distinction. In four cases, log coffin graves were shown to have been marked on the surface with a spread of quartz pebbles, in a context where surface marking of graves was exceedingly rare.

The next major reorientation of the site took place in the eighth century with the construction of a series of timber churches and a clay-bonded stone mortuary chapel, all oriented SW – NE (Hill 1997, 134-82). In this latest phase of burial, log coffins and long cists became rare and were replaced by simple earth-dug graves, and, less frequently, plank-built timber coffins and chest burials. The latest log coffin was associated with the mortuary chapel, and sealed by a tenth-century destruction layer. Overall, it seems the mortuary ritual practiced at Whithorn incorporated various types of grave lining, and log coffins occur across three different phases of use, with the majority appearing in the row-grave phase, and dwindling after the establishment of church buildings on site.

7.2.3 Thornybank, Midlothian

Thornybank is a row-grave cemetery containing 108 individuals, all oriented SW – NE and with 30 radiocarbon dates clustering mainly in the fifth to seventh centuries (Rees 2002). The organisation was very similar to the middle phase of the Whithorn cemetery, except there was no evidence for contemporary settlement. The dominant

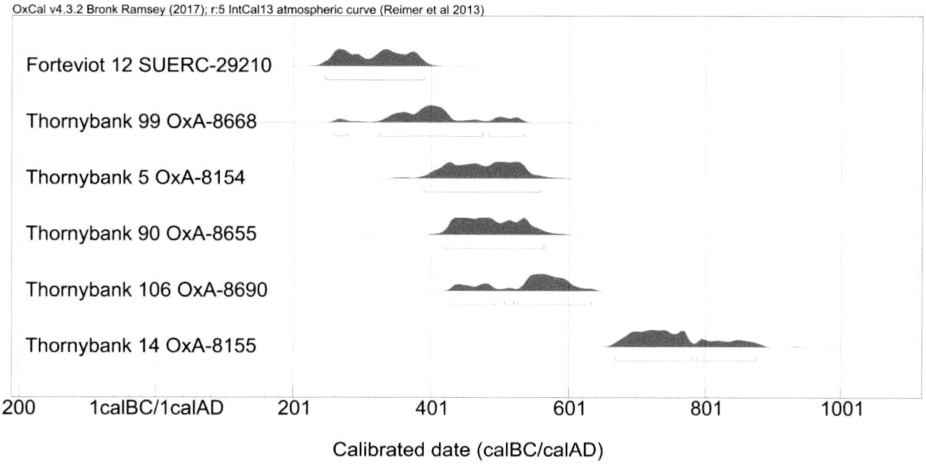

Illustration 7.3 Plot of available radiocarbon dates from log coffins in Scotland using OxCal v4.3.2.

grave type was the long cist, with 63 instances as opposed to the 45 graves with an organic grave lining. While long cists tended to have shallow grave cuts, coffins appeared in markedly deep oval-shaped graves, as much as 1.3m below the surface, a distinction already seen at Whithorn. No wood survived in these graves, but the best-preserved examples retained coffin and body stains. The coffin stains were generally of a rectangular, straight-sided plan with square corners but were u-shaped in profile, indicative of logs sawed at the ends. Most coffin graves also used boulder settings to keep the round-bottomed coffins upright, which would not be necessary for cadavers wrapped in organic material. Finally, the stains often had irregular shapes, including one slightly crescentic coffin. For all these reasons the excavator argues that these 45 graves were likely to be log coffins (Rees 2002, 332-3). However as no lid was preserved on site, it is also possible that some of the shallower graves could be on wooden biers made from hollowed logs.

Log coffins tended to cluster together in the centre of the site, but also occurred in rows alongside long cists. Bones from five log coffins were radiocarbon dated (Illus 7.3), showing they spanned the lifetime of the cemetery, including the latest date from the site. It is also worth noting that there were three 'special' graves in this cemetery, and all three were in log coffins. These included two in square ditched enclosures, and one within a four-post setting. One of the square enclosures preserved traces of a timber sill-beam construction, indicating a mausoleum or *cella memoriae* similar to those found in late Roman and Early Medieval sites in southwest Britain and Wales (Brassil et al 1991; Webster and Brunning 2004). This structure is currently unique to Thornybank in Scotland, but four-post settings around graves are found at Forteviot, Perthshire (Campbell et al, this volume) and similar 'mortuary houses' are attested in Anglo-Saxon England, though primarily associated with cremation burials (Hogarth 1973; Meyers Emery and Williams 2017). The second square enclosure was of a rather different form, with a very wide (1m) ditch around an infant-sized log coffin; the ditch in this case contained blocks of stone which may be the remains of a kerb or cairn. While log coffins appear to have been somewhat interchangeable with long cists at Thornybank, it is significant that they were linked with all three of the more elaborate graves.

7.2.4 Redcastle, Angus

Redcastle is a cemetery of nine barrows and nine flat graves looking out over the North Sea, with radiocarbon dates ranging from the second to the eighth century (Alexander 2005). The burial monuments included seven square barrows with causewayed corners, and two annular ditched barrows. These kinds of monuments are seen as typically 'Pictish' and generally dated to the fifth to seventh centuries (Maldonado 2013, 5), so this site was a long-standing mortuary arena, reserved for infrequent but carefully managed funerary events. The central graves of the barrows were in long cists except in one instance, square barrow 5, which contained a log coffin, again attested by soil stain and u-shaped profile rather than preserved wood, bearing a possible adult oriented W – E. Unusually, the base of the grave pit had only been paved with sandstone slabs at head end, and capstones only at foot end. The log coffin was one of only a few graves here, but except for the odd arrangement of paving and capstones it was not otherwise treated any differently from the long cists.

7.2.5 Forteviot, Perthshire

The ritual landscape and cemetery at Forteviot have been described in detail (Campbell et al, this volume; Maldonado 2017). In summary, the burials at Forteviot appear along the edges of a major ceremonial centre of the first millennium AD, which would become a royal palace and monastery from at least the eighth or ninth century. There were two log coffins found amongst the 24 excavated burials scattered across the site: one in a square barrow (SB3), and the other in a flat grave (UGr12). As at Redcastle, the burials at Forteviot have a wide date range spanning the first millennium AD.

The log coffins were identified due to the size and shape of the grave cut and soil stains, and in one case preserved wood. Based on the uninterrupted square ditch of SB3 in site B it is argued this could be a later Iron Age barrow paralleled at Boysack Mills, described above. Two spreads of quartz pebbles were found at the head and foot ends of the grave, but it is not clear whether they were within or above the coffin. The second log coffin, UGr12 in Site K, was an unmarked grave oriented W – E, with a deep, neatly rectangular grave cut with vertical sides, very different from the shallow, oval grave cuts seen elsewhere at Forteviot. Charred wood was preserved in situ, allowing for the identification as oak; it is possible the charring relates either to burning to help hollow out the oak trunk, or as a purification ritual (cf Hirst and Clark 2009, 477). The charring of the coffin joins a wide array of evidence for fire-related ceremonial activity at Forteviot confirmed by the SERF project excavations (Campbell et al, this volume). No bone was preserved but charcoal from the coffin was dated to the later Iron Age or early Pictish period (Illus 7.3). The only other evidence for burning the inside of a log coffin comes from a much later child's burial at St Nicholas Kirk, Aberdeen (see below, 7.2.7).

7.2.6 Iona, Argyll and Bute

The monastery of Iona was founded in AD 563 by St Columba (d. AD 597). The oldest surviving structure is the foundation of the small stone-built chapel known as St Columba's Shrine, which dates to c 800 (Ó Carragáin 2003, 136, 144). Excavations in 1976 outside the chapel revealed a sequence of six intercutting graves abutting the south wall and clearly postdating its construction (Redknap 1977). These graves were all sealed under a Late Medieval paving layer. The lowest grave was a simple earth-dug pit, disturbed by a later grave containing the rounded bottom of a small, child-sized log coffin of alder preserved by waterlogging. This grave was in turn disturbed by a grave using a nailed plank coffin. The excavator argued for a date ranging from the construction of the chapel to the twelfth century for these coffined burials. It is worth noting that log coffins were being used here at the heart of the monastic complex, the shrine of the founder, just as the elegy for Bridei portrayed the Pictish king being buried at Iona in a log coffin of oak (see above).

7.2.7 St Nicholas Kirk, Aberdeen

Excavations in the East Kirk of St Nicholas revealed a twelfth-century buttressed stone church overlying an earlier apse-ended church (Stones 2008). Twenty graves of infants and children were radially aligned along the outside of this apse, and a further cluster of graves east of these were probably contemporary. At least three of this latter group were in log coffins, all apparently for children; one coffin, partially charred and containing a child of 6 to 8 years of age, has been radiocarbon dated to the early eleventh century (Alison Cameron pers comm). However, the site has not yet been published and post-excavation analysis is currently ongoing.

7.2.8 Undated and possible examples

Aside from the issue of poor preservation of organic material, another problem may be the lack of recognised log coffins in Early Medieval Scotland until relatively recently: the Whithorn cemetery was excavated 1984-1991 and not published until 1997; Thornybank was excavated in 1996 and published in 2002. As such it will be worth reinterpreting older excavations which showed traces of organic linings for log coffins that may have been overlooked. For instance, at the long cist cemetery of Hallow Hill, St Andrews, Fife, 'boulder cists' lined with cobbles (Proudfoot 1996, 407) may instead be chocking stones similar to those seen underneath log coffins at Thornybank and Forteviot.

There are also antiquarian accounts of log coffins which may date to the Medieval period, but must remain tentative. Two W – E log coffins bearing a male and a female found at Castlehill, Edinburgh in 1850 have entered the literature as Late Medieval due to their description as having head niches like Medieval sarcophagi (Mowat 1996, 463-4; Parker Pearson et al 2013, 29; Wilson 1851, 463-4; Zimmermann 1992, 84). At Cairngall, Aberdeenshire, two W – E oak coffins, one with a flat plank lid, were found in a 'tumulus' in 1813 while cutting peat, with projections at either end for carrying, reminiscent of the wooden 'troughs' used as body-bearers at Mucking and elsewhere (Donald 1845; cf Hirst and Clark 2009, 470). Log coffins thought to be Bronze Age have occasionally been dated to the Early Medieval period in northern England (Melton et al 2016, 387), and similarity of form means that dating museum samples should be a future priority.

7.3 Summary of dating evidence

There are only very few radiocarbon dates available for log coffins in Scotland (summarised in Illus 7.3 which does not include unpublished data from St Nicholas Kirk,

Aberdeen, A. Cameron, pers comm). However, what we have makes it clear that the bulk of these belong to the fifth to seventh centuries, which is the period for which we have the most excavated burial evidence (Maldonado 2013); in this respect, log coffins should not be seen as outliers but generally part of mainstream funerary practice. The examples from Boysack Mills and Forteviot are likely to date to the early centuries AD, such that log coffins join square barrows and long cists as examples of grave types which originated in the Iron Age but flourished in the Early Medieval period (Maldonado 2013, 3-6). In line with general trends, the Whithorn log coffins became rarer after the seventh century, but notably reappeared through several major reorganisations of the site while long cists disappeared. The instance at Iona has a *terminus post quem* of c AD 800, the construction date of St Columba's Shrine, but as the examples from Aberdeen show, log coffins continued in sporadic use as late as the twelfth century. There is now a wider context for these later log coffins from ecclesiastical sites: a series of mainly antiquarian finds from England north of the Humber have been identified as Early Medieval log coffins, and where dated seem to be of middle or late Saxon date (McComish 2015; Melton et al 2016, 387; Mui 2015). At time of writing, a large cemetery with 81 log coffins from Great Ryburgh, Norfolk has also been provisionally assigned a middle Saxon monastic context (Hilts 2016).

The log coffins from Scotland can thus be seen to span the first millennium AD, with examples from each of Zimmermann's 'Merovingian', 'Carolingian' and 'High Medieval' periods (1992, 100-1), with rare instances in the Iron Age just as log coffins began to reappear elsewhere in northern Europe (cf Andersen et al 1991). The 'Carolingian' phase now seems to map onto a widespread but discontinuous fashion for log coffins at ecclesiastical sites as seen from the Netherlands to Scandinavia, and now increasingly from northern Britain (Gräslund 1981, 44; Lanting and Van der Plicht 2012; McComish 2015, 306-7). This is not to say that those labels have any significance in a Scottish context, but rather to show that log coffins appear and go out of use at similar times across north-west Europe, with no need to presume any migration or diffusion from a specific origin.

7.4 Demographics and social status

There is very little reliable demographic information for log coffins due to poor preservation. At Whithorn it was possible to tell that log coffins were mainly used for adult males, although this was only apparent in four instances, in an already male-dominated cemetery. Aside from these well-preserved examples, there were also two possible females, three unsexed adults, one sub-adult and two children in log coffins (Cardy 1997). At Thornybank, sexing was not possible for the log coffin graves, but based on grave length there were an estimated 27 adults, 7 juveniles and 11 infant/neonates (Rees 2002, 350-2).

It is significant that log coffins were used in square-enclosed graves in four of the seven sites in which they appear, and were placed in prestigious locations near a church or chapel in three others. Clustering of log coffins within a cemetery was also seen at Thornybank and Whithorn. However, whether these can all uncritically be taken to signify 'elite' or higher status within each cemetery is debatable, though most of these sites are themselves high-status. While there is evidence that log coffins often appeared in more elaborate graves, dozens of instances at Thornybank and Whithorn show that log coffins were also interchangeable with long cists, and were available to all ages and genders. This fits in with the early Anglo-Saxon log coffins (summarised above, 7.1), which were used in high-profile elite graves at Sutton Hoo but also across the demographic range at Mucking.

7.5 Coffins as grave furnishings

Given the broad parallels in the use of log coffins across Britain, it should now be difficult to sustain discussion of the Scottish material as separate from the Anglo-Saxon or Welsh data. The interpretation of Anglo-Saxon instances of log coffin burial traditionally leads to a 'pagan' Germanic cultural background. Without resorting to migration as an explanation, how are we to account for these concordances? An alternative approach would be to highlight the active role of the grave lining – the tree-trunk – in the transformation of the body and the memory of the deceased.

In Early Medieval Scotland, by far the most common grave type was the long cist, in which the body was lined with upright slabs of stone (Maldonado 2016). Log coffins appeared at the same time and in the same cemeteries as long cists, and in rare occasions, composite wood and stone linings have been detected (Hill 1997, 72-3). While the log coffin would have required significantly more labour to produce (Knol et al 1996, 298-9), the 'natural' appearance of a hollowed tree trunk parallels the use of undressed slabs gathered into long cists. As such, long cists and log coffins can be seen as cognate rather than opposed practices of reassembling the elements of the landscape as part of the funerary ritual.

Along with Ireland and western Britain, Scotland's mortuary remains form part of a spectrum of 'unfurnished' burial practices in this period, characterised by the absence of grave goods (Longley 2009; O'Brien 2009). However, grave goods are not the only way of investing in mortuary practices, and there is evidence for a wide variety of funerary monuments, structures and architecture both above and below ground in use across the first millennium AD in Scotland. These range from stone and earth monuments such as mounds and cairns, to timber structures mainly attested by postholes and soil stains such as the four-post 'mortuary house' and plank-built burial enclosure found at Thornybank, Midlothian (Rees 2002, 335-9). Aside from this it is clear that the excavated burial record represents only a small proportion of the actual population, and thanks to recent finds at Forteviot, Perthshire (Campbell et al, this volume) it is likely that cremation was also practiced into the Early Medieval period, and so cremation pyres represent another use of timber related to funerary contexts that remains archaeologically invisible (Meyers Emery and Williams 2017). As such, the arbitrary distinction between 'furnished' and 'unfurnished' graves is not helpful as a method of assessing investment of labour and resources into mortuary practice and commemoration, and the author has recently made the case for considering long cists as a form of grave furnishing (Maldonado 2013, 14-15; 2016).

Studies in Anglo-Saxon contexts have argued that linings of stone, wood and other materials should be seen not as a backdrop for the body but as material culture which needed to be sourced and arranged as part of the funerary ritual, and patterns in their use reveal they played an active role in the transformation of the memory of the dead (Harrington 2007; Thompson 2004, 107-12; Williams 2006, 141-4). By studying how the grave was made and how the body was prepared, such graves can provide a wealth of information on funerary ritual and social identity (Buckberry 2010; Williams 2006, 102-16).

Mortuary rituals are primarily concerned with the recasting of personhood for the dead from living kin to ancestral spirit through the handling of the body (Hertz 1960; Metcalf and Huntington 1991). As exemplified in recent studies of Anglo-Saxon period mortuary practices, the Early Medieval body was continually refashioned throughout the life cycle as signalled by age- and gender-specific material culture worn by the living and the dead (Crawford 1993; Stoodley 2000). In life as in death, the body was permeable, subject to supernatural forces which could be managed through the funerary process (Dickinson 2005; Thompson 2004, 92-131). The living were also at risk of pollution or haunting from the improperly managed dead, as revealed both through the contemporary literature and mortuary archaeology (Blair 2009; Reynolds 2009). The use of material culture in mortuary contexts can be understood as ways of managing these potential threats to the social order at the time of death. It has been argued that decorated log coffins such as those at Oberflacht were apotropaic, defending the dead from spiritual attack to which bodies were vulnerable as they decayed (Schiek 1992, 35-40).

Recent work has turned attention to the role of emotion in the funerary ritual, and its role in reorienting the memory of the deceased (Harris 2010; Williams 2007b). The mnemonic and emotional capacity of the cadaver can be mediated through practices of display and concealment during the preparation, deposition and committal of the body (Tarlow 2002; Williams 2006). In particular, grave linings, wrappings and coverings produced a multisensory effect on the mourners which served to heighten some aspects of the performance of the burial ritual while masking or downplaying the putrefaction of the corpse (Harrington 2007; Maldonado 2016; Mui 2015; Williams 2011). The use of coffins, as with any other covering or vessel, should be interpreted according to their affective role in selectively recreating and obliterating the memory of the deceased (Nugent and Williams 2012; Williams 2006, 121-34).

The above discussion has by necessity relied on examples from outside of Scotland, as such ideas have yet to be applied widely in this context. A notable exception is the work of Howard Williams. By focusing on mnemonic practice in the construction of the grave, Williams (2006, 141-4) has pointed out the parallels between 'unfurnished' long cists prevalent in the north with 'furnished' graves elsewhere in Britain. He has also discussed long cists and stone cairn monuments as evidence for a form of relational personhood, in which the 'individual' grave can be seen as the construction of kinship between the living and the long dead (Williams 2007a, 156-60). Taking these ideas forward, the current author has recently shown the complexity of meanings which can be communicated by the plain stone grave linings in long cists, the most common form of grave type in Scotland in this period (Maldonado 2016). The deployment of hard stone in place of the dress and weaponry found further south would appear to be a significant difference between 'Anglo-Saxon' and 'Celtic' parts of Britain. However, the appearance of log coffins across these perceived cultural boundaries would seem to upset this distinction. The use of long cists and log coffins together in the same cemeteries in Scotland seems to further undermine the conceptual distinction between these types of grave furnishing.

7.6 Log coffins and the afterlife

This article has barely scratched the surface of the interpretive potential of this peculiar form of grave furnishing. To date, no comprehensive review of the occurrence of log coffin burial in Britain has taken place, making it difficult to situate these in the insular context. However, the comparative approach used here points out significant parallels between Scotland and log coffins across north-west Europe that demand future targeted analysis.

Due to the poor survival of wood, the log coffin has been seen as a rare and extraordinary mortuary practice, one which traditionally has required some external prompt such as migration or diffusion of ideas. It is impossible to know how many more log coffins have been lost to time and insensitive excavation techniques. What is clear is that log coffins had a long currency that spanned the first millennium AD; like long cists and barrow burial, log coffins were an adaptation of existing Iron Age practices rather than 'intrusive' rites introduced from outside. They seem to have been adopted by early Christians, and may have developed a religious significance over time, but given the diversity of contexts and time periods involved, no single interpretation of their function will apply.

A way forward is to draw attention to the log coffin, and any grave lining, as an active agent in the transformation of the deceased. A wider concern for apotropaic defence against supernatural forces besieging the body as it decayed should be considered, as has been demonstrated primarily for organic linings in early Alammanic and late Saxon graves (Schiek 1992, 35-40; Thompson 2004). What has not yet been considered is the materiality of wood in a Scottish context; coffins are not the only uses of timber related to the mortuary arena, and any discussion of the wood as a material will have to take into account the sourcing of timber for biers, pyres and mortuary structures (eg Meyers Emery and Williams 2017; Williams 2004; 2006). The term 'coffin' itself carries significant baggage, and an appreciation of the range of vessels that might be represented by the round-bottomed organic linings discussed here opens up a variety of other interpretive possibilities, including dugout logboats, biers and troughs. In a Scottish context, the long cist has been interpreted less as a 'coffin' or protective container than a way to aid in the transformation of bodily essences into earthly substances (Maldonado 2016). These and other interpretations help us think of the funerary vessel as a negotiation of the personhood of the dead, a structuring role that depends on the cosmological position of the dead with regard to ancestral essences in the landscape. It is unlikely that their function in the burial rite and their cultural significance will have remained static throughout the period, but the fact that log coffins appear go out of use after the twelfth century indicates a fundamental rupture with past practice at that time.

The Scottish burial evidence, not despite but because of its lack of traditional 'grave goods', allows us to focus more attention on the wood, stone and earth which make up the grave. The use of wood and stone grave linings alongside each other on the same site shows considerable experimentation and multivocality in the cemeteries of the period. Such insights show that these graves were hardly 'unfurnished', and the Scottish material shows that attention to the efficacious role of the architecture of the burial should be considered as part of mortuary analysis elsewhere.

Acknowledgments
Thanks especially to Alice Blackwell for encouraging the completion of this article, and for Ewan Campbell for inspiring me to put this research together. Mark Hall, Howard Williams, Brian Costello, Anouk Busset, Susanna Harris, Kate Forsyth, Stephen Harrison and Paul Duffy all helped procure sources and provided ideas. All errors remain my own.

Bibliography
Alexander, D 2005 'Redcastle, Lunan Bay, Angus: the excavation of an Iron Age timber-lined souterrain and a Pictish barrow cemetery', *Proceedings of the Society of Antiquaries of Scotland*, 135, 41-118.

Andersen, S H, Lind, B and Crumlin-Pedersen, O 1991 *Slusegårdgravpladsen III: Gravformer og gravskikke, Bådgravene*. Jysk Arkcologisk Selskabs Skrifter 14.3. Aarhus: Jysk Arkcologisk Selskabs.

Bärenfänger, R 1988 *Siedlungs- und Bestattungsplätze des 8. bis 10. Jahrhunderts in Niedersachsen und Bremen*. BAR International Series 398. Oxford: British Archaeological Reports.

Blair, J 2009 'The dangerous dead in Early Medieval England', *in* Baxter, S, Karkov, C Nelson, J L and Pelteret, D (eds) *Early Medieval studies in memory of Patrick Wormald*, 539-59. Aldershot: Ashgate.

Brassil, K S, Owen, W G and Britnell, W J 1991 'Prehistoric and Early Medieval cemeteries at Tandderwen, near Denbigh, Clwyd', *Archaeological Journal* 148, 46-97.

Buckberry, J 2010 'Cemetery diversity in the mid to late Anglo-Saxon period in Lincolnshire and Yorkshire', in Buckberry, J and Cherryson, A K (eds) *Burial in later Anglo-Saxon England c 650-1100* AD, 1-25. Oxford: Oxbow.

Campbell, E 2007 *Continental and Mediterranean imports to Atlantic Britain and Ireland,* AD *400-800*. CBA Research Report 157. York: Council for British Archaeology.

Cardy, A 1997 'The human bones', *in* Hill, 519-62.

Carver, M 2005 *Sutton Hoo: a seventh-century princely burial ground and its context.* London: British Museum Press.

Crawford, S 1993 'Children, death and the afterlife in Anglo-Saxon England', *Anglo-Saxon Studies in Archaeology and History* 6, 83-91.

Dickinson, T M 2005 'Symbols of protection: the significance of animal-ornamented shields in early Anglo-Saxon England', *Medieval Archaeology* 49, 109-63.

Donald, W 1845 'Parish of Peterhead', *New Statistical Account of Scotland, v. 12,* 344-96. Edinburgh: William Blackwood and Sons.

Edwards, N (ed) 2009 *The archaeology of the Early Medieval Celtic churches*. Society of Medieval Archaeology Monograph 29. Leeds: Maney.

Filmer-Sankey, W and Pestell, T 2001 *Snape Anglo-Saxon cemetery: excavations and surveys 1824-1992*. East Anglian Archaeology Report 95. Ipswich.

Forsyth, K 2009 'The Latinus Stone: Whithorn's earliest Christian monument', *in* Murray, J (ed) *St Ninian and the earliest Christianity in Scotland*, 19-41. BAR British Series 483. Oxford: Archaeopress.

Gräslund, A-S 1981 *Birka IV: the burial customs. A study of the graves on Björkö.* Stockholm: Almqvist and Wiksells.

Harrington, S 2007 'Soft furnished burial: an assessment of the role of textiles in early Anglo-Saxon inhumations, with particular reference to East Kent', *in* Semple, S and Williams, H (eds) *Early Medieval mortuary practices. Anglo-Saxon Studies in Archaeology and History* 14, 110-16.

Harris, O 2010 'Emotional and mnemonic geographies at Hambledon Hill: texturing Neolithic places with bodies and bones', *Cambridge Archaeological Journal* 20(3), 357-71.

Herbert, M and Ó Riain, P (eds) 1988 *Betha Adamnáin: the Irish Life of Adamnán*. London: Irish Texts Society.

Hertz, R 1960 'A contribution to the study of the collective representation of death', *in* Needham, R and Needham, C (eds) *Death and the right hand*, 29-86. Glencoe, IL: The Free Press.

Hill, P 1997 *Whithorn and St Ninian: the excavation of a monastic town, 1984-91*. Stroud: Sutton.

Hilts, C 2016 'Great Ryburgh: a remarkable Anglo-Saxon cemetery revealed', *Current Archaeology* 322, 18-24.

Hirst, S and Clark, D 2009 *Excavations at Mucking: volume 3, the Anglo-Saxon cemeteries*. London: Museum of London Archaeology.

Hogarth, A C 1973 'Structural features in Anglo-Saxon graves', *Archaeological Journal* 130, 104-19.

Knol, E, Prummel, W, Uytterschaut, H, Hoogland, M, Casparie, W, De Langen, G, Kramer, E and Schelvis, J 1996 'The Early Medieval cemetery of Oosterbeintum (Friesland)', *Palaeohistoria* 37/38, 245-416.

Lanting, J N and Van der Plicht, J 2012 'De 14C-chronologie van de Nederlandse pre- en protohistorie VI: Romeinse tijd en Merovingische periode, deel B: aanvullingen, toelichtingen en 14C-dateringen', *Palaeohistoria* 53/54, 283-391.

Longley, D 2009 'Early Medieval burial in Wales', *in* Edwards, 105-34.

Maldonado, A 2011 'Christianity and burial in Late Iron Age Scotland, AD 400-650', unpublished PhD thesis, University of Glasgow.

Maldonado, A 2013 'Burial in Early Medieval Scotland: new questions', *Medieval Archaeology* 57, 1-34.

Maldonado, A 2016 'Materialising the afterlife: the long cist in Early Medieval Scotland', *in* Pierce, E, Russell, A, Maldonado, A and Campbell, L (eds) *Creating material worlds: the uses of identity in archaeology*, 39-62. Oxford: Oxbow.

Maldonado, A 2017 'Barrows and the conversion of the landscape at Forteviot, Perthshire', *in* Edwards, N, Ní Mhaonaigh, M and Flechner, R (eds) *Transforming landscapes of belief in the Early Medieval insular world and beyond. Converting the Isles II*, 319-50. CELAMA 23. Turnhout: Brepols.

McComish, J M 2015 'The pre-Conquest coffins from 12-18 Swinegate and 18 Back Swinegate', *Web Report 2015/46* [accessed May 2016]. Available at: <http://www.yorkarchaeology.co.uk/resources/publications/web-publications/>

Melton, N, Montgomery, J, Roberts, B W, Cook, G and Harris, S 2016 'On the curious date of the Rylstone log-coffin burial', *Proceedings of the Prehistoric Society* 82, 383-92.

Metcalf, P and Huntington, R 1991 *Celebrations of death: the anthropology of mortuary ritual*. Second edition. Cambridge: Cambridge University Press.

Meyers Emery, K and Williams, H 2017 'A place to rest your (burnt) bones? Mortuary houses in early Anglo-Saxon England', *Archaeological Journal* 175(1), 55-86.
Mowat, R 1996 *The logboats of Scotland*. Oxford: Oxbow.
Mui, S 2015 'Life after death: shrouded burials in later Anglo-Saxon England', *Archaeological Review from Cambridge* 30(1), 150-6.
Murray, D and Ralston, I B M 1997 'The excavation of a square-ditched barrow and other cropmarks at Boysack Mills, Inverkeilor, Angus', *Proceedings of the Society of Antiquaries of Scotland* 127, 359-86.
Nordeide, S W 2011 *The Viking Age as a period of religious transformation: the Christianization of Norway from* AD *560-1150/1200*. Studies in Viking and Medieval Scandinavia 2. Brepols: Turnhout.
Nugent, R and Williams, H 2012 'Sighted surfaces: ocular agency in early Anglo-Saxon cremation burials', *in* Back Danielsson, I-M, Fahlander, F and Sjöstrand, Y (eds) *Encountering imagery: materialities, perceptions, relations*, 187-208. Stockholm: Stockholm Studies in Archaeology 57.
O'Brien, E 2009 'Pagan or Christian? Burial in Ireland during the fifth to eighth centuries AD', *in* Edwards, 135-54.
Ó Carragáin, T 2003 'The architectural setting of the cult of relics in Early Medieval Ireland', *Journal of the Royal Society of Antiquaries of Ireland* 133, 130-76.
Päffgen, B and Hoeke, B 2004 'Sarg', *in* Hoops, J (ed) *Reallexikon der Germanischen Altertumskunde* 26, 470-83. Berlin: Walter de Gruyter.
Parker Pearson, M, Sheridan, A and Needham, S 2013 'Bronze Age tree-trunk coffin graves in Britain', *in* Melton, N, Montgomery, J and Knüsel, C (eds) *Gristhorpe Man: a life and death in the Bronze Age*, 29-66. Oxford: Oxbow.
Proudfoot, E 1996 'Excavations at the long cist cemetery on the Hallow Hill, St Andrews, Fife, 1975-7', *Proceedings of the Society of Antiquaries of Scotland* 126, 387-454.
Redknap, M 1977 'Excavation at Iona Abbey, 1976', *Proceedings of the Society of Antiquaries of Scotland* 108, 228-53.
Rees, A R 2002 'A first millennium AD cemetery, rectangular Bronze Age structure and late prehistoric settlement at Thornybank, Midlothian', *Proceedings of the Society of Antiquaries of Scotland* 132, 313-55.
Reynolds, A 2009 *Anglo-Saxon deviant burial customs*. Oxford: Oxford University Press.
Salin, E 1952 *La civilisation mérovingienne, d'après les sépultures, les textes et le laboratoire. Deuxième partie : Les sépultures*. Paris: A and J Picard.
Schiek, S 1992 *Das Gräberfeld der Merowingerzeit bei Oberflacht (Gemeinde Seitingen-Oberflacht, Lkr. Tuttlingen)*. Forschungen und Berichte zur Vor- und Frühgeschichte in Baden-Württemberg Bd. 41/1. Stuttgart: K. Theiss.
Scull, C 2011 'Foreign identities in burials at the seventh-century English emporia', *in* Brookes, S, Harrington, S and Reynolds, A (eds) *Studies in early Anglo-Saxon art and archaeology: papers in honour of Martin G Welch*, 82-7. BAR British Series 527. Oxford: Archaeopress.
Stead, I M 1991 *Iron Age cemeteries in East Yorkshire: excavations at Burton Fleming, Rudston, Garton-on-the-Wolds, and Kirkburn*. London: English Heritage.

Stones, J (ed) 2008 *East Kirk of St Nicholas project 2006*, interim report, second edition. Aberdeen: Aberdeen City Council Archaeology Unit. Available at: http://www.aberdeencity.gov.uk/education_learning/local_history/kirk_stnicholas/loc_arch-kirknicholas.asp

Stoodley, N 2000 'From the cradle to the grave: age organization and the early Anglo-Saxon burial rite', *World Archaeology* 31(3), 456-72.

Tarlow, S 2002 'The aesthetic corpse in nineteenth-century Britain', *in* Hamilakis, Y, Pluciennik, M and Tarlow, S (eds) *Thinking through the body: archaeologies of corporeality*, 85-97. London: Plenum.

Thompson, V 2004 *Dying and death in later Anglo-Saxon England*. Rochester, NY: Woodbridge.

Toop, N-J 2005 'Dialogues of power: early Christian monumentality around the northern Irish Sea AD 400-1000', unpublished PhD thesis, University of York.

Webster, C J and Brunning, R A 2004 'A seventh-century AD cemetery at Stoneage Barton Farm, Bishop's Lydeard, Somerset and square-ditched burials in post-Roman Britain', *Archaeological Journal* 161, 54-81.

Williams, H 2004 'Death warmed up: the agency of bodies and bones in early Anglo-Saxon cremation rites', *Journal of Material Culture* 9(3), 263-91.

Williams, H 2006 *Death and memory in Early Medieval Britain*. Cambridge Studies in Archaeology. Cambridge: Cambridge University Press.

Williams, H 2007a 'Depicting the dead: commemoration through cists, cairns and symbols in Early Medieval Britain', *Cambridge Archaeological Journal* 17(2), 145-64.

Williams, H 2007b 'The emotive force of Early Medieval mortuary practices', *Archaeological Review from Cambridge* 22(1), 107-23.

Williams, H 2011 'The sense of being seen: ocular effects at Sutton Hoo', *Journal of Social Archaeology* 11(1), 99-121.

Wilson, D 1851 *The archaeology and prehistoric annals of Scotland*. Edinburgh: Sutherland and Knox.

Zimmermann, K 1992 *Baumsarg und Totenbaum: zu einer Bestattung unter dem Berner Münster, Acta Bernensia 11*. Bern: Stämpfli.

8

Medieval European land assessment, Fortriu, and the *dabhach*

Alasdair Ross

8.1 Introduction

The history of investigations into the different units of Medieval land assessment in Scotland follows a long and convoluted path. Yet, over 243 years since people first began to discuss them in print (Pennant 1998, 316), there is still no consensus about the when, who, and why such units were first introduced. Disagreement has also arisen about perceived differences within single types of land assessment, leading to excessive and convoluted disputes about inter-relationships, typology, and even ethnicity (Robertson 1862, ii, 271; Elder-Levie 1931, 99-110; Barrow 1962, 133; Dodgshon 1980, 49-50; Ross 2006, 57-74). To an outside observer, this debate must often seem oddly introverted. To be fair, not all of the controversy has been caused by historians; Medieval Scottish records are generally poor in comparison to other European countries and the fact that Scotland once possessed at least ten different units of land assessment within its current borders has merely served to stir already murky waters. Indeed, perhaps one of the great conundrums in Scottish Medieval history is why its rulers never introduced a truly common unit of land assessment across the whole country.

In contrast, during the last decade or so both North Atlantic and European studies in land assessment have burgeoned as researchers have realised the fundamental importance of such units to the formation of an apparatus of state in their respective countries. This paper will firstly provide a brief overview of some of this North Atlantic and European material and then examine one of the most common units of land assessment found in Medieval Scotland, the Pictish *dabhach* (pl. *dabhaichean*), within the broader context of this research.

in: Blackwell, A.E. (ed.) 2019: *Scotland in Early Medieval Europe*, Leiden: Sidestone Press, pp. 135-148.

8.2 Medieval European land assessment

Much research has been undertaken in Norway over the last decade in relation to Medieval administrative systems and state formation. One area of particular focus has been Hardanger, part of the early tenth century Gulathing law province. The Gulathing Law, surviving in written form from the thirteenth century – but much older – lists in descending order four units of land organisation, the *fylki*, *fjórðungr*, áttungr, and *skipreiða*. The three Medieval *fylkir*, *Horðafylki*, *Sygnafylki*, and *Firðafylki*, are thought to have comprised the original core of the province (Hobæk 2013, 64-75). Like some units of land assessment found in Scotland, so the *fylki* could be divided into quarters (*fjórðungr*) and eighths (áttungr) but it is perhaps the *skipreiður* that are of more immediate interest. These units of assessment were part of the naval defence system called the *leiðangr*, introduced during the tenth century and also allegedly found in the Northern Isles (Williams 2004, 68-9), in which each *skipreiða* was obliged to build and supply a warship. Claims that the two were introduced simultaneously are disputed but it seems to be generally accepted that *skipreiður* were first introduced in Gulathing during the tenth century and thereafter across the entire kingdom. In addition, *skipreiður* quickly came to function as fiscal and administrative units for more general tax assessment. According to Hobæk, the *fjórðungr* of Hardanger was divided into five *skipreiður*, the equivalent of exactly ten local communities that also formed ten Medieval parishes: Ulvik, Eidfjord, Granvin, Kinsarvik, Ullensvang, Odda, Røldal, Jondal, Vikøy, and Øystese. Interestingly, these ten parishes also formed nine judicial *-tinget* districts, Øystesetinget comprising the two parishes of Vikøy, and Øystese (Hobæk 2013, 65-8).

Similar research has also been undertaken in the landscape of Vicken, located in the Oslo fjord region. There, Ødegaard has argued that the area originally comprised three *fylki* that were subsequently united at the beginning of the eleventh century into the Borgarthing law province after the establishment of a *lawthing* in the town of Borg c 1016 (Ødegaard 2013, 42-63). Vicken also possessed *skipreiður* established during the tenth century: forty-eight of these were listed in 1277, and an occasional correlation between Medieval parish boundaries and *fjórðungr* boundaries has already been noted. To complicate matters further, here the *skipreiður* may have been mapped on top of an earlier system of land assessment, the Danish *herað*, whose extents often match topographical borders (Ødegaard 2013, 44-8).

It has, however, already been recognised that both taxes and duties varied between the constituent parts of Medieval Norway and the taxation of Härjedalen is a case in point. There, though sixteenth-century tax registers have to be relied upon as evidence for Medieval taxation, it has been argued that even then the tax system was still quite primitive when compared against other regions, with either squirrels or their equivalent in money being due in tax. Because taxation via land assessment had been introduced throughout most of Norway by the end of the thirteenth century, Holm argues that Härjedalen, with its very basic form of squirrel taxation, remained on the periphery of the core of royal power (Holm 2010, 229-51).

In Sweden, on the other hand, there seems to have been almost as much academic controversy generated over various systems of land assessment as has occurred in Scotland. For example, in 1296 the seemingly new judicial-administrative entity called Uppland contained three *folkland* (Attundaland, Tiundaland, and Fjädrundaland) which were clearly much older divisions of land. In turn, each *folkland* was divided into *hundare* (nominally the district of a chieftain and his one hundred men). Other units of assessment also existed alongside sub-divisions of *hundare*: half *hundare*, *hundarefjärdinger*, *hundaresåtting*, *skeppslagar*, *socknar* (parishes), *tolfter*, and *tredingar*. In Svealand, the *hundare* seem to have existed as a *ting* (court) region, as a tax district, and in the organisation of the military *ledung* (military fleet levy). In the mid-fourteenth century, during the reign of King Magnus Eriksson, the *hundare* (possibly in name only) was replaced by the *härad*, which meant that both Svealand and Götaland were assessed in the same way. These reforms were clearly an imposition of conformity in nomenclature by a state authority, though some regional variation remained. The author also noted that the boundaries of these *hundare*, or *härader*, remained constant throughout the late-thirteenth, fourteenth, and fifteenth centuries and that there was wide variation in their size and wealth (Line 2007, 206-24). Lindquist has further refined this argument and suggested that the development of the Medieval Swedish realm occurred in three phases. The first phase, until c 980, was characterized by the demanding of tributes as part of an economy based upon plunder. The second phase, to 1250, involved the conversion of kings to Christianity with increased control over territory, modes of production, and men and the appearance of a new economic system based upon internal appropriation. The final phase, beginning c 1250, saw the emergence of a state with institutionalized political power, administrative literacy, legislation, and the imposition of permanent taxes (Lindkvist 2010, 251-61; Lindkvist 2011, 265-78).

Perhaps unsurprisingly, traces of Scandinavian units of land assessment can also be found in England, specifically in the Danelaw. There, Baker and Brookes have argued that the hundredal pattern of the Southern Danelaw, as it existed in 1086, demonstrates a complex evolution that preserves earlier elements of both Norse and English administrative landscapes. Essentially, they argue that the Scandinavian landscape organisation of midland England seems to be a reflection of groupings of troops ruled from a central settlement. The basic administrative unit was the *wapentake* (ON *vápnatak*) with such groups of troops perhaps capable of being organized into territorially based armies equivalent to *fylki*. They also note, however, that this administrative system may well have used a pre-existing Mercian structure, perhaps as early as eighth century in date; a case of adaptation rather than re-organization (Baker and Brookes 2013, 76-95).

Moving across the North Atlantic, the Faroe Isles were settled by the Norse in the ninth century AD. There, one or multiple *fyrndarbýlingur* (an 'old farm' which could be sub-divided into farmsteads and households) formed the eighty-five *bygðir* (settlements) that comprised the colony. Many of the latter possessed their own church and were also parishes. According to Vésteinsson, the concept of the *fyrndarbýlingur* is closely related to an Icelandic taxable unit of land assessment that could also contain multiple farmsteads, the *lögbýli* – a taxable unit of a certain value that contained any number of farmsteads and households (Vésteinsson 2006, 91).

Iceland is another part of the North Atlantic world where a lot of research has recently been undertaken in relation to landscape division and settlement. Iceland has a number of different terms for clusters of settlements including þorp (village) and *hverfi* (hamlet or neighbourhood). The latter sometimes has a dual meaning as either a cluster of farms or as a neighbourhood (Vésteinsson 2006, 102). Here too, parishes were a later development of the twelfth and thirteenth centuries and there were two main types.

One was akin to an estate parish, where the parish comprised either a single estate, or a single core estate with smaller ancillary estates attached to that core. The other type was where the parish church was attached to a less wealthy farm or in areas where there were major single estates (Vésteinsson 2006, 107-8).

In other parts of Medieval Europe these processes were different still. In order to achieve their goal of surveying and controlling new lands as their empire expanded, the Carolingian emperors introduced a standardised system of land organisation called the *mansus* (pl. *mansi*) as a means of tax-levying and warrior-recruitment from c 780. Essentially, this amounted to the managed exploitation of land through the mechanism of small units of land assessment whereby it became possible to calculate the tax contribution of each property holder. This standardisation transformed the Carolingian production structure and it ultimately proved to be a hugely successful method of cultivating land and organising labour and army service (Sonnlechner 2004, 43-4).

This process was a clear attempt to establish order upon the Carolingian European landscape and its inhabitants by getting rid of diversity and imposing standard dues and obligations. Sonnlechner has further suggested that the whole system was underpinned by the development of an agro-ecological system which integrated livestock pasturing into land husbandry, thereby ensuring the proper fertilisation of field systems. In this model *mansi* became the production units of larger nodes of seignorial exploitation. In addition, the *mansus* was a flexible fiscal and administrative unit of differing size and producing different renders that could be imposed upon a range of different ecologies from the Paris basin to the high Alps of Salzburg and Provence (Sonnlechner 2004, 44-7).

Moving south-west again, in Medieval Castile the standard term for the units of administration was *Alfoz* (pl. *alfoces*) and they formed the territorial framework of governance. They seem to have been created in the late ninth or early tenth centuries out of supralocal territories and the free population in these units were subject to jurisdiction, work renders, and military obligations (Escalona 2006, 143-66), just like the *mansus*, *hundare*, *skipreiður*, and the *dabhach*.

In the eastern Alps, the Slovene territories of *Carnolia* and *Carantania* had been affected by the collapse of the Avar khaganate in the late eighth century which caused widespread social and ethnic restructuring (Štih 2010, 154). Key figures seem to have the Župani, who constituted a special class and who governed župe (sing. župa) into which most of the Slavic population was organised. This seems to have been a unit of population greater than a single family unit. But like Scotland, Medieval historians of this area only have few sources upon which to draw information so it is a difficult process to precisely understand the structures of the area. Historians still do not know how big a župa was, how many there were, their internal structures, or their respective shares of population. Nevertheless, their society was structured and key to the development of land assessment were elders who aided the transition from a Slavic economy based upon the *zadruga* (large family) to one based upon the *mansus* (Štih 2010, 167). Accordingly, by the ninth and tenth centuries, many populations widely spread across both Europe and the North Atlantic lived and paid taxes according to regulated systems of land assessment. While each of these units may have possessed different names, they essentially performed identical purposes.

8.3 The *dabhach*

The first attempt to undertake a supra-regional study of Medieval Scottish units of land assessment was completed in the mid-1980s yet it was deeply unsatisfactory because it mostly utilised only published primary sources, leaving a huge evidence gap (Easson 1986). This has recently been rectified but to date only half of the country has been covered in any detail (Bangor-Jones 1986; Raven 2005; Ross 2015). Even more surprising is that, until recently, most of the Medieval land assessments in Scotland had not been contextualised using research from across Europe. Many earlier debates about land assessment and the *dabhach* in Scotland could perhaps be described as rather myopic in nature, obsessed as many of them were with hypothetical tubs of grain (Jackson 1972, 116-17).

Most have thought the *dabhach* Pictish (pre-900) in origin, mainly because its distribution pattern generally matches the area of the historical Pictland. But such comparisons are rather inexact because we know so little about the historic extent(s) of Pictland across the centuries of its existence, never mind the fact that 'Pictland' may never have been a homogenous realm except in the minds of kings who occasionally ruled both 'northern' and 'southern' Picts. Like the 'kingdom of the Picts', the distribution of *dabhaichean* is nuanced and the extent of these nuances is only now becoming clear. In part, perhaps previous investigations were inadvertently hampered because 'Pictish Studies' were long tagged as being 'problematic' in nature (Wainwright 1955; but see Driscoll et al 2011).

Recently the *dabhach* has been comprehensively surveyed across an area of northern Scotland that stretches from Huntly in the north-east westwards to the Outer Hebrides, and from the Cairngorm plateau northwards to Cape Wrath, utilising historical evidence culled from over 1000 years of written records and maps (Ross 2015). The products of this survey are discussed in detail elsewhere but a number of key points can be taken from it for the purposes of this article.

First, the *dabhach* debuts in the historical record in the longer version of the St Andrews foundation (Account B) which is thought to have been written c 850 during the Pictish historic period. Indeed, an old stratum in this text lists several place-names, some of which are given two names; what looks like the Pictish name is then followed by the Gaelic version. One such example is contained in the following section: *Inde transierunt montana, scilicet Moneth, et uenerunt ad locum qui uocabatur Doldocha nunc autem dictus Chendrohedalian* (Then they crossed the mountains, ie the Mounth, and came to a place which was called *Doldauha* but is now called Kindrochit-Alian). The latter place-name represents Kindrochit, now Castletown of Braemar in Deeside, a property that belonged to the Medieval cathedral of St Andrews.

Within the place-name *Doldocha*, *Dol-* (field or water meadow) was the Pictish form of the element thereafter borrowed into Scottish Gaelic as *Dail-*. The second element of this Pictish place-name, *-docha*, likely represents Middle Irish *dabcha*, the genitive singular of *dabhach*. If Taylor's interpretation is correct, it looks as though the term *dabhach* must have been in use during the Pictish historic period (Taylor and Márkus 2009, 564-92). By any reckoning this is a very thin sliver of evidence upon which to argue that the landscape of the kingdom of the Picts had been perambulated and divided into *dabhaichean* before it ended c 900, yet it is all we currently have until the insertion of pre-charter property records into the Book of Deer between c 1130 and c 1150 (Broun 2008, 313). By the twelfth century, when Scottish records begin to appear more regularly, the *dabhach* was already a recognised and common feature of land transactions. But unlike units of land assessment elsewhere in Europe, across northern Scotland the *dabhach* remained in active use and seemingly unchanged across the entire range of ecological zones until c 1800, by which time many had fallen prey to the processes of agricultural improvement as estates were cleared and enclosure created new patterns across different landscapes (Caird 1980, 203-22); the last few units disappeared from estate rentals in the early twentieth century.

Second, across the survey area two different types of *dabhach* are found: the first I have termed as 'self-contained' because all of the different elements of that type of *dabhach* are contained within a single defined area; the second as 'scattered' because the *dabhach* can be composed of as many as four different portions that are physically separated from each other in the landscape, sometimes by distances of up to 30km. Both types look to have contained every resource that a group of settlements needed to survive throughout the year, ranging from meadow through to rough grazing (Ross 2015, 68). Unfortunately, the mechanism by which just one of these areas of settlement was chosen to lend its name to a particular *dabhach* is currently unknown.

Each of these different types of *dabhach* could be fractionalised, with halves, quarters, and eighths being the most common divisions. But even here there was great diversity in size. For example, the two half-*dabhaichean* that comprised the *dabhach* of Crathie in the parish of Laggan (Badenoch) were respectively 40km^2 and 10km^2 in size. In Sutherland, the two half-*dabhaichean* that together comprised the *dabhach* of Mudale in Strath Naver were respectively 89km^2 and 50km^2 (NRS RS38/3/348; RS37/5; GD84/1/32/5). Such disparity in size brings into sharp focus the fact that it was the availability of and access to natural resources that determined the size of each *dabhach* and its constituent parts, nothing else.

But it is equally important to realise that the landscape of northern Scotland was not entirely divided into *dabhaichean*. Very rarely in the landscape appear upland areas described (post 1100) as 'forest' that remain *dabhach*-free but which were used in common by the inhabitants of *dabhaichean* who otherwise had no access to high mountain grazings, most regularly by those who lived in *dabhaichean* along coast lines. Few of these upland areas have been identified to date but they amount to the high Medieval 'forests' of Strathavon, Glenmore, and Freevater. Perhaps the closest analogy to these 'forests' are the Medieval Cumbrian vaccaries identified by Angus Winchester (Winchester 1987, 42-3).

The third point is perhaps the most important. According to the available historical evidence, through time only one new *dabhach* was ever created across the whole of the survey area. This occurred in the lordship of Badenoch in 1639 while it was temporarily under the control of the earl of Argyll. Contemporary documentation is quite clear that this new unit of land assessment was created by taking land from an adjacent *dabhach*, thereby reducing it in status, and that it had been done for personal greed. In any event, the new creation only lasted for a few years before the marquis of Huntly regained his lordship and restored the status quo (NRS GD44/41/22/2; GD44/10/10). Taken together, this evidence overwhelmingly suggests that the *dabhach* was a permanent feature across many landscapes, doubtless helped by the fact that their boundaries regularly followed landscape features like rivers and ridges.

This permanence is also highlighted by the relationship between the *dabhach* and the parish. Other than in parts of Caithness and some of the Outer Hebrides, for which information is now entirely absent, across the whole of the survey area of Moray, Ross, Sutherland, and Caithness each Medieval parish (bar one which also contained a three plough land) was comprised of an exact number of *dabhaichean*. The key to understanding this relationship lies in tracking the detached portions of parishes. Across the area of the survey Medieval parishes could possess up to five detached portions of land. In every case these detached portions were either an exact multiple of *dabhaichean*, a single *dabhach*, or an exact fraction of a *dabhach*, indicating an intimate relationship between *dabhach* boundaries and parochial boundaries (Ross 2015, 71-2). Trying to decide which preceded the other is slightly more difficult.

The first scenario is that parishes were created at an unknown point in time and then subsequently divided into *dabhaichean*. This is an entirely logical proposition and something similar has been argued for the units of land assessment in the Northern Isles when they were under Scandinavian rule. Sarah Jane Gibbon has recently investigated the formation of parishes in Orkney in some detail and argued that they date from a twelfth-century ecclesiastic and secular reorganisation of the Orcadian landscape predicated upon the foundation of St Magnus cathedral in Kirkwall. During this reorganisation each Orcadian parish was subsequently divided into a set number of ON *eyrislands* (ouncelands – a fiscal unit for assessing taxation) (Gibbon 2007, 235-50).

However, given the dating of the St Andrews foundation legend and its mention of a *dabhach*, suggesting the same for mainland Scotland would firstly require that parishes across much of the kingdom of the Picts had been formed before c 850. Given the numbers of detached parochial portions this is also quite a messy solution. It either requires that some of the *dabhaichean* being laid out in each parish did not possess sufficient resources and so required lands elsewhere, or someone deciding that a particular parish did not possess a sufficient number of *dabhaichean* and so it was granted others (or fractions of others) elsewhere, often located some distance away from the original parish. Either way, we are looking at many potential lawsuits as pieces of land were taken from one community and given to another in order to satisfy the basic requirements of *dabhaichean* as they were created within each new parish.

The second scenario is more logical. This suggests that *dabhaichean* preceded the formation of parishes and the latter were subsequently superimposed onto a pre-existing *dabhach* pattern of secular assessment. Using this argument, the apparent anomaly of the detached portions disappears because the only reason why some Medieval parishes possessed detached portions of land was because those same detached portions already belonged to the 'scattered' *dabhaichean* in those newly created parishes. Rather than break up pre-existing units of land assessment during the period of parish formation in northern Scotland, whenever that might have been, the detached portions of any *dabhaichean* in a particular parish were also included in that parish. For what it is worth, whenever a northern parish was split into two new parishes during the survey period, the cleavage always occurred along *dabhach* boundaries. For example, when the twenty *dabhach* parish of Tarbat in Easter Ross was divided into the two new parishes of Tarbat and Fearn by the Reformed Church in 1628, each of the two new ecclesiastic divisions received exactly ten *dabhaichean*:

> The bishop and whole diocese agree to the division of the parish of Tarbat into the parishes of Tarbat and Fearn, the tithes [...] for each church to be decided on information from the owners of property there. Each church is to have ten dawaches (considerable tract of land; a small district including several oxgangs) of land. Signed: Mr. Will. Lauder. 1632 Nov. 15 Chanonry (NRS, SP46/129, fo.164r).

Given the clear relationship between the *dabhach* and the parish it is unsurprising that there are also close links between *dabhaichean* and secular units of lordship. Wherever we look across northern Scotland, Medieval lordships were divided into exact numbers of *dabhaichean*, as were thanages. The lordship of Badenoch comprised sixty *dabhaichean*; the lordship of Abernethy (Inverness) thirteen; and the thanage of Cromarty six.

Finally, across the full chronological range of documents relating to *dabhaichean* in northern Scotland, there are various types of service demanded by the crown and lords from these units of land assessment. The first of these burdens spans almost the entire historical period and relates to army service, specifically the widespread European assumption that during hosting each house and its land would produce a warrior (Duncan 1975, 110, 379-80; Taylor 2011, 166-234). The oldest reference to army service and other burdens in Scotland is again found in the Version B of the St Andrews foundation legend, written c 850:

> *Rex uero hunc locum, scilicet Chilrimonith, dedit Deo et Sancto Andree eius apostolo, cum aquis, cum agris, cum pratis, cum pascuis, cum moris, cum nemoribus in elemosinam perpetuo; et tanta libertate illum locum donauit ut illius inhabitatores liberi et quieti semper existerent de exercitu et de operibus castellorum et pontium et de inquietacione omnium secularium exactionum* (Taylor and Márkus 2009, 573).

> And the king [Unuist son of Uurguist, king of the Picts, c 729-61] gave this place, that is Kilrymont, to God and St Andrew his apostle, with waters, with fields, with meadows, with pastures, with muirs, with woods in alms for ever; and he endowed that place with such liberty that its inhabitants will always be free and quit of hosting, and of castle and bridge work, and of the trouble of all secular exactions.

It is entirely possible that this is an accurate record even if it might be a later addition: many other nascent kingdoms in Europe, like Mercia, also exacted similar levies during the eighth century (Stevenson 1914, 689-703). Similar demands to those expressed in the St Andrews foundation legend appear in other royal documents, specifically those from to the respective reigns of Kings Macbethad mac Findlaích (1040-57) and Malcolm IV (1153-65). In these latter cases religious communities were variously freed from the burdens of bridge repair, castles, military service, and hunting (Thomson 1841, 114; Barrow 1960, no 213). Taken together, these later Scottish references again seem very familiar to the *trinoda necessitas* (bridge work, fortress work, and hosting) recorded from the eighth century in Mercia and Kent and later across the whole of the developing Anglo-Saxon kingdoms in England, and the three burdens of bridge work, army service, and watch duty found in the Carolingian Empire (Stevenson 1914, 689-703). Nor was the military service imposed on *dabhaichean* solely limited to fighting men. A 1304 document ordered that every *dabhach* in the lordship of Garmoran (including Knoydart, Moidart, and Ardnamurchan) would furnish a galley of twenty oars, and in 1343 two charters required the recipients to supply ships of twenty-six and twenty oars respectively for *dabhaichean* in Glenelg and Assynt (Bain 1884, no 1633; Megaw 1979, 75; Webster 1982, nos 486 and 487).

But by far the most common burdens imposed on *dabhaichean* were local as they were assessed for secular services and exactions, payable to the lord. One of the most common local services that can be traced concerns carriage service; others included arriage/harriage (the delivery of documents), hunting service (usually four men per *dabhach* for a specified period), road service, harvest service, fuel service (cutting peat), and building service. Interestingly, the evidence shows that local burdens due from each *dabhach* were not automatically exacted each year but could instead be carried-over by the superior lord for future use. This is logical as it would aid long-term demesne planning and allow superior lords to make strategic decisions about the uses to which their local reserves of manpower and the associated burdens might best be put. The final point to make here is that any *dabhach* could be picked up, transported across the North Sea, and put down in a number of other Medieval European countries. The people living there would instantly have recognised the *dabhach* for what it was: a common unit of land assessment imposed by a superior authority as an effective way to assess and raise taxation, and to aid in a state building process.

8.4 The *dabhach* and Fortriu

Almost ten years ago Alex Woolf trashed the mental image Medieval historians possessed about the location of the powerful Pictish kingdom of Fortriu. By marshalling disparate pieces of evidence he effectively argued that it was not based in southern-central Scotland but north of the Mounth in northern Scotland (Woolf 2006, 195-7). The key to this are the *Verturiones* whose name passed into Gaelic as **Foirtrenn* (genitive *Fortrenn*, 'of *Fortriu') and into English as *Waerteras*. Their seventh-century kings rose to eventually dominate both Northern and Southern Pictland and who can forget that Bredei son of Bili, king of Fortriu, 'destroyed' the Orkney Islands in 682 (Mac Airt and Mac Niocaill 1983, 682.4; Fraser 2009, 50)?

The immediate problem is this: although the last mention of Fortriu in the Gaelic Annals dates to 918, and its people survive as a distinct entity in English sources until the late tenth century, historians currently have no means of estimating its territorial extent. This raises a new set of questions. If it is assumed for the sake of argument that the historical kingdom of Fortriu once occupied the whole of north Scotland, by what mechanism did that kingdom subsequently shatter into individual provinces like Caithness, Ross, and Moray before the end of the eleventh century as the regnal and political focus of the kingdom of Alba increasingly shifted southwards? Were these provinces originally named parts of Fortriu? If they were, how did Fortriu disappear without seeming to leave any trace in the place-names of those same areas? Essentially, there is no current way of telling just how far west, south, and east Fortriu may once have extended and how that varied across time.

Fraser has plausibly suggested that by 700 the Pictish kingdom of Atholl might have been the southern part of a diphyletic kingdom of Fortriu with rival 'colleague-kings' in both Atholl and Moray before the rise of Onuist son of Vurguist from the Mearns in 728 to dominate Fortriu and all of the Picts (Fraser 2009, 101-2, 225, 292). But this still leaves unclear the status of regions like Mar, Banff, Buchan, and Kincardine and their position in relation to the northern kingdom of the Verturiones. Nevertheless, given what is currently known about Fortriu and its location in north Britain, together with the almost complete population of that same part of north Britain by the *dabhach*, it is now surely worth exploring in greater depth the idea that the *dabhach* was the unit of land assessment employed by the rulers of Fortriu as a fairly standard European means of calculating military service and raising taxation across the lands under their authority (Ross 2015, 198).

Although a second survey of *dabhaichean*, this time for Banff, Buchan, Aberdeenshire, Mar, the Mearns, Angus, Atholl, and Fife, has begun it is already reasonably safe to state that there are some glaringly obvious differences between some of these areas and northern Scotland. Only Mar (so far) seemingly replicates the longevity of *dabhaichean* found further north. Most important is the fact that *dabhaichean* remain in use as viable units of land assessment far longer in the north than elsewhere in Scotland, even though there is no obvious landscape-related or climatic reason to explain this discrepancy. Again at a regional level, while there are *dabhaichean* present in Atholl they seem to form distinct clusters at key geographic points (like the southern end of Glen Tilt or the junction of the Rivers Tay and Tummel) rather than being omni-present across the entire landscape. What exactly these patterns might mean is also worth investigating. It might even be possible to contextualize them using the ritual murder of Talorcan, the Pictish king of Atholl, by the effective ruler of Fortriu in 739, which may have been followed by the absorption of Atholl into the Verturian kingdom of the Picts (Mac Airt and Mac Niocaill 1983, 739.7; Fraser 2009, 100-3).

Perhaps odder is the fact that while the *dabhaichean* of Braemar and Invercauld (in Mar) stretched southwards to Cairnwell and the summit of Glas Maol at 1068m, *dabhaichean* seem to be absent from large parts of the landscape on the southern side of the Cairnwell watershed. One interpretation might be that this is evidence of a political boundary but there are other possible solutions worth exploring because *dabhaichean* do occasionally appear elsewhere in Perthshire. Equally, how can the almost total absence of *dabhaichean* from Fife, Strathearn and Menteith be explained away, bearing in mind the small and solitary cluster of four *dabhaichean* in the Forth Valley that likely comprised the Medieval parish of Tillicoultry (RMS II 1984, no 3641). Evaluating and then interpreting the patterns of *dabhaichean* in the area of this second survey will likely lead to many more new insights.

What is clear is that the *dabhach* is no longer a 'Pictish problem'. By opening both it, and the patterns it created across so many different Pictish landscapes to wider contextualization across Europe and the North Atlantic, many more answers to the hitherto intractable puzzle of the Medieval state building process in North Britain will likely become apparent. More research of this type will also eventually allow us to look backwards in time and question why and how some areas of early Medieval settlement achieved pre-eminence over their neighbours by being chosen to lend their names to these new units of Pictish land assessment.

Documentary sources

National Records of Scotland (NRS).

NRS, GD44/10/10, Gordon Castle Muniments. Titles to Land: Lands in Lordship of Badenoch, Inverness-shire and in Barony of Kincardine, Inverness-shire, 1338-1776.

NRS, GD44/41/22/2, Gordon Castle Muniments. Arguiles Papers, 1640-86.

NRS, RS38/3/348, Particular Register of Sasines etc for Inverness, Ross, Sutherland and Cromarty: Second Series, 4 Aug 1665-4 Mar 1670.

NRS, RS37/5, Particular Register of Sasines etc for Inverness, Ross, Sutherland and Cromarty: First Series, 11 Apr 1632-30 Nov 1636.

NRS, SP46, State Papers.

NRS, GD84/1/32/5, Papers of the Mackay Family, Lords Reay, 1714.

References

Bain, G 1884 *Calendar of Documents Relating to Scotland* 5 vols. Edinburgh: Neill and Company.

Baker, J and Brookes, S 2013 'Governance at the Anglo-Scandinavian interface: hundredal organization in the southern Danelaw', *Journal of the North Atlantic* Special Volume 5, 76-95.

Bangor-Jones, M 1986 'Land assessments and settlement history in Sutherland and Easter Ross', *in* Baldwin, J R (ed) *Firthlands of Ross and Sutherland*, 153-68. Edinburgh: The Scottish Society for Northern Studies.

Barrow, G W S 1960 *Regesta Regum Scottorum I: The Acts of Malcolm IV*. Edinburgh: Edinburgh University Press.

Barrow, G W S 1962 'Rural settlement in central and eastern Scotland: the Medieval evidence', *Scottish Studies* 6, 123-44.

Broun, D 2008 'The property records in the Book of Deer as a source for early Scottish society', *in* Forsyth, K (ed) *Studies on the Book of Deer*, 313-62. Bodmin: Four Courts Press.

Caird, J B 1980 'The reshaped agricultural landscape', *in* Parry and Slater, 203-22.

Dodgshon, R A 1980 'Medieval settlement and colonisation', *in* Parry and Slater, 45-68.

Driscoll, S T, Geddes J and Hall, M A (eds) 2011 *Pictish progress: new studies on northern Britain in the Early Middle Ages*. Leiden: Brill.

Duncan, A A M 1975 *Scotland: the making of the kingdom*. Edinburgh: Oliver and Boyd.

Easson, A R 1986 'Systems of land assessment in Scotland before 1400', unpublished PhD thesis, University of Edinburgh.

Elder-Levie, W 1931 'The Scottish Davach or Dauch', *Scottish Gaelic Studies* 3(2), 99-110.

Escalona, J 2006 'Mapping scale change: hierarchization and fission in Castilian rural communities during the tenth and eleventh centuries', *in* Davies, W, Halsall, G and Reynolds, A (eds) *People and space in the Middle Ages, 300-1300*, 143-66. Turnhout: Brepols.

Fraser, J 2009 *From Caledonia to Pictland. Scotland to 795*. Edinburgh: Edinburgh University Press.

Gibbon, S J 2007 'Medieval parish formation in Orkney', *in* Ballin Smith, B, Taylor, S and Williams, G (eds) *West over sea: studies in Scandinavian sea-borne expansion and settlement before 1300: a festschrift in honour of Dr Barbara E Crawford*, 235-50. Leiden: Brill.

Hobæk, H 2013 'Tracing Medieval administrative systems: Hardanger, Western Norway', *Journal of the North Atlantic* Special Volume 5, 64-75.

Holm, O 2010 'The integration of Härjedalen into the Norwegian kingdom', *in* Imsen, 229-51.

Imsen, S (ed) 2010 *The Norwegian domination and the Norse world c1100-c1400*. Trondheim: Tapir Academic Press.

Imsen, S (ed) 2011 *Taxes, tributes and tributary lands in the making of the Scandinavian kingdoms in the Middle Ages*. Trondheim: Tapir Academic Press.

Jackson, K H 1972 *The Gaelic notes in the Book of Deer*. Cambridge: Cambridge University Press.

Lindkvist, T 2010 'The making of a Greater Sweden', *in* Imsen, 251-61.

Lindkvist, T 2011 'Taxation systems in Medieval Sweden', *in* Imsen, 265-78.

Line, P 2007 *Kingship and state formation in Sweden, 1130-1290*. Leiden: Brill.

Mac Airt, S and Mac Niocaill, G (ed and trans) 1983 *The Annals of Ulster (to* AD *1131)*. Dublin: Dublin Institute for Advanced Studies.

Megaw, B 1979 'Notes on Pennyland and *Dabhach* in south-western Scotland', *Scottish Studies* 23, 75-7.

Ødegaard, M 2013 'State formation, administrative areas and *Thing* sites in the Borgarthing law province, southeast Norway', *Journal of the North Atlantic* Special Volume 5, 42-63.

Parry, M L and Slater, T R (eds) *The making of the Scottish countryside*. Trowbridge: Croom Helm.

Pennant, T 1998 *A tour in Scotland and voyage to the Hebrides 1772*. Edinburgh: Birlinn.

Raven, J 2005 'Medieval landscapes and lordship in South Uist', unpublished PhD thesis, University of Glasgow.

Robertson, E W 1862 *Scotland under her early kings* 2 vols. Edinburgh: Edmonston and Douglas.

Ross, A 2006 'The *Dabhach* in Moray: a new look at an old tub', *in* Woolf, A (ed) *Landscape and environment*, 57-74. St Andrews: Committee for Dark Age Studies.

Ross, A 2015 *Land assessment and lordship in Medieval northern Scotland*. Turnhout: Brepols.

Sonnlechner, C 2004 'The establishment of new units of production in Carolingian times: making Early Medieval sources relevant for environmental history', *Viator* 35, 21-37.

Stevenson, W H 1914 '*Trinodas necessitas*', *English Historical Review* 29, 689-703.

Štih, P 2010 *The Middle Ages between the eastern Alps and the northern Adriatic*. Leiden: Brill.

Taylor, A 2011 'Common burdens in the *Regnum Scottorum*: the evidence of charter diplomatic' *in* Broun, D (ed) *The reality behind charter diplomatic in Anglo-Norman Britain: studies by Broun, Dauvit, Davies, John Reuben, Sharpe, Richard, and Taylor, Alice*, 166-234. Glasgow: Centre for Scottish and Celtic Studies.

Taylor, S with Márkus, G 2009 *The place-names of Fife*. Vol. iii, Donington: Shaun Tyas.

Thomson, T 1841 *Liber Cartarum Prioratus Sancti Andree in Scotia, E Registro Ipso In Archivis Baronum De Panmure Hodie Asservato*. Edinburgh: Bannatyne Club.

Vésteinsson, O 2006 'Communities of dispersed settlements: social organisation at the ground level in tenth- to thirteenth-century Iceland', *in* Davies, Halsall and Reynolds, 87-114.

Wainwright F T (ed) 1955 *The problem of the Picts*. Edinburgh: Thomas Nelson and Sons.

Winchester, A J 1987 *Landscape and society in Medieval Cumbria*. Edinburgh: John Donald.

Webster, B 1982 *Regesta Regum Scottorum* VI: *The Acts of David II*. Edinburgh: Edinburgh University Press.

Williams, G 2004 'Land assessment and the silver economy of Norse Scotland', *in* Williams, G and Bibire, P (eds) *Sagas, saints and settlements*, 65-104. Leiden: Brill.

Woolf, A 2006 'Dún Nechtain, Fortriu and the Geography of the Picts', *Scottish Historical Review* 85, 182-201.

9

Ideas of origins and ethnicity in Early Medieval Scotland

Nicholas Evans

In all societies of the world, including those of Early Medieval Scotland, the preservation, creation and transmission of accounts of the past are important activities, whether it takes place in an oral or written context, whether perceptions are dominated by recent events or distant history. Early history may not seem obviously important, but this is because our understanding of the remote past is often more deeply embedded in our identity, being the unacknowledged foundation upon which perceptions of more recent events are constructed. The representation of history is not static, but fluid. It changes as societies develop, because people focus on and enhance more relevant aspects and discard or downplay elements which are no longer so pertinent or conflict with dominant political and social narratives.

This has important consequences, because texts about the past and our interpretations of them have often formed one basis for our understanding of the origins of Europe's peoples and 'nations' (Geary 2002, 1-40, 155-74). Historical accounts are thought to reflect more the perceptions, aspirations and nature of societies at the time of writing than the eras they are describing (Fraser 2009, 1-6). Some current scholarship would go as far as to regard a person's ethnic identity as largely a matter of choice, with the result that such identities can be formed relatively rapidly by people of disparate backgrounds, though the ability to become part of or leave a group can be overstated (Heather 2009, 12-28). What is clear is that viewing ethnic groups as entities with unchanging defining characteristics is mistaken, even if particular facets of an ethnic group are focussed on as markers of membership.

However, that does not negate the usefulness of accounts of the early history of these groups. Susan Reynolds (1983) has argued that such texts have their own significance, reflecting the existence of political communities, such as a kingdom, but also sometimes regional or local units with separate administrative identities because they had their own leaders, assemblies or laws. When such a political community was created, so was an account creating a single origin for it, while obsolete political units, often identified with particular ethnic groups, faded into obscurity or were actively

in: Blackwell, A.E. (ed.) 2019: *Scotland in Early Medieval Europe*, Leiden: Sidestone Press, pp. 149-160.

rejected. Especially after AD 900, when regnal administrative authority was growing, the political community in question was usually also a kingdom, regarded as the default European type of government in the Medieval period. However, where local or regional autonomy was strong, or where separate institutions and laws remained, for instance in areas of the Carolingian empire such as Bavaria, Alemannia (in south-west Germany and northern Switzerland), and Lombardic Italy, different ethnic identities could persist for centuries, even after earlier kingdoms were subsumed into a larger polity (Reynolds 1997, 250, 258-302; Geary 2002, 151-5). There was, therefore, no simple correlation of kingdoms and peoples, since it depended to a considerable extent on the nature of the kingdom, although Reynolds (1983, 318-3) has suggested that from the tenth century onwards more integrated realms in legal and political terms tended to result in the replacement of regional origin accounts with single accounts for larger kingdoms. Nevertheless, it is likely that the overall correspondence of origin legends with kingdoms is also found earlier than this, since new regimes created impressive backgrounds for themselves in preceding centuries (Geary 2002, 77-9, 108, 117), so it is legitimate to consider origin accounts for particular peoples throughout the Early Medieval period.

In addition, the variations in these texts could represent not only the different circumstances of each people and kingdom, but also patterns of Medieval ethnic thought. The current dominant view among scholars is that Medieval people were not racist in the sense that ancestry – biological descent from the same source – and physical attributes (such as skin or hair colour) were not regarded as the only determinants of ethnic group membership. Descent, especially directly from an important male ancestor, was often an important facet, but often outsiders could become part of another ethnic group, especially wealthy and powerful people (for instance, Geary 2002, 126, 137). Language, customs, and laws were also considered significant (Reynolds 1997, 254-9; Bartlett 2001, 45, 47-54; Geary 2002, 153-5), while the environment was sometimes thought to shape the personality of a people (Bartlett 2001, 45-7). Whether this was also the case in Early Medieval northern Britain has not attracted much discussion to date. If historical texts, such as origin-legends and king-lists, reflected perceptions of or aspirations for current societies, then some of the variation should relate to what was thought to matter in defining particular groups.

We are fortunate to have a number of texts of this type relating to the ethnic groups and kingdoms of Early Medieval Scotland – the Picts, Gaels, Britons, the Bernicians of Anglo-Saxon Northumbria, and Scandinavians – which allow us to study how people regarded themselves. How representative these are of what once existed is difficult to know. Most Early Medieval texts from northern Britain no longer survive (Hughes 1980; Forsyth 1998), and what remains is a selection, comprising works of interest to outsiders like Bede, or relevant in support of various secular and ecclesiastical statements later in Scotland (Evans 2011, 59-61). Therefore, any analysis of our sources for northern Britain should be somewhat tentative, although we can gain assistance from a comparative methodology, considering wider British, Gaelic and English and continental contexts.

What does survive indicates that ethnicity was indeed an important means of distinguishing people in Britain and Ireland in historical texts, as is indicated by the histories of the period, such as Bede's *Ecclesiastical History of the English People*

(Colgrave and Mynors 1969) and the Welsh *Historia Brittonum* (Morris 1980), which tend to divide people foremost by ethnicity. The evidence early historical texts provide for customs, legal systems, and the supposed character of the different peoples of northern Britain is outwith the scope of this study, although these sources do sometimes provide important evidence relating to these aspects of identity (see Pohl 1997; 1998 for broader studies; Fraser 2009, 375-9, for comments on Pictish identity). What follows focuses on the significance of ancestry and language. It avoids the issue of the role of Christianity, which scholars are increasingly arguing had an important role for identity formation in Ireland (Flanagan 2010, 106-8) and among the Anglo-Saxons (Howe 1989), and may have shaped the whole ethnic framework of the Middle Ages (Pohl 2013).

The ethnic groups of northern Britain have accounts of origins which vary considerably but follow models found across Europe. Reynolds (1983, 375-9) has grouped the origin-legends of Medieval Christian Europe into four main groups: those tracing origins back to classical characters and groups, particularly the Trojans; those with connections to Biblical, usually Old Testament, figures; those based on the 'Table of Nations', a sixth-century Byzantine or Ostrogothic Italian text which listed peoples of Europe descended from three sons of a certain Alaneus; and finally explanations based on the idea of migration from a Germanic homeland.

By the time of *Historia Brittonum* (written in 829 or 830), there were alternative origins for the Britons (Dumville, 1994). One view was that they derived from Brutus, a descendant of Aeneas who left the Trojan colony in Italy as an exile and came to Britain. Another, based on the 'Table of Nations', made them brother peoples of the Franks, Romans and Alemans, but with Biblical ancestry. The idea of Trojan ancestry may be reflected in the genealogy of the Britons of Strathclyde, found in Harley MS 3859 (dating from c 1100, but with contents compiled 950 x 88), which traces the ancestry of the mid-late ninth-century Rhun, son of Arthgal. According to this genealogy (Bartrum 1966, 10), their earliest ancestor was a certain *Confer*, to whom a note was added which was probably intended to mean that he came from Litau, *Latium* around Rome, and was linked to *mor meton*, the 'middle sea', meaning the Mediterranean (Evans 2008, 28, n 99). This could potentially be related to Bede's statement that, according to tradition, the Britons came to Britain from Armorica in north-west France, since the word *Litau* could also mean Brittany, as well as the Continent more generally (Koch 1991, 21), but the genealogy seems to prefer a more Mediterranean, perhaps classical, background for the Strathclyders. This would be consistent with the self-perception that they were descendants of the Romano-Britons, who also claimed ancestry from the Trojan settlers in *Latium* who later founded Rome. Therefore, this supports the view that the northern Britons had an identity formed in distinction to their neighbours, especially the Picts, who had remained unconquered by the Romans (Fraser 2009, 47-9).

For the rulers of Bernicia and Orkney, their ancestry was in the Germanic-speaking regions of Europe. The earls of Orkney were traced back to the earls of Møre in Norway, and earlier to the far north of Scandinavia, although it is difficult to know how many elements of these accounts date to before 1100, rather than reflecting later concerns (Crawford 2013, 80-7, 90-9). The Bernicians, whose territory extended from the River Tees to the Firth of Forth, traced descent from their dynastic founder Ida who supposedly settled at Bamburgh in the mid-sixth century. Bede stated that the Northumbrians were Angles, a group he thought came from the land of *Angelus* (Colgrave and Mynors 1969, 50-1). Moreover, Northumbrian genealogies continue beyond Ida back to Woden, ancestor of most Anglo-Saxon dynasties, although in the Anglo-Saxon Chronicle the line went back further to Geat ('God') (Whitelock 1979, 156). Presumably these figures were explained as great ancestors turned into gods by pagans. The importance of ancestry is indicated by the Northumbrian succession, even after the kingship was contested between the royal lines of Bernicia and Deira in the seventh century (Yorke 1990, 74-81). In the eighth century, when multiple kindreds contested the kingship, often with doubtful claims to royal ancestry, a genealogical linkage to the Ida dynasty was still necessary to strengthen claims to power (ibid, 86-94).

For the Gaels we have genealogies for a number of kindreds in Dál Riata, mainly in the texts *Cethrí Prímchenéla Dáil Riata* (Dumville 2000) and *Míniugud Senchusa Fher nAlban* (Bannerman 1974, 27-156; Dumville 2002), covering more than just the dominant groups of this region. We have less evidence in the tenth and eleventh centuries for the kingdom of Alba, the Gaelic successor to the Pictish overkingship. However, genealogies do exist for the dominant royal line descended from Cináed mac Ailpín (842/3-76), for territories in Alba, linking them to the royal kindred, and for the eleventh-century rulers of Moray (Broun 1999, 173-93; Woolf 2007, 226-8). All these genealogies trace ancestry back to the Dál Riata, and through them back to Ireland. The Irish portrayed themselves as migrants who arrived from Spain in the ancient period, having previously travelled in the Middle East, Egypt, south-eastern Europe, and 'Scythia', in accounts based substantially on Biblical precedents and earlier writers like Isidore of Seville (Carey 1994). The justification of the status of particular groups in Alba through familial connections going back to the deep past suggests that ancestry continued to be significant in Gaelic society in northern Britain after 900, and that Irish origins were still desirable.

In contrast, no genealogies of the Picts survive, a fact that could be connected with the lack of father-to-son succession at least before 730, a feature of kingship also found in Visigothic Spain (Evans 2008, 14-43). A potential explanation is that Pictish genealogies were not copied later due to cultural, linguistic and political shifts. For instance, no genealogy survives for the dynasty of Onuist son of Uurguist (732-61) which broke the previous succession system (Evans 2008, 43-7) and dominated the Pictish over-kingship from 732 to 839 (Broun 2000). However, while the lack of evidence renders any inferences from absence highly tentative, the general lack of stated genealogical connections to predecessors, even in the pre-Christian section of the Pictish king-lists (apart from implicit fraternal relationship when brothers succeeded each other) where we might expect ideological statements, is perhaps significant. In other Early Medieval king-lists (for instance, for the kingships of Leinster and Tara in Ireland, see Charles-Edwards 2000, 454-8, 482-7, 491-4, 499-507) we sometimes can discern processes of inclusion and exclusion of kings so that particular dynasties came to be depicted as dominating kingdoms more than they did in reality. Does the seeming lack of Pictish genealogical interest support the idea that dynastic ancestry was not such an important element for the Pictish overkingship?

Instead of statements of dynastic ancestry, what we have are expressions of regnal continuity from the deep ancient past, back to the founder, Cruithne (the Gaelic for 'Pict') son of Cinge. Moreover, in the ninth-century longer Pictish king-list, the territorial, rather than dynastic, aspect of the kingship was increasingly stressed. An addition to the longer king-list (probably made 862 x 876) explained that after Cruithne took the land of the Picts, his seven sons, all of whom had the names of territories, ruled in succession to each other before being followed by seemingly unrelated kings (Anderson 2011, 245; Broun 2007, 75-9). A similar account can be found in Wales, where the sons of the ancestral figure Cunedda had names of regions, and each were the ancestors of Gwynedd's royal and local rulers (Morris 1980, 37, 79; Bartrum 1966, 9-13). Such accounts legitimised situations in which a number of territories or peoples were being brought under the control of a single kingdom by stressing the ancientness and continuity of the larger unit in spite of the existence of constituent, and perhaps once independent, parts. However, unlike the Gwynedd account, the Pictish king-list particularly focussed on the territorial dimension by avoiding genealogical connections with later dynasties. The Pictish king-list also does not provide comprehensive coverage of the kingdom's lands (Broun 2007, 78-9), but the sons still symbolically denote the wider Pictish realm. This is evidence for the idea, continued in the successor kingdom of Alba, that the Pictish kingdom comprised all of Britain from the Firth of Forth to Caithness (Broun 2007, 79-80). For the Picts, then, the evidence we do have indicates that the over-kingship did not employ dynastic ancestry in the same way as elsewhere in northern Britain.

Accounts of early history, therefore, could indicate that ancestry was significant for royal dynasties in northern Britain among the Gaels, Anglo-Saxons and maybe Britons, but to a lesser extent for the Pictish overkingship. While we cannot be sure what the majority of people regarded as intrinsic to their identity, historical texts usually focused on the elite as the heart of an ethnic group or kindred. The creation and destruction of peoples was primarily explained in terms of elite groups in society. For example, the disappearance of the Picts came to be explained through the idea that Cináed mac Ailpín undertook a massacre of the Pictish nobility at Scone (Anderson 1922 vol I, 273-4; Anderson 2011, 195-8). This is a common European phenomenon, for instance found in the slaughter of Britons in *Historia Brittonum* by the Anglo-Saxon Hengest and Horsa (Morris 1980, 32, 72-3). While it would be a mistake to infer from this that ethnic identity was thought to reside solely in the upper echelons, in a hierarchical society they were certainly regarded as pivotal. The nobility acted as representatives for all non-ecclesiastical people in a locality (Reynolds 1997, 302-5), so it would be natural to link royal and aristocratic kindreds closely to ethnicity.

That ancestry was important does not mean, however, that to be properly Gaelic, British, Pictish or English you needed to be of 'pure' stock, with descent solely from a single ethnic group. Agnatic unilineal ancestry (that is, directly back in the male line) was usually key to a person's familial and ethnic identity (except perhaps among the Picts), but connections with other peoples, often through the female line, could also be significant enough to deserve comment. Our surviving sources provide a number of instances where there was ethnic inter-marriage, with beneficial or at least no obvious negative connotations. For instance, *Míniugud Senchusa Fher nAlban* states that a member of Cenél nÓenguso had a Pictish mother (Dumville 2002, 202), and it can inferred that the Pictish royal dynasty in the seventh century inter-married with the royal dynasties of Bernicia and Dumbarton Rock (Evans 2008, 26, 27). In the mid-tenth century St Cathroe not only had a connection with the ruling dynasty of Alba where he originated, but also had royal relatives in Strathclyde and Scandinavian Northumbria (Dumville 2001). As with modern royal families, such wide dynastic connections presumably increased Cathroe's prestige, giving him an international dimension.

Moreover, according to Bede's account of the Pictish settlement in Britain (Colgrave and Mynors 1969, 16-19), the Early Medieval Picts were the product of inter-marriage between Pictish men, who had neglected to bring along anyone of the opposite sex on their travels, and Gaelic women from Ireland. Debate about this origin legend has centred on whether Bede's statement implies that Pictish royal succession went through the female line when the issue was in doubt. This has been argued (for instance, Anderson 2011, 165-78, 191-6; Miller 1982; see Evans 2008, 1, for lists) to describe a practice of Pictish matrilineal succession; that while only men could rule the Pictish over-kingdom, legitimacy was derived from an unbroken line of women of the royal dynasty (therefore, ruling out a claim based on being the son of a king's daughter). As it stands, there are plausible grounds for arguing (Woolf 1998; Ross 1999) that the source of Bede's account was a response to a particular need to legitimise Pictish kings (Bridei and Nectan, sons of Derilei) in the late seventh and early eighth centuries who had claims through their mother's line. Moreover, the later Gaelic accounts which contain more explicit statements of Pictish matrilineal succession could plausibly have developed Bede's account, rather than being independent evidence. On the other hand, when the evidence for succession to the Pictish over-kingship is analysed (Evans 2008), the result does not rule out matrilineal practice before the 730s, although after then patrilineal ancestry becomes a significant factor in determining who became king.

Further study of this issue is required, but we can still draw one relevant conclusion from Bede's text, in addition to inferring that there was a Pictish royal dynasty. Since Bede probably used a Pictish source, it would seem unlikely that the Picts were considered any less Pictish or worthy as a result of the ancient inter-marriage between Picts and Gaels, although it did mean that Gaels could legitimately be regarded as part of their society. The overall picture is that while common descent was significant for ethnic groups in northern Britain, they were open to inter-marriage with incomers without the same ancestry. It was the quality of the ancestors in terms of status and character, rather than their purity of descent, which was most important.

One notable characteristic of ethnicity in Early Medieval Britain and Ireland is that, when compared to the rest of Christian Europe, it displays less correspondence with kingdoms. Among the Britons and Gaels, as well as perhaps the Picts, and the English before the tenth century, there were multiple kingdoms in the areas of each ethnic group, usually with structures of overlordship defining loose and changeable relationships between kings. Political alliances could cross ethnic boundaries, as James Fraser (2005) has suggested for the Gaelic Cenél Comgaill and the British kingdom of Dumbarton Rock in the seventh century. Language, and probably shared cultural and societal norms, such as legal structures, which were shared by the inhabitants of a number of kingdoms, meant that 'British', 'Gaelic', and 'English' supra-regnal identities could co-exist with a strong loyalty to a particular kingdom, as well as other secular and ecclesiastical local, kindred and familial connections.

These broader ethnic identities could form the ideological basis for wider hegemonies, promoted in titles, which often reflected aspirations rather than practical reality, as with the statement added in 1005 to the Book of Armagh proclaiming Brian mac Cennétig, king of Munster and overlord of Ireland, as *imperator Scottorum*, 'emperor of the Gaels' (Woolf 2007, 225). In some cases, the idea of a common identity (for instance, of the Picts or English) could became a force for regnal unity after military expansion had taken place, even if the concept had originally been artificial. However, in this period, kings of such polities could not necessarily impose a common culture and identity on their realms, even if this was desired; for example, many of Cornwall's inhabitants remained speakers of Cornish (a Brittonic language close to Breton and Welsh) into the modern era, long after its conquest by the kingdom of Wessex in the ninth century (Charles-Edwards 2013, 341-2), and the inhabitants of the kingdom of the Scots were still divided frequently in documents into its constituent peoples and territories into the thirteenth century (Broun 2007, 7-11, 126-7).

In what became Scotland, the ethnic situation was particularly complex, containing all the main ethnic groups of the British Isles. We only have fragmentary evidence for how different groups co-existed inside kingdoms. Thomas Charles-Edwards (2008, 185-8) has argued that in Pictland in the eighth and ninth centuries, and in twelfth- and thirteenth-century Alba, the existence of multiple languages in a kingdom was probably regarded as unproblematic, but that in Alba from the tenth century the demise of the Pictish language indicates desire for a polity with a single language and presumably ethnic identity. This theory would imply that language was not so significant for identity in periods when diversity was more in favour (or when the imposition of a single language or culture was not practical politically), such as the Pictish era. As we have seen, Gaels were significant protagonists in the Pictish settlement tale, and their influence was even reflected in the use of the Gaelic word Cruithne for the Picts' ancestor figure. In another context, the division of Anglo-Saxon Bernicia into the kingdoms of the Scots and English after a considerable period in which local earls tried to prevent outside interference indicates that shared language and maybe culture was not necessarily the prime determinant of loyalty (Aird 2010).

The part of Bernicia in Alba – the Lothians and the Borders – remained English for centuries after its incorporation, presumably because significant aspects of its pre-existing culture remained. Nevertheless, after their dynasties disappeared the origin accounts of the kingdoms of Bernicia and also Strathclyde ceased to be preserved in manuscripts in Scotland. Elements of their history could be utilised for contemporary purposes, as was the case when the bishops of Glasgow in the twelfth century stressed their British identity in order to gain special status within the Church (Broun 2007, 124-57), but the origin accounts of kingdoms no longer served an important contemporary purpose.

In terms of the transition from Pictland to Alba (and Scotia), it is likely that processes of Gaelicisation came to a climax in the late ninth and early tenth centuries due to Scandinavian pressure and conquest, resulting in the replacement of Pictish language and identity with a Gaelic one (cf Woolf 2007). This was accompanied by new names for the kingdom: Gaelic *Alba*, Latin *Albania* (and later *Scotia*, Old English *Scottas* for the people from the 920s), with the inhabitants called *Goídil* ('Gaels') and *Albanaig* in Gaelic, and *Scotti* in Latin (Broun 2007, 80-7; Charles-Edwards 2008, 170-1). However, the idea of Alba did not lead to the creation of a completely new, separate, ethnic identity.

A potential ancestor figure, *Albanus*, included after 829/30 in *Historia Brittonum* had been adopted by the late eleventh century in the poem *Duan Albanach* (Jackson 1957, 129) as the first settler in Britain from whom the kingdom of Alba was named, but not as the ancestor of the kings or people since Gaelic origins were preferred (Evans 2015). Given the dominance of the Gaelic language in Alba, cultural connections with Ireland, and pre-existing historical texts for Dál Riata, Gaelic ancestry presumably had a strong plausability and resonance which was not possible to ignore or supplant.

Nevertheless, the Picts retained a significant place in perceptions of Alba up to the late eleventh century, since Pictish origin accounts continued to be copied and in one case the longer king-list was updated to include the kings of Alba up to the contemporary reign of Máel Coluim III (1058-93). However, these origin accounts usually state that the Gaels replaced the Picts or took their land, so since the version of the king-list which continues to Máel Coluim III does not provide a statement that he was a Pict, it may simply indicate that his kingdom of Alba was considered the successor of the Pictish realm. Therefore, the interest in the Picts in this later period was not based on perceived ethnic descent from them, but on the continuity of the kingdom and its territory (Broun 2007, 54-61). In addition, the origins of some important ecclesiastical centres, such as St Andrews and Abernethy, was situated temporally in reigns of particular Pictish kings found in texts such as the Pictish king-lists, providing a further reason to copy such documents (Evans 2011, 60-1). Less certain written evidence that Alba's royal centres were regarded as having Pictish origins may have been another factor. The settlement accounts of the Picts and Dál Riata do not mention the establishment of particular strongholds, but the implication of the 'Treachery of Scone' tale is that that centre at least was thought to have existed before Cináed mac Ailpín's destruction of the Picts. The late tenth-century continental 'Life of Cathroe' (Dumville 2001) implies anachronistically that the centre of *Bellathor*, as well as Iona and *Rigmonadh* (St Andrews), was already in existence when the Gaels arrived in Britain. The Picts were no longer ancestors, but they were still significant as founders.

Overall, the evidence from Early Medieval Scotland supports to some extent Reynolds's theory that origin accounts correspond to contemporary kingdoms, since these accounts focus mainly on ruling dynasties and polities. However, these texts also placed the community of the realm in the context of wider ethnic groups usually not encompassed by single kingdoms. These accounts produced and reflected affinities existing between the inhabitants of Scotland and peoples throughout the Insular world in Britain, Ireland and Brittonic-speaking Brittany. The explanation for the continued significance of these wider identities, even after the creation and expansion of the kingship of Alba could potentially be that cultural and social practices, including common legal and poetic traditions, provided connections which bound speakers of particular languages together. However, while these broader ethnic groups had importance, and ancestry was generally significant for legitimising rule, membership did not exclude the inclusion of outsiders of suitable standing, nor prevent loyalties and alliances being formed with elites from other ethnic groups. Over time, as Alba incorporated the polities of earlier peoples, the origin accounts of extinct dynasties faded from memory, but the ethnic identities of the regions of Scotland remained in the consciousness, for the kingdom remained for centuries a diverse entity in many respect with institutions and territories traced back to the Early Medieval era.

References

Aird, W M 2010 'Northumbria and the making of the kingdom of the English', *in* Tsurushima, H (ed) *Nations in Medieval Britain*, 45-60. Donington: Shaun Tyas.

Anderson, A O 1922 *Early sources of Scottish history.* Vol 1; Edinburgh: Oliver and Boyd.

Anderson, M O 2011 *Kings and kingship in early Scotland.* Edinburgh: John Donald (reprint of 1980 second edition).

Bannerman, J 1974 *Studies in the history of Dalriada.* Edinburgh: Scottish Academic Press.

Bartlett, R 2001 (Winter) 'Medieval and Modern concepts of race and ethnicity', *Journal of Medieval and Early Modern Studies* 31.1, 39-56.

Bartrum, P 1966, *Early Welsh genealogical tracts.* Cardiff: University of Wales Press.

Broun, D 1999 *The Irish identity of the Kingdom of the Scots in the twelfth and thirteenth centuries.* Woodbridge: Boydell.

Broun, D 2000 'The seven kingdoms in *De situ Albanie*: a record of Pictish political geography or imaginary map of ancient Alba?', *in* Cowan, E J and McDonald, R A (eds) *Alba. Celtic Scotland in the Medieval era*, 24-42. East Linton: Tuckwell Press.

Broun, D 2007, *Scottish independence and the idea of Britain from the Picts to Alexander III.* Edinburgh: Edinburgh University Press.

Carey, J 1994 *The Irish national origin-legend: synthetic pseudohistory.* Cambridge: Department of Anglo-Saxon, Norse and Celtic, University of Cambridge (Quiggin Pamphlet).

Charles-Edwards, T M 2000 *Early Christian Ireland.* Cambridge: Cambridge University Press.

Charles-Edwards, T M 2008 'Picts and Scots. A review of Alex Woolf, *From Pictland to Alba 789-1070*', *The Innes Review* 59, 168-88.

Charles-Edwards, T M 2013 *Wales and the Britons 350-1064.* Oxford: Oxford University Press.

Colgrave, B and Mynors, R A B (eds and trans) 1969 *Bede's ecclesiastical history of the English people.* Oxford: Clarendon Press.

Crawford, B E 2013 *The northern earldoms. Orkney and Caithness from* AD *870 to 1470.* Edinburgh: John Donald.

Dumville, D N 1994 '*Historia Brittonum*: an Insular history from the Carolingian age', *in* Scharer, A and Scheibelreiter, G (eds) *Historiographie im frühen Mittelalter*, 406-34. Wien: R Oldenbourg.

Dumville, D N 2000 '*Cethri prímchenéla Dáil Riata*', *Scottish Gaelic Studies* 20, 170-91.

Dumville, D N 2001 'St Cathróe of Metz and the hagiography of exoticism', *in* Carey, J, Herbert, M and Ó Riain, P (eds) *Studies in Irish hagiography. Saints and scholars*, 172-88. Dublin: Four Courts.

Dumville, D N 2002 'Ireland and north Britain in the earlier Middle Ages: contexts for *Míniugud Senchasa Fher nAlban*', *in* Ó Baoill, C and McGuire, N R (eds) *Rannsachadh na Gàidhlig 2000*, 185-211. Aberdeen: Clò Gaidhealach.

Evans, N 2008 'Royal succession and kingship among the Picts', *The Innes Review* 59, 1-48.

Evans, N 2011 'Ideology, literacy, and matriliny: approaches to Medieval texts on the Pictish past', *in* Driscoll, S T, Hall, M, and Geddes, J (eds) *Pictish progress. New studies on northern Britain in the Early Middle Ages*, 45-65. Leiden: Brill.

Evans, N J 2015 'Cultural contacts and ethnic origins in Viking Age Wales and Northern Britain: the case of Albanus, Britain's first inhabitant and Scottish ancestor', *Journal of Medieval History* 41:2 (June), 131-54.

Flanagan, M-T 2010 'Strategies of distinction: defining nations in Medieval Ireland', *in* Tsurushima, H (ed) *Nations in Medieval Britain*, 104-20. Donington: Shaun Tyas.

Forsyth, K 1998 'Literacy in Pictland', *in* Pryce, H (ed) *Literacy in Celtic societies*, 39-61. Cambridge: Cambridge University Press.

Fraser, J E 2005 'Strangers on the Clyde: Cenél Comgaill, Clyde Rock and the bishops of Kingarth', *The Innes Review* 56, 102-20.

Fraser, J E 2009 *From Caledonia to Pictland. Scotland to 795*. Edinburgh: Edinburgh University Press.

Geary, P J 2002 *The myth of nations. The Medieval origins of Europe.* Oxford: Princeton University Press.

Heather, P 2009 *Empires and barbarians.* London: Macmillan.

Howe, N 1989 *Migration and mythmaking in Anglo-Saxon England.* New Haven: Yale University Press.

Hughes, K 1980 'Where are the writings of early Scotland?', *in* Dumville, D (ed) *Celtic Britain in the Early Middle Ages. Studies in Scottish and Welsh sources*, 1-21. Woodbridge: Boydell.

Jackson, K 1957 'The Duan Albanach', *Scottish Historical Review* 36, 125-37.

Koch, J 1991 'Ériu, Alba, and Letha: when was the language ancestral to Gaelic first spoken in Ireland?', *Emania* 9, 17-27.

Miller, M 1982 '"Matriliny by treaty": the Pictish foundation-legend', *in* Whitelock, D, McKitterick, R and Dumville, D (eds) *Ireland in Early Mediaeval Europe. Studies in memory of Kathleen Hughes*,133-61. Cambridge: Cambridge University Press.

Morris, J (ed and trans) 1980 *Nennius. British history and the Welsh annals.* London: Phillimore.

Pohl, W 1997 'Ethnic names and identities in the British Isles: a comparative perspective', *in* Hines, J (ed) *The Anglo-Saxons from the Migration period to the eighth century: an ethnographic perspective*, 7-40. Woodbridge: Boydell.

Pohl, W 1998 'Telling the difference: signs of ethnic identity', *in* Pohl, W and Reimitz, H (eds) *Strategies of distinction. The construction of ethnic communities, 300-800*, 17-69. Leiden: Brill.

Pohl, W 2013 'Christian and barbarian identities in the Early Medieval west: introduction', *in* Pohl, W and Heydemann, G (eds) *Post-Roman transitions. Christian and barbarian identities in the Early Medieval west*, 1-46. Turnhout: Brepols.

Reynolds, S 1983 'Medieval *Origines Gentium* and the community of the realm', *History* 68, 375-90.

Reynolds, S 1997 *Kingdoms and communities in western Europe 900-1300.* Oxford: Oxford University Press. Revised edition.

Ross, A 1999 'Pictish matriliny?', *Northern Studies* 34, 11-22.

Whitelock, D (ed) 1979 *English historical documents c 500-1042.* London: Eyre Methuen. Second edition.

Woolf, A 1998 'Pictish matriliny reconsidered', *The Innes Review* 49, 147-67.

Woolf, A 2007 *From Pictland to Alba 789-1070.* Edinburgh: Edinburgh University Press.

Yorke, B 1990 *Kings and kingdoms of early Anglo-Saxon England.* London: Routledge.